Storage Networks

DANIEL J. WORDEN

Storage Networks

ISBN-13 (pbk): 978-1-59059-298-4
ISBN-10 (pbk): 1-59059-298-0

Printed and bound in the United States of America (POD)

Trademarked names may appear in this book. Rather than use a trademark symbol with every occurrence of a trademarked name, we use the names only in an editorial fashion and to the benefit of the trademark owner, with no intention of infringement of the trademark.

Lead Editor: Jim Sumser

Technical Reviewer: Jonathan Hassell

Editorial Board: Steve Anglin, Dan Appleman, Ewan Buckingham, Gary Cornell, Tony Davis, John Franklin, Jason Gilmore, Chris Mills, Steven Rycroft, Dominic Shakeshaft, Jim Sumser, Karen Watterson, Gavin Wray, John Zukowski

Assistant Publisher: Grace Wong

Project Manager: Beth Christmas

Copy Manager: Nicole LeClerc

Copy Editor: Ami Knox

Production Manager: Kari Brooks

Production Editor: Janet Vail

Compositor: Diana Van Winkle

Proofreader: Elizabeth Berry

Indexer: Valerie Perry

Artist: Kinetic Publishing

Cover Designer: Kurt Krames

Manufacturing Manager: Tom Debolski

Distributed to the book trade in the United States by Springer-Verlag New York, Inc., 233 Spring Street, 6th Floor, New York, NY 10013 and outside the United States by Springer-Verlag GmbH & Co. KG, Tiergartenstr. 17, 69112 Heidelberg, Germany.

In the United States: phone 1-800-SPRINGER, e-mail orders@springer-ny.com, or visit http://www.springer-ny.com. Outside the United States: fax +49 6221 345229, e-mail orders@springer.de, or visit http://www.springer.de.

For information on translations, please contact Apress directly at 2560 Ninth Street, Suite 219, Berkeley, CA 94710. Phone 510-549-5930, fax 510-549-5939, e-mail info@apress.com, or visit http://www.apress.com.

For my brothers:
John Ulrich—Thanks for making our payroll, so many times!
Verner Ulrich—Your compassion is an inspiration.
Tom Ulrich—Working as an executive with your direction was a career high point.
Viggo Ulrich—My son is a better man because you were "in loco parentis."
Bill Ulrich—You go to impressive distances to set such a good example.
Stephen Worden—How could I ever forget OokaDokah?
Donald Worden—Even as an eight-year-old, you could always out-quip me.

Contents at a Glance

Contents

About the Author

 **Daniel Worden** has been an IT manager, architect, and administrator since 1982. He obtained his first Unix root account in 1984 working with Pyramid and Sun equipment. His first exposure to fibre channel attached storage arrays was in 1996 while providing systems administration services to a multinational oil company. He has also been hands-on in retail, hospital, and video production environments.

During the 1990s, Daniel and his wife Marie built a 25-employee software and services company, which they sold to a publicly traded firm in 2001. He currently offers his consulting skills for interesting projects as they arise. Recently, he published a series of tutorials on autonomic computing tools.

Storage Networks is his fifth computer book. Previous work has been translated into Chinese and Japanese. More information about the author is available at http://daniel.worden.net.

About the Technical Reviewer

 **Jonathan Hassell** is a systems administrator and IT consultant residing in Raleigh, NC. He is currently employed by one of the largest departments on campus at North Carolina State University, supporting a computing environment that consists of Windows NT, 2000, XP, Server 2003, Sun Solaris, and HP-UX machines.

Hassell has extensive experience in networking technologies and Internet connectivity. He currently runs his own web hosting business, Enable Hosting, based out of Charlotte, NC. He is involved in all facets of the business, including finances, marketing, operating decisions, and customer relations.

Jonathan's previously published work includes *RADIUS*, published by O'Reilly and Associates; and *Hardening Windows*, published by Apress. He has also written monthly columns for the Windows 2000 Magazine Network and WindowsITSecurity.com. His work has been published in CMP's *Publish* magazine and Pinnacle's *Linux AppDev* newsletter, and he is a frequent contributor to *SecurityFocus*, the leading online security magazine, and *PC Pro*, a renowned computing magazine in the United Kingdom.

Hassell's latest book, *Managing Windows Server 2003*, will be published by O'Reilly and Associates in early 2004.

Acknowledgments

IN THE CREATION of a work like this book, there are a great many people involved, none more than Jim Sumser, in every step from the initial gleam on. I couldn't possibly thank everyone by name who contributed in important ways to the writing, editing, and production of this book. Thank you all!

I would like to take this opportunity to doff my cap in thanks to the entire Apress team—you are a truly exceptional group: Ami Knox, for your improvements to my prose, punctuation, and capitalization, grazie, mille grazie; Beth Christmas, from expediting my contract through the most genteel and effective project shepherding I've ever before enjoyed; Jonathan Hassell, your even-handed praise and critique both encouraged and challenged me to bring out my best in this book; and two more "Js" on the team, Janet Vail in Production and Julie Miller in Marketing—thank you both for your efforts.

Alexander Worden's keen eye and deft hand resulted in some of the better diagrams in the book—thanks, kiddo.

Carla Bayha, without your introduction to Studio B, no one would be reading this. Thanks so much. And thank you, Laura Lewin, though agents never get the thanks they deserve.

The greatest acknowledgement goes to Marie, my spouse and partner, for the myriad ways she was and continues to be the best helpmeet ever, and to those family and friends who encouraged and supported me through this process.

Of course, for all the support and diligent review by others, any flaws in conception or construction of this book remain my responsibility alone.

Introduction

THANK YOU FOR picking up *Storage Networks*. When I was initially approached about writing this book, my first thought was the Fortune 500 market for Storage Area Networks (SANs) was pretty well serviced already. Then it dawned on me that twin revolutions in both storage and network technologies were opening up new opportunities and simultaneously presenting a variety of new issues for IT professionals to overcome.

This book, *Storage Networks*, is the result of my efforts to make sense of the explosion of products that increase network speed, link more nodes, and store ever-greater amounts of data over geographically disparate areas.

More than anything else, my objective for this book was to organize those issues and break them down into comprehensible, related pieces. I wanted to evaluate the components of Storage Area Network solutions so you, the Reader, would be better equipped to plan, implement, and administer this critical resource in your own environment.

To accomplish this, I felt I had to link theory and practice, SAN and NAS, Ethernet and Fibre Channel into a cohesive treatment of the technologies as an integrated set. A tall order to be sure.

Along the way, my review of technology standards in one chapter led me later to the selection of certain configuration options in proof-of-concept testing. These allowed me to achieve returns in performance tuning of 20 percent and more.

The theoretical concept informs the practical approach, and this book reflects that dynamic.

Rather than get immersed in the depth and breadth of any one component of storage networks, my aim here was to pull it all together for you. I wanted to deal with the "down and in" detail of each layer of the ISO network model as it applies to storage networks, and relate that to an "up and out" review of vendor offerings, data life cycle, and business considerations.

By the time you finish the book, I expect you'll be comfortable with the barrage of tech-spec numbers associated with any storage network product, and be better able to determine how it could fit within your environment.

If you're someone who's been tasked with implementing or administering a storage network, I kept your interests firmly in mind as well. Likewise, I hoped to appeal to anyone looking to get grounded in the technologies for the first time. Those of you with many years of experience in the field may also find a few gaps in your knowledge of disk and networking technology filled in.

Where possible, I related ideas and concepts to products on the market when I wrote the book, but I made an effort to make the discussion relevant beyond the latest release from any particular vendor. You should find the book applicable to Storage Area Network technology for quite some time to come.

In any case, this book was meant to be read rather than referenced, and I hope you find it an instructive companion on your way to grappling with storage network technology.

—Daniel J. Worden

CHAPTER 1

A Walk Around the Technology

IN THIS CHAPTER, I take you on a tour through the various components that make up a storage subsystem, paying particular attention to identifying areas of contention and bottlenecks. You'll learn the true definition of "bandwidth" and get a look at several areas that can affect the real data transfer rate through a system and across a network.

This chapter explores the role of specifications as a means of encouraging interoperability. I review several of the most useful standards for evaluating storage networks and appraising offerings from different vendors.

As befits an introductory chapter, I begin with the fundamental concepts and take you through the internals of representative storage network systems, and the paths bits take through them. Then I layer on general networking concepts, with specific attention to contributions to the increase in throughput and how that enables storage networks.

Emerging protocols such as iSCSI and 10 Gigabit Ethernet are covered in the context of where they fit in the overall scheme of storage network options and how they affect design and deployment decisions today and possibly in the future.

By the end of this chapter, you should have a feel for the end-to-end path a data packet has to travel as part of even the simplest storage solution, as well as the standards and products involved in large-scale networked storage solutions.

Getting Started

Like everything digital these days, Storage Area Networks (SANs) are inherently complex. This makes them difficult to manage, in part because of the sheer number of contributing components offered by different vendors. Add to this the need to layer software and procedures on top of a SAN in order to gain the expected benefits, and, for many, storage network components represent a jumble of puzzle pieces.

The premise of this book is that you can more quickly understand SAN technology, in theory and practice, if I organize my approach a bit differently. Whereas many technology authors start at the "big picture" and drill down, I'm going to take a different approach and start from the foundation and work up.

Yet, even within this basic approach, a couple of wrinkles need to be ironed out from the beginning. Storage Area Networks are, on an important level, less about storage and more about networking. The good news is that by limiting the scope of the network to storage, I can contain some of the complexity around networks in general and cover the material with a view to one particular kind of application.

The other piece of good news is that, although outside of the mainframe environment SANs are relatively new (say post–Windows 95), Local Area Networks are not. So I propose to start there.

The Network Is the Computer–Again

Sun Microsystems used to say, "The Network is the Computer." Sun's marketing material in 1987 was printed with this slogan when the company was promoting clusters of engineering workstations, and Sun resurrected it in the late 1990s when it was promoting the Internet as the network to bring everything together. It's interesting to me that the performance of my old Sun 3/50, 10Base-2 network, with its little black RG-58u coaxial cable, has about the same throughput and ping speed as my current Southwest Bell ADSL modem and wireless network. Old LAN performance equates to new small office/home office Wide Area Network (WAN) performance.

That observation isn't made idly; it's a recurring theme as I show you the different offerings for interconnecting storage subsystems. Network speeds and distances are increasing steadily, if not exponentially. If today's local access becomes tomorrow's WAN access, when it comes to storage and disk access, you can start to think "outside of the box."

The Network is the Computer: That's the motif for this chapter. Keeping that motto front and center, let's go through the process of how a generic network is created, and then layer on top of that the specific considerations that go into creating a storage network.

Class and Instance

One of the things that object-oriented programming maintains is that you approach software from the perspective of first defining a class, and after that you can create a concrete example or instance of something that belongs to that class. A *class* is a description of a collection of objects with common attributes, behavior, and responsibilities. Your dog Fido is an instance of the class pet. An iSCSI card is an instance of the class network controller. TCP/IP is an instance of the class protocol.

In networking, you start first with a specification and after that is published (or even a little before), a bunch of vendors run out and create products. So before you can even start at the ground level and work up, you have to identify the specifications that govern a storage network and its constituent parts. I think of this as pulling out all the puzzle pieces with straight lines and forming the outer perimeter of the puzzle first.

The point to remember is that without a specification or defined class for networking components, there wouldn't be implemented instances in the form of interoperable products. Even products ostensibly built to standards may not work and play well with those from competitors, depending on how well a particular standard has been defined. As you'll see, this is rife in some areas of storage networks. To better appreciate how this can happen, we have to start with some of the relevant specifications and consider the role they have in understanding storage network components.

In the Beginning—There Was the ISO/ITU/OSI Network Model

The seven-layer ISO/ITU/OSI network model, which I'll refer to from this point on as the ISO model, was a breakthrough in computing when it was first published in 1978. Of course, those with a love of esoterica could argue that IBM's SNA standard announced in 1974, or the work done by Honeywell a few years before, were more important stepping-stones than the committee agreement. But as a step toward nonproprietary, interoperable product development to spec, it was quite significant indeed. For the practical purpose of understanding how storage networks are designed, built, and managed, you'll find the seven-layer model quite useful in organizing the options and understanding their implications.

For those who slept through that class, the ISO model consists of the seven layers shown in Figure 1-1.

OSI Network Model
Application
Presentation
Session
Transport
Network
Data Link
Physical

Figure 1-1. The ISO/ITU/OSI network reference model

The ground from which you'll build is the physical layer, particularly, fiber-optic cable and Category 5 (Cat 5) and higher twisted-pair copper wire. Generally, a network by definition requires more than a single computer. However, by agreeing that the network is the computer, you can approach understanding storage networks as if you were building a single computer out of subsystems: processors, memory, storage, and the means to link them all together. The extrapolation of this is that the computing resources of your entire campus, hospital, organization, or corporation can be treated as a single computer and managed accordingly.

One of the beneficial side effects of taking this approach should be an introduction to, or refresher of, the basic underlying technical considerations that must be addressed in the design of a storage network. In this chapter, I look at the various ways that bits are moved around a computer, identify the ones that impact storage and, I hope, link those concepts to the various products and topologies that make up a potential Storage Area Network.

With this goal in mind, let's review the components that make up any given hardware environment.

SAN Components

To understand how to manage a storage network, or a collection of SANs as a single logical entity, you have to first identify its components. As part of this book's approach, you'll look first at the most simple implementation of a disk subsystem. You'll see how the addition of new components adds functionality, at the expense of complexity, as you go through this process.

In Figure 1-2, you can see the constituent parts of any disk storage subsystem:

- Hard disk

- Controller

- Bus

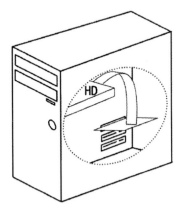

Figure 1-2. Direct attached server storage

A Network Attached Storage (NAS) appliance isn't really very different. A generic NAS is shown in Figure 1-3.

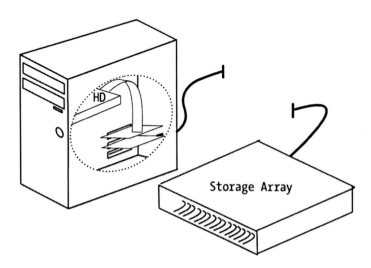

Figure 1-3. Network Attached Storage appliance

By moving the storage subsystem across the network, you can replace the controller card with a network interface card (NIC) or what is more appropriately referred to as a *host bus adapter* (HBA).

In a typical NAS or SAN configuration, more than one connection exists between the storage device and the server. I'll discuss multiple servers after I've covered the entire stack for a single server configuration.

Let's trace the journey of a single text file as it's retrieved by a client workstation (see Figure 1-4). If Unix is your home environment, consider an example of using the more utility to view the contents of File.txt. If you think in Windows, imagine that you double-clicked File.txt in Explorer and WordPad has requested it.

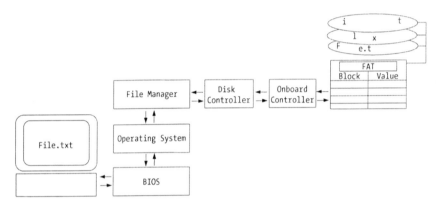

Figure 1-4. Path of a file request

As you can see, the application program sends the requested file name to the OS, which passes the request to the underlying file manager. The file manager then checks the status of the file and permissions before carrying out the request. This is to say, it looks at the file allocation table to determine the physical address of the logical file name File.txt. The hard disk heads move to the location of the file, read the bytes of which it's made up, and transfer those through the bus to RAM. The I/O processor within the OS is notified of the location in RAM and the bytes sent to the screen for your review.

The disk storage system then performs the electromechanical work of reading and passing along the bytes representing the file to the OS, which stores it in RAM and passes the first part of the file along to the standard out device, in this case the terminal by way of more or the WordPad application under Windows.

It's not a big leap to see that in a client/server environment, the disk and OS can be separated from the client by a network.

Virtually everyone has participated in this type of configuration and you probably have more than a little experience in its design, installation, and support. Of course, we're only part of the way along the path to even the most simplistic storage network.

To separate the client from the server, you need a new set of services, as shown in Figure 1-5. Specifically, you now have to manage the translation of the file through the network card of the client, the network port, and services of the server; and then invoke the process described in the previous three figures. (Again, I know this may be rudimentary to you, but explaining multivendor storage arrays, switches, operating systems, buses, and later host bus adapters requires I define and illustrate the fundamental terms.)

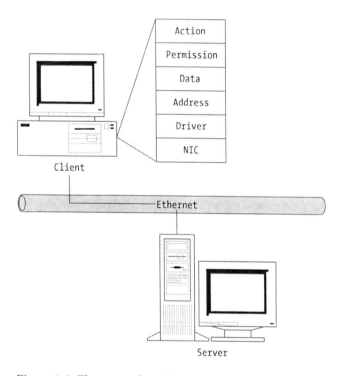

Figure 1-5. The network and protocols

At a generic level, a server-attached disk subsystem accessed by a client across the network is pretty straightforward. Let's assume that the network protocol is TCP/IP. Add to that assumption that you're using Gigabit Ethernet (GbE) over Cat 5 copper wire, and you have a good baseline for determining file access speeds over the Local Area Network. We'll have to come up with other metrics for dealing with multiple users and different types of file access, such as database transactions, but for now, let's consider that a 100-megabyte (MB) file is the baseline.

You could use the theoretical throughput speeds or even ping time to get some idea of the relative performance of the network. However, by considering file load times in increments of a single megabyte, and then looking at the appetite for storage and file size profiles, the practical work expected of a storage subsystem is going to become pretty clear. And by using this approach, you'll end up with a good rule of thumb for when determining whether direct-attached storage, network-attached storage, or a SAN is the right configuration for your particular job of work.

Benchmarking Data Throughput

Informal benchmark results abound, typically involving an FTP transfer measured with a stopwatch. A 100-megabyte file transfer that takes 80 seconds over 11-Mbps wireless will complete in a little more than 10 seconds over 100Base-T. With 1000Base-T you could expect it to be done in a second. The problem is in knowing whether you are gaining an insight into the fundamental performance characteristics of the pipeline or benchmarking behavior of the network cards.

I bring this up because no matter what assertion gets made regarding benchmarking network performance, the methodology can be called into question and the conclusions rejected. The point I want to underscore is that while I'm going to identify rules of thumb for predicting or measuring system performance, too many variables exist to be able to come up with a generic, reliable formula.

Frequently you hear the term *bandwidth* used to refer to the volume of data that can be processed by a given computing component. In an electrical engineering sense, bandwidth is the range of frequencies used in analog signals. Common use of the term refers to bits per second and is really a measure of the data rate or throughput.

Network cards handle the data transferred over the network in a way directly analogous to the way a controller card handles the data transfer. In each case, the performance of the card is directly affected by the bus, which in turn is measured by data throughput rate (bits per second) and clock speed (megahertz rate). In a Storage Area Network, a key component is the host bus adapter, which is really a network card. The addition of this feature is depicted in Figure 1-6.

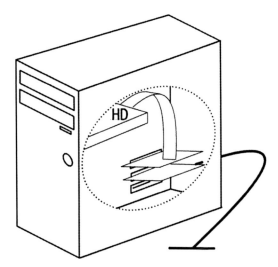

Figure 1-6. A channel-attached storage array

But before I go too far with this analogy, let's not forget that a typical network interface card relies on the server CPU for some processing. Here I'd like to give honorable mention to the MicroChannel architecture. One of the attractions of that model was the inclusion of bus master network cards, which didn't interrupt the CPU when handling network traffic. The intelligence was built into the controller card itself. That is closer conceptually to the way a host bus adapter card works in a SAN. The HBA doesn't require work to be done by the CPU, and as such its performance isn't limited by the bus speed into which it's plugged.

This offloading of work to dedicated cards and appliances is the cornerstone concept of a physical Storage Area Network. Bear in mind that although I compare it to a traditional network card, the HBA isn't as affected by server bus characteristics. Its overall performance is more affected by the speed of the network of which it's a part.

This configuration is more typical of a SAN rather than Network Attached Storage, primarily because a SAN is channel attached by way of a switch. These switches form *fabrics,* and they are responsible for performing the work of routing the stream of bytes requested for reading or writing to the appropriate storage device. Unlike a direct-attached disk or a network-attached storage array, a SAN has different paths that can be taken from the disk to the server, and a switch manages that process to optimize and balance the workload. I'll get to that a bit later in this chapter in the section titled "Topologies."

Get on the Bus

Let's get back to the bus for a bit. In this section, you'll take a tour of the internal considerations for moving data from one subsystem to another. The reason for the level of detail is to provide an insight into the factors that affect the host bus adapter and network cards that can be used for communicating to a storage network.

A shared bus is the mechanism at the heart of traditional computers for sharing data across all subsystems—storage, processor, memory, display, and other peripherals. The bus operates like a stretch of expressway in a heavily populated metropolitan area. The bytes get on the bus, and then follow a path through it until they reach the intended exit. Like a highway, access is shared and contention has to be managed.

The number of lanes in the expressway corresponds to the data path. The PC AT from years ago made the astonishing (or so it seemed at the time) leap from 8 bits to 16 bits. The original PCI bus was 32 bits wide. Some proprietary architectures have wider data paths.

There are several problems with this approach. One is that the fundamental capability for moving bits along a bus isn't keeping pace with either processing power, networking speeds, or file size growth, as you can see in Figure 1-7.

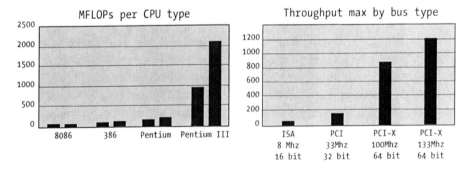

Figure 1-7. Comparison of bus and processor performance increases

Like a processor, a bus also has a clock speed that governs its performance. To continue with the expressway analogy, you have a speed limit. When congestion occurs, traffic slows, both in the real world and within the system. This maximum becomes theoretical, and bits move at whatever crawl is sustainable given the volume and contention.

The significant difference between these two technologies is that every 5 years or so, you see an order of magnitude (ten times) increase in processing power, whereas system buses have measured performance improvement at a rate more like doubling every 4 years. The net result is that servers can now process a much higher volume than can be moved between subsystems—specifically storage, with the controllers passing data between subsystems via the server's bus.

Murphy, Moore, and Metcalf's Law

Storage networks incorporate two of the most popular laws observed by someone whose last name starts with *M*. No, I don't mean Murphy. Moore's Law relates to CPU processing power, as reflected in the number of transistors contained on a silicon chip. George Moore wrote in 1965 (as many of you have heard countless times) that the number of transistors on a square inch of silicon will double every 12 months. Moore went on to discuss other trends that affected computing power, and later revised the trend to approximately 18 months. The sense of Moore's Law is that computing power doubles every 18 months while production costs hold steady.

Robert Metcalfe, the notional creator of Ethernet, defined his own law, not coincidentally known as MetCalfe's Law. It states that the utility of a network is the square of the number of connected nodes.

As you'll see in the succeeding chapters, these two trends greatly affect Storage Area Networks: Moore's Law by bringing ever increasing computing power cost effectively and Metcalfe's by pointing to the utility gained by increasing connectivity.

There are two models for implementing internal bus architectures—an internal and external bus. The internal bus is best demonstrated by the motherboard approach. The CPU, disk controllers, and memory slots are integrated into a single board. The external bus, for example PCI, is integrated with the motherboard to allow the insertion of other special-purpose cards. Desktop PCs are a prevalent example of this architecture.

The other approach is with a backplane, where each subsystem is segregated and communicates across the external bus. Chassis for supporting multiple single-board computers, such as blade servers, are an example of this architecture.

Industry Standard System Bus Architectures

Although there may be myriad server vendors in situ across corporate America and the rest of the world, practically speaking, only a handful of vendors account for most of the server environments generating the demand for storage, including the following:

- Apple

- Compaq

- Dell

- International Business Machines Corporation (IBM)

- Hewlett-Packard (HP)

- Silicon Graphics, Inc. (SGI)

- Sun Microsystems

I suppose I'll hear from Tandem, Hitachi, Amdahl, and other folks, but the point here is to identify the major players and look at their system bus architectures before moving on to a review of host bus adapters.

The most popular bus architecture, at least in terms of units sold, is the Peripheral Component Interconnect (PCI) bus. The PCI bus found in most desktop PCs is configured with a 32-bit data path at 33 megahertz (MHz) and a bandwidth of up to 133 megabytes per second (MBps).

This isn't fast enough for transfers between memory and processors, so different standards have emerged for those, specifically JEDEC for 168-pin 64-bit dual inline memory modules (DIMMs) whose 66 MHz, 100 MHz, and 133 MHz clock rates make up most of the memory installed in a lot of Pentium- or Athlon-based systems. CPU socket definitions are defined by the CPU vendors and, like memory, are designed to accommodate more pins and higher transfer rates between the subsystems.

To help understand the interrelationships, visualize a garden-variety Windows 2000 server, with three different bus standards built into the motherboard: socket 478 for the Pentium IV; two 512MB, 184-pin PC2700 DDR SDRAM DIMMs snapped into the memory slots; and a 64-bit PCI bus at 66 MHz with slots for four cards. In this scenario, the slowest bus with the lowest transfer capability is the PCI bus, which is going to be used to house the storage controller and network cards.

The PCI-X architecture is the extended definition of the PCI bus specification, which allows for a 64-bit data path at 133 MHz. The spec allows different speeds to be supported in multiple buses, which means matching the right bus to the optimized storage controller card could be an issue when deciding what equipment is right for your site.

The Compaq ProLiant DL760 was one of the first implementations of a PCI-X–enabled server on the market.

Proprietary Bus Architectures

SGI has historically offered one of the top-performing backplanes in a server environment. Their niche has been visualization computing—the art and science of converting 2-D data into a 3-D simulator environment. Think of it as presenting fighter jet tactics as a stream of graphics—in real time. This is a particularly demanding computing environment, and SGI has long architected its products to support it.

Competition being the driving force that it is, other server vendors weren't prepared to cede the battle and walk away from this market. HP, IBM, and Sun all offer serious hardware for high-performance computing (HPC). These offerings typically sport their own proprietary operating systems, whether HP-UX, Solaris, or AIX (though Linux is available on most, if not all, platforms), and the internal architectures have been customized accordingly.

PCI is offered in virtually all main servers, but host bus adapter cards are also available for proprietary buses as described in Table 1-1.

Table 1-1. Proprietary Bus Architectures—Past and Present

Architecture	Description
SBUS	Incorporated into Sun SPARCStations beginning in 1989.
MBUS	Featured in Sun SPARCServers, a multiprocessor bus architecture first released in 1991 that became obsolete in 1997.
MCA	Initially developed for the PS2 personal computer, MCA found a new home in the RS/6000. This 32-bit bus supports automatic configuration of inserted cards and multiple bus master cards. All of this was pretty aggressive in 1987, and although it disappeared from the PC scene years ago, it continued as the bus architecture for many RS/6000 models.
GIO	This 32- and 64-bit bus architecture is found in SGI Indy Workstation machines.

(continued)

Table 1-1. Proprietary Bus Architectures—Past and Present (continued)

Architecture	Description
HIO	Another SGI offering, for the Onyx line with a system bus 256 bits wide and a sustained throughput of 1.2GB, the High-Speed I/O (HIO) subsystem delivers 320 MBps.
PMC	PCI mezzanine cards are used to incrementally add processing power to existing servers via their PCI cards.
VME Bus	Originally found in pre-SPARC systems from 1987 to 1992, VME bus is a 32-bit data path capable of accessing 64 bits' worth of addresses and transferring 320 MBps. Although not found in general-purpose servers any longer, it's used in some embedded systems.

The main point is that even in a straightforward implementation of a single-server implementation of a Storage Area Network, start by identifying your bus architecture. With that knowledge, and having selected a physical medium to be your system's backbone, you are ready to go shopping for an HBA—unless of course you want to adopt a newer interconnection model, like InfiniBand.

InfiniBand

There have been many failed attempts to introduce a widely accepted standard for clustering servers and devices over the years. InfiniBand is a new specification for point-to-point interconnection incorporating switches and fabrics. An Infini-Band configuration includes host channel adapters, target channel adapters, and InfiniBand-aware switches to link them. The specification is backed by a diverse set of industry "heavy hitters," and even with the withdrawal of Intel and Microsoft from the trade association in 2003, widespread investment by vendors is already occurring.

In 2003 and 2004, IBM and Sun announced InfiniBand strategies, resurrecting hopes that the technology will take hold and grow to take on an increasingly important role in storage network solutions. To date, most InfiniBand implementations have been in HPC applications at universities.

Whether InfiniBand ever serves as a replacement for the PCI bus is a discussion for future directions, which appears in the last chapter of the book. At this point, I only wish to introduce the importance of switching and its characteristics in contrast to bus and backplane approaches.

InfiniBand communication channels scale from 500 megabits per second (Mbps) to 40 gigabits per second (Gbps) and are ideal for both server interconnection and support for storage networks. Products based on the InfiniBand 1x spec communicate at 2.5 Gbps and the 4x specification supports bursts of up to 10 Gbps.

InfiniBand has several layers, as shown in Figure 1-8.

OSI Network Model
Application
Presentation
Session
Transport
Network
Data Link
Physical

InfiniBand Layers
Upperlayer Protocol Mapping
Transport
Network
Link and Encoding
PHY

Figure 1-8. The InfiniBand stack

The transport services API encapsulates the lower level communications equivalent to ISO layers 2 and 3. Intelligent I/O looks after message handling between devices and the operating system device drivers. Virtual Interconnect efficiently handles application-to-application communication.

By incorporating InfiniBand blade servers, the PCI bus can be completely bypassed, optimizing performance and consumption of other resources such as space and power.

Host Bus Adapters

One of the main objectives of this book is to resolve some of the complexity involved in understanding Storage Area Networks. I want to do this by layering compatible sets of products together. Now that I've introduced the relationships between the components within the server, we can apply the same principles to evaluating SAN components that go outside the server—the first feature of either a NAS or a SAN.

The component that links the server with the storage subsystem is the host bus adapter. There are three main kinds of HBAs on the market at the present time—Fibre Channel, iSCSI, and Gigabit Ethernet.

Some sources will define a SAN as necessarily channel attached. That is, a system must have Fibre Channel to be a SAN. In the next breath, however, iSCSI and Gigabit Ethernet get discussed as aggressive new ways of connecting external storage subsystems to servers. This tells me that I need to treat any network scheme that links storage to servers, promoting high availability, performance, and single-desk administration, as within the scope of this book.

To work within the approach I've laid out at the beginning, I need to map a few HBAs and their protocols onto the ISO model.

Gigabit Ethernet

Not that long ago, Ethernet was doomed (it was said) to be restricted to the 10 Mbps of 10Base-T. Then a breakthrough occurred with the introduction of 100Base-T, or 100 Mbps over twisted-pair Cat 5 cable. In 1998, 1000Base-T became standardized, and products followed into the market. The 10 Gigabit Ethernet specification is expected to support development of cards to replace ATM and SONET networks and take advantage of the fiber-optic cable laid for those installations.

This means that with no change to the physical network installed, or the supporting CSMA/CD and MAC protocol, Ethernets can already handle two and soon three orders of magnitude more volume and speed than they could 10 years ago.

Gigabit Ethernet can run for distances of 100 meters over copper but is also available over fiber-optic cable, with similar distances and constraints as Fibre Channel backbones.

In Figure 1-9, you can see the mapping of Gigabit Ethernet to the OSI model.

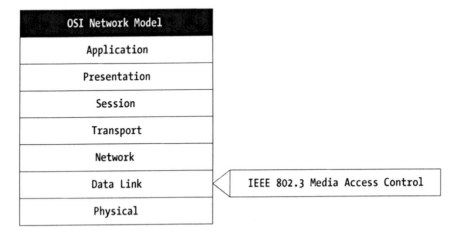

Figure 1-9. Gigabit Ethernet layers

Gigabit Ethernet, as defined in the IEEE 802.3 specification, handles the translation of the data link layer to the physical Ethernet protocol, which, as I've already noted, may be copper wire or fiber-optic cable. The upper layers are unaffected by the decision to go Ethernet, and the drivers for managing the network and transport layers also don't have to be specifically written to support the deployment of Gigabit Ethernet. Specific device drivers for the server and SAN have to be loaded, but this is to make the storage services available to the OS and applications, rather than as a result of deciding to implement Gigabit Ethernet.

One potential advantage offered by Gigabit Ethernet is a greater likelihood of interoperability between components developed by different vendors. This would be a reflection of the greater experience vendors have with Ethernet protocols, in no small part due to the much greater volume of Ethernet installations in the world.

A typical Gigabit Ethernet SAN configuration over copper wire might be for sharing tape and backup servers across a data center, especially where the existing infrastructure is limited to 100Base-T and file sizes are large enough to cause delays and network congestion.

One of the drawbacks of Gigabit Ethernet is the potential requirement for much of the TCP/IP processing to be handled by the CPU, but many vendors are now offering this functionality as part of their HBAs. It pays to check.

iSCSI

iSCSI (pronounced eye-scuzzy) is a transport protocol that allows the iSCSI host bus adapter to use existing Ethernet media as the link between the server and storage resources. In 2002, Hitachi Alacritech and Nishan Systems announced they used their existing components to achieve data transfer rates of 218 MBps.

iSCSI can be used with existing Gigabit Ethernet infrastructure or coexist with Fibre Channel SAN equipment. For installations that haven't previously installed SAN capabilities, iSCSI offers lower cost integration of storage management devices and appliances.

With Windows 2000 server and client support announced by Microsoft in the summer of 2003, iSCSI was positioned to make significant inroads for MS Exchange sites needing improved backup and availability.

As you move up the ISO stack, security considerations are introduced. At the lowest levels, you're primarily concerned with physical carrier characteristics, the effect of distances on signal propagation, the need for repeaters, and managing collisions and contention, for example. Although bus mastering allows for offloading CPU cycles to dedicated functions in the HBA, not all of these adapters handle security. Those that don't handle this function have an impact on SAN performance at either the storage controller, the CPU of the server, or both.

iSCSI has been criticized as a candidate for SAN-enabling technology because of its reliance on TCP/IP, which is vulnerable to the interception of network transmissions and having them read by a packet analyzer.

To get around this, some HBA vendors are offering IPSec and other encrypt/decrypt capabilities on their boards.

Fibre Channel

The first segregated storage arrays made available to Unix servers were Fibre Channel devices operating at a theoretical throughput of 100 MBps. In the mid-1990s, this technology supported remote copying, mirroring, and arrays of more than two-dozen disk devices. The first such device I worked with was the Sun Disk Array, and it contained 30 9GB barracuda hard disks. It was awesome, especially compared to the FastSCSI network I built to support an all-digital video production application that was limited to 20 feet of SCSI cable and no more than seven devices. Of course, iSCSI has been developed to eliminate the distance and device restrictions, but I bring this historical recollection up to show the roots of the competing architectures and just how far ahead FDDI has consistently been the enabling SAN technology.

So what has Fibre Channel done lately? Today, Fibre Channel SANs support terabytes of disk and transfer rates of up to 2 Gbps. This translates to a 2.5-terabyte-per-hour backup, for example. By the end of 2003, for the largest volumes of data to be handled in the least amount of time, Fibre Channel SANs were still the performance leaders.

The Fibre Channel model is similar to the OSI model with the notable difference of more detailed layers, which are described in Table 1-2.

Table 1-2. Fibre Channel Layers

Layer	Description
FC-4	Upper layer protocol mapping (exposes interface between FC and upper layers)
FC-3	Common services (file encryption, compression)
FC-2	Framing (encapsulation of data, flow control)
FC-1	Transmission (defines arrangement of data sets and their encoding and decoding)
FC-0	Physical (signaling, addresses media, ports, and cabling)

These layers actually correspond to the bottom three layers of the OSI model, as depicted in Figure 1-10.

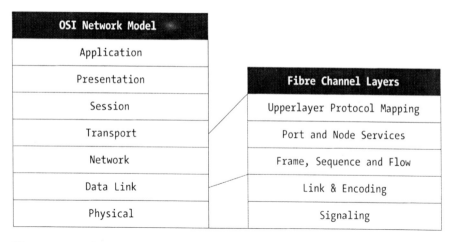

Figure 1-10. Fibre Channel layers mapped to the OSI reference model

Although there are many providers of HBAs, the market for Fibre Channel HBAs is dominated by Emulex (45 percent of the market in 2002) and QLogic (30.8 percent of the 2002 market). As you'll see in subsequent chapters, there is a great deal of partnering in the industry. Storage network vendors try to build interoperable solutions while contributing as much value and extracting as much margin as they can. Contracting out to other manufacturers is commonplace, and places an additional burden on interoperability as products incorporate complex components to achieve higher performance.

Putting Together the Hardware Puzzle

You've now seen all of the major concepts involved in moving data around inside a server. The bus architecture has significant drawbacks when it comes to managing transfers of large amounts of data. The solution to this problem comes to us from the telephony side of technology in the form of switches. This technology grew out of the need to connect many different callers across the country and around the world, with high quality and reliability—much higher, in fact, than computer users have demanded until recently.

Moving the processing out from the CPU to the controller card is an effective way of gaining performance efficiencies. The data no longer has to traipse through the server as part of being handled, unless that data has been requested specifically by the server OS for some particular application task.

This principle goes further with Network Attached Storage and Storage Area Networks. In an NAS environment, the buffering, caching, and physical I/O to disk is handled by a dedicated, optimized appliance, with little or no impact on the host bus adapter.

Topologies

Regardless of which HBA you decide is right for you, the topology of your SAN is the next consideration. The two options are point-to-point or switched. Both Fibre Channel and Gigabit Ethernet support either, but Fibre Channel supports an additional topology called *arbitrated loop*. These topologies are shown in Figures 1-11, 1-12, and 1-13.

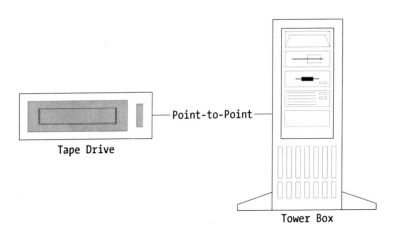

Figure 1-11. Point-to-point storage network topology

In Figure 1-11, you can see how a storage device and server connect in a point-to-point network. Another example of a typical point-to-point topology connects a server and an offline storage device such as a tape drive (see Figure 1-12).

The switch allows multiple devices to interconnect dynamically, as shown in Figure 1-13.

All devices on the loop share the same throughput capacity.

I go into technical detail on topologies in Chapter 3. However, it seems that it might be a good idea to at least generally introduce how these networks function from the perspective of options and implications.

Those of us who grew up in the "Duck and Cover" era no doubt remember the famous red phone linking the White House and the Kremlin. This is to me the classic point-to-point dedicated link. Always there, always ready, never any interruptions. However, I've been told that one of the biggest problems with being old enough to have 20-plus years' experience working with computers is that one (I won't say I) sometimes has difficulty being relevant to the younger generation. For those of you who don't remember Duck and Cover, ask your grandfathers about those "Fall Out" shelter signs. Really, it's fascinating.

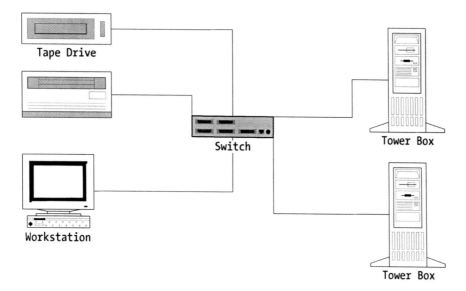

Figure 1-12. Switched storage network topology

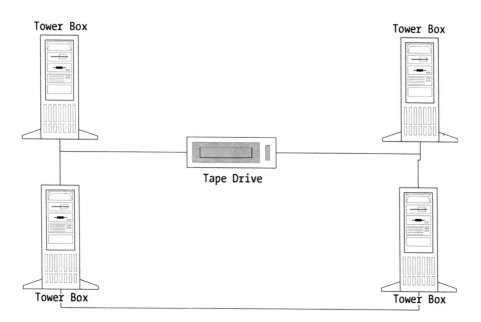

Figure 1-13. An arbitrated loop topology in a Fibre Channel implementation

Instead, let's look at the Dark Ages of the Internet, when people actually used dial-up lines. The network in this case is the phone system. When you dialed up your Internet service provider, you established a point-to-point link. But because it wasn't always on, it wasn't dedicated. If while connected to the Internet you established a chat session with several people, you could consider that a loop. The capability of the line was shared or arbitrated across the connected parties depending on who was typing and who was reading. Using the same phone to make a call is like a switched network. You can get to any address anywhere, be forwarded or put on hold, and leave voicemail at any number—unlike dialing your ISP, which was your telephone number always connecting to the ISP's telephone number.

To extend the metaphor, consider that the phone in your house is like a bus topology. If you pick up the phone and someone else is on the line, you are in contention for the service. "Get off the phone, I need to make an important call" is an example of contention arbitration by priority.

Like any technology, every combination has its features and benefits. One of the main themes of this book is matching the capabilities and costs of storage networks to your particular set of requirements.

Networked Storage: NAS Is SAN Spelled Backwards

Network Attached Storage has been described by some vendors as file oriented: Ethernet-based general storage that can be quickly and easily installed. SAN technology deals more effectively with block-oriented I/O characteristic of database access and online transactions. I believe that with the introduction of iSCSI over both Fibre and Gigabit Ethernet, and perhaps even more important, the introduction of SAN file systems, a more practical differentiation is whether a SAN is segregated or not segregated.

Segregation in this case is the extent to which your storage network is accessible to clients and servers, resulting in shared network traffic. By that definition, a NAS is any storage network configuration where the assets are directly addressable. A SAN, conversely, is formally segregated, and intelligence is deployed in the arrays, switches, and routers to isolate and secure the storage devices.

This isn't to imply that a NAS configuration is insecure (although it may be) or that a SAN solution isn't easily accessed (although it too may be). The purpose of this rule of thumb description is to help clarify the convergence of Fibre Channel and Ethernet technologies as well as copper and fiber-optic cabling media. You can consolidate your direct-attached storage into a wide variety of alternatives. The point I'm making here is that traditional NAS/SAN distinctions are less about the technologies employed and more about the topologies deployed.

As I'll cover in Chapter 12, the business case for SAN technology doesn't have to revolve around many servers accessing hordes of disk. You can just as effectively design and build a storage network as a way of building a high-performance disk subsystem for an imaging, database, or message store application such as Microsoft Exchange or Lotus Domino. One key advantage in that scenario would be the ability to add in shared backup services without affecting server performance.

In both cases, I'm describing networked storage. What I really want to do is to make it easier for you to understand what storage networks are, how they work, and what they can do for you. As a starting point, let's assume the TLA (or three-letter acronym) NAS translates to a nonsegregated storage network and that SAN refers to a segregated storage network. These topologies are compared later in Figure 1-14.

One of the promises from storage vendors is that they can be in and out, with the NAS up and running, in about an hour. This implies they either have a truly terrific training program or the technology is more straightforward than we typically think of with a SAN.

Offerings such as HP's StorageWorks NAS 1000s is a Windows-powered appliance that supports both CIFS for Microsoft clients and NFS for Unix. Basic features include snapshot backup, replication, and volume expansion services.

NAS implementations are tied into the production LAN, and they contribute to the volume of activity on the network, which, like any additional contention, can affect performance.

SAN—Switched Network Storage

In return for the cost of complexity and higher sticker price, a SAN moves the network traffic away from the production network, while still providing access to data stores to multiple servers and their clients. This is accomplished with switching technology.

In a SAN, another term for these interconnected switches is the *fabric*.

Fibre Channel switches are designed to be self-configuring. When a device, such as an HBA or storage array, is connected to a fabric, it's assigned a unique 24-bit address. As more switches are added, addressing conflicts can occur, and this adds to the implementation complexity that has been traditionally associated with a SAN over a NAS.

The key benefit is the ability for any given server to access any given data store via the fabric. Add to this the ability to extend the distances between switches outside the local area, and to administer all of the devices in the storage subsystem from a single console.

The frontrunners for fabric technology include Brocade and McData. These two companies drive standards and have partners who incorporate their switches into overall solutions.

NAS Gateway

One of the latest additions to the SAN and NAS landscape, this type of gateway provides IP connectivity and file system services to servers, while taking advantage of SAN resources and management software behind the scenes. The IP connectivity allows servers or clients to take advantage of Fibre Channel–based storage without being directly connected via a Fibre Channel HBA.

A configuration combining NAS and SAN resource access through a NAS gateway is depicted in Figure 1-14.

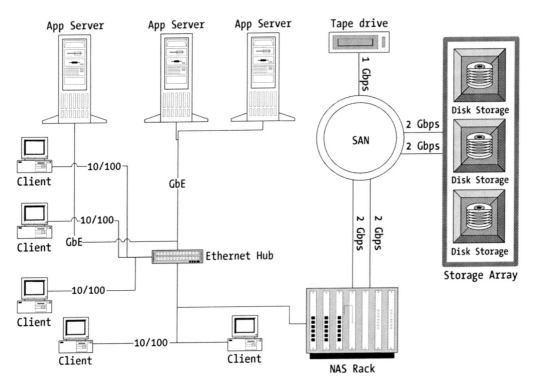

Figure 1-14. A typical NAS gateway configuration including GbE and SAN technologies

Writing to Disk

You should be somewhat comfortable with the high-level treatment of HBAs and switches, NAS and SAN configurations, and the role of the protocol in moving bits from the server through the network. At some point, the file or the transaction must be physically written out to an electromechanical disk or another kind of stable storage device.

Like the sections on host bus adapters and fabrics, I would like to point out that there is a different set of vendors who dominate the market for the provision of storage devices. And like the considerations surrounding the choice of adapter, there is an equally diverse array of options for disks.

A few short years ago, interoperability between different vendors of storage devices at the operational level, complete with integration of switches and adapters from a different set of vendors, was more wishful thinking than practical. As networked storage capacity has surpassed shipments of server-attached disks, the commitment to certifying multiple vendors has become more of an action item.

As much as you might like to design a storage network that assumes disk is a commodity—as in JBOD (short for "Just a Bunch Of Disks"), real-world compatibility issues are a very real threat. Ongoing upgradeability of firmware versions, introduction of new servers and software—all of these very real operational requirements mitigate away from best-of-breed buying towards a "known-good-configuration" orientation. I'll identify those certified product sets as we progress through the book.

There are several key offerings that need to be introduced as part of the component descriptions for networked storage. These include storage offerings from market leaders EMC, Hitachi, and HP. As a result of my own experience, I'll add in some description of the IBM Shark and Storage Tank equipment as well in Chapter 2.

A Word on Disks

In the same way that I spent a certain amount of time reviewing the behavior of buses and adapter cards, I think it's appropriate to review the few major disk technologies from the ground up. These include SCSI, ATA, and serial ATA.

ATA Disk Drives

I would imagine that pretty much every reader of this book has, in one incarnation or another, installed a hard disk on a system. Those IDE drives incorporated the parallel ATA technology. Serial ATA is quickly pushing these drives to the side, especially for networked storage. In this world, Seagate and Maxtor are the first companies to deliver serial ATA drives, with Western Digital playing catch-up. (Or leapfrog if you prefer.)

Disk drives are electromechanical devices comprised of platters that spin, for purposes of this discussion, at speeds of 7200 revolutions per minute (rpm), and heads positioned over the platters that seek locations with an average access time of 9 milliseconds.

The Serial ATA interface is capable of a top short burst of bandwidth of 150 MBps, whereas the older ATA/100 technology maxes out at 100 MBps.

Serial ATA drives, priced lower and for somewhat less demanding applications than the transactional block I/O found in SANS, tend to be used for online backup, image storage, and NAS configurations. Some controllers support a mix of ATA and SCSI drives.

SCSI

Traditionally, SCSI drives were the big capacity, high-performance drives on the market. In 2002, ATA took the lead in storage capacity per drive. Now the various offerings compete on price/performance and warranty/reliability features. From a performance standpoint, Fujitsu offers a 15,000 rpm rotational speed that reduces average seek time to 3.3 milliseconds. These Ultra320 SCSI drives allow transfer rates of up to 320 MBps, with internal transfer rates rated at 118.2 MBps. The external transfer rate refers to the speed at which bits are moved after they come off the platter. A more telling indicator is the lower internal transfer rate. As for reliability, SCSI drive manufacturers frequently offer a 5-year warranty, and these drives are priced accordingly.

Connecting the Dots

If you consider the server to be point B and the storage array or disk to be point A, you naturally need a way of connecting the two in order to replace direct-attached storage. As promised earlier in this chapter, here is where I introduce the switch.

But before I can do that, I need to refresh your understanding of how a network functions vis-a-vis that switch. There are considerations regarding switch performance that are just as important as those governing the selection of the right HBA.

When I mentioned my old 10Base-2 Ethernet network and its little black cable, no doubt some of you who are newer to IT thought this was merely nostalgic. In fact, the migration of Ethernet from coaxial cable to twisted-pair cable introduces some concepts that are critical to planning and designing a storage network.

As you may already know, Ethernet is a broadcast-based protocol. It sends out addressed collections of bits (datagrams), and these are picked up and processed by the addressee. The original design of Ethernet was along this long black cable in a bus topology. (And yes, this is the same bus configuration that figures in my discussion of server internals.)

The problem, very quickly experienced by those of us who had to "fish" cable along conduit, was that as more stations were added, performance dropped considerably. Ethernet devices could only transmit when the coast was clear—the Carrier Sense, Multiple Access part of CSMA/CD.

Along came 10Base-T with its twisted-pair cable, which among other things meant we could have the wires from each workstation go directly to the wiring closet or computer room instead of meandering around the ceiling.

The central device in this topology was the *hub*, also known as a *port concentrator*. The point I want to make here is that a hub/concentrator is not a switch or router. By using switches or routers, you may do away with the need for a hub, but the internal processing and that impact on performance is directly relevant to understanding a storage network.

Ethernet by specification is half duplex. It listens and transmits on the same channel, and from a CSMA/CD standpoint this means the coast must be clear in each direction. To extend the expressway analogy, every big city I've ever driven through has at least one of those hated exits that is also the entrance for other cars. This works fine as long as traffic is light, but during rush hour, it can be nerve-wracking to get into the far right lane just as someone else barreling along at 75 miles per hour (I drive on the LBJ in Dallas) wants to occupy the same space you do on the left before they run out of lane.

Twisted-pair cable took care of this by segregating the transmit and receive signals on specific wires. If nothing else, 10Base-T allowed for a more civilized exit and entrance for packets and reduced contention, thereby increasing overall network performance.

But wait, these packets worked (and still do) in a broadcast mode. This means that although they don't need to run from one end of the coaxial cable to other, pushing off the terminator like a swimmer hitting the end of the pool, they need to be propagated from the concentrator out to the other attached devices.

The highest point of contention then moved from packets through the wire to activity in the hub. These hubs worked as store and forward repeaters. The signals went from the sending device to the hub where a copy was made, and the signal boosted and sent out on the receive line to all the other connected devices. The hub would retransmit if a collision occurred, and once successfully received, an acknowledgment was sent back to the hub and the buffer cleared of those packets.

A switch does something quite different. A switch maintains an address pool, and it does the work of identifying the port to which the address is connected. In this way, a switch manages the interconnection of significantly more devices, and the efficient throughput of traffic, by taking back the work that had been previously downloaded to the adapter cards.

A switch works at layer 2 of the ISO model; it more or less dumbly moves the packets from point to point. A router on the other hand handles packets at network layer 3, which allows it to provide additional services such as filtering and translation from one link type to another. A common example of a router is found in a basic home network with the PCs connected via a built-in 10/100 switch or wireless link and the ADSL modem connected in the uplink port. When a participant on the Ethernet accesses the Internet, the packets are translated from the subscriber link and the modem to the Ethernet hub, and for 10/100 wired clients, the address is directed by the switch to the correct port. Wireless clients are handled by the broadcast nature of wireless in a manner like a hub. The transmitted packets are sent to all stations for rejection by the wireless cards if not for them and receipt by the addressee.

I like this hybrid example as it shows the roles of routers, switches, and hubs, as well as points us in the direction of where bottlenecks can occur.

There is a place for both hubs and switches in various Ethernet topologies, depending on the application. If you think of the behavior of a NAS as being similar to a hub-based network implementation and the SAN as incorporating switched functionality, you see the reason why it's important to understand the bus versus star, switched versus concentrated topologies.

The inexpensive routers are appropriate and popular for home and small office environments. But as experience has shown, they aren't scalable beyond a certain point given their broadcasting to all stations. For scalability, a switching technology is required.

Switches themselves, as a class, might be the right answer when planning a storage network, but all switches aren't created equal. The cornerstone value proposition of the switch is the ability to provide full throughput for each port, even as the number of ports in use climbs.

This means that internally, the switch must be able to receive a stream of packets at, say, a 100Base-T, and write them out at the 1000Base-T speed of the server, even while managing the handling of incoming and outgoing datagrams from other ports, and simultaneously looking up the addresses in its address table.

The capacity of the switch is affected by its internal design, which includes a backplane. As I show you different switch offerings and capabilities, you'll see that these differences in architecture affect scalability and performance, just as they do in a workstation or server.

Switch Technology

Switch technology is used in Ethernet and Fibre Channel networks. A *switch* is a box with ports to which cables are connected. Logic is held in an Application-Specific Integrated Circuit (ASIC) in order to maximize the throughput of the bits from one port to another. A switch has a backplane along which it moves these bits from port to port.

However, the throughput of any given switch is governed by more than the number of ports times the speed supported by each port. Unlike a hub, switches don't broadcast; they instead inspect the address of the packet and send it to the appropriate port.

Moving the inspection and forwarding logic onto a chip, the ASIC greatly increases the efficiency of the switch. Offloading the processing from a CPU once again proves its value. The type of inspection and ways in which forwarding is determined can be related back to the OSI model.

Layer 2 Switches   Data Link

As I identified earlier, layer 2 in the OSI model is where the data link occurs. In Ethernet, this is where the Media Access Control (MAC) address of the recipient is used to match to a port. For more than 15 years, Ethernet device manufacturers have been building cards with unique addresses—the MAC address. The green data link light on a switch indicates that the MAC address has been successfully added to a table in the switch. A Fibre Channel fabric uses a similar addressing scheme so the behavior of the two types of switches is consistent with this description.

Layer 3 Switches   Network

Layer 3 switches calculate the route to send packets along based on the logical address assigned to the data packet. An IP address would be an example of a logical address. This becomes significant as subnets and internetwork connections become more complex with larger numbers of devices. A traditional router also performs this service, but does so in software, which tends to result in slower throughput.

Layer 4 Switches   Transport

This kind of switch relies on the IP from the layer below it, but adds flow control and reliable delivery through the usage of protocols such as TCP and UDP. By looking at the port number, as well as the IP address, routing decisions can be taken on the type of service. Web pages requested for port 80, for example, might be best stored on a NAS file system where a relational database port could be directed to a block I/O device on a SAN. Prioritization is another service that may be beneficial—web pages for browsing might be a distant third priority when contending with a database query for a patient record, for example.

Comparing Switch Layers: Performance and Service

The lower the layer, the closer the logic is to the hardware, and the result is faster throughput, which means more ports capable of higher sustained rates of transfer. As switches have evolved, more intelligence has been put into the ASICs, resulting in layer 3 switches that have the performance characteristics previously obtained only by layer 2 switches.

Layer 4 switches allow for more intelligence in the network—moving past brute-force techniques to enhance network speed. The problem posed by more intelligence is the increase in management skills required to take advantage of that intelligence.

This brings us to the next major feature of a storage network—the software needed to manage and administer it.

As you can see from the discussion on buses and backplanes, the decision of which switch or what HBA to buy isn't a trivial one. Price alone is hardly the way to go about it. But like server technology generally, the cost isn't simply the sticker price on the gear. There is also the amount of time that must be invested in the care and feeding of any network—and storage networks intensify this requirement.

Orchestrating the Arrangement

The management of these complex devices and interconnections can be summed up in a five-point list:

1. Storage resource management (SRM)

2. Storage network management

3. Policy management

4. Data management

5. Virtualization

Let's take a closer look at these areas of management.

Storage Device and Network Resource Management

This is essentially product management, where the products are the disk arrays, network appliances, and tape libraries. A wide range of tools is available to give an administrator insight into the utilization of storage assets. Job monitoring and notification as well as reporting are key elements of SRM.

Managing the network is generally a discrete SRM function, with specific attention paid to network utilization, identifying bottlenecks, and optimizing resources in place, as well as helping plan for upgrades as driven by demand.

Data and Policy Management

These tools enforce decisions that govern the amount of data users can store, and how it will be grouped and accessed as well as protected. Latency in delivering data is a key factor for containing storage costs, and policy management automates the process of moving data into less costly storage. Recoverability requirements are defined as part of the data management practice, and these thresholds trigger policies for data groups.

Virtualization

Virtualization is to storage networks what Logical Volume Management (LVM) is to server-attached storage. It's a way to declare and modify disk resources to servers without handling everything at the physical level. Early in my career as a database administrator, I had to physically carve up raw disk partitions, declare them to the database engine with their slash-dev address, and decide specifically which ones to mirror. When LVM showed up in HP-UX, I was amazed at how much easier my job was. This meant I could administer more servers in the same amount of time, and therein is the value proposition of virtualization. The same number of administrators can manage an ever-expanding network of connections and devices.

John Cordelis, Total Storage Manager for IBM Canada, says, "What we want to see administrators do is use Storage Tank, install volumes on every server at their maximum size, say 2 terabytes. Then, as they use it, they can simply add more devices to the Tank without having to reconfigure their volumes server side."

Other vendors have similar ideas. HP, EMC, and Network Appliance all offer storage virtualization at the disk or hardware level. VERITAS has a virtualization offering at the host level.

A storage network is almost never from a single vendor; it's made up of components from a number of providers. The overall solution must fit the unique requirements of each site while conforming to the general standards in order to interoperate. It's a fine line and a great deal to expect. The concepts that I've introduced in this chapter will help you design a storage network that is optimized for the kinds of usage you expect, and allow you to tailor that design as your needs change.

Summary

For some, this chapter will have been a straightforward review of standards and products involved in different networked storage solutions. For others, the comparison of Fibre Channel and Ethernet in the context of OSI layers may be a new way to sort out the different components and their behavior.

How bits move within a computer and across a network are the key elements that any storage network designer or administrator has to understand. Contention makes for bottlenecks that affect performance, and the need to integrate software, hardware, and services from many vendors introduces complexity—which is difficult to manage. Virtualization is turning many of the products into logical resources that can be more easily administered, after the installation is designed and the equipment acquired.

"From the ground up" implies that we appreciate the importance of the things we plug in to make up a storage network. From this chapter, you should be able to more easily segregate fiber from copper, Ethernet from SCSI, and Network Attached Storage from a Storage Area Network.

The cornerstone concepts to take from this chapter relate to the digital data transfer rate (aka bandwidth) and how it's calculated. Theoretical throughput is theoretically interesting. From this chapter, you should have a better sense of how to measure the capacity of each link in the storage subsystem chain and evaluate its impact on your data stores.

The network is indeed the computer, and the move to storage networks is an evolutionary step in enterprise computing. In this chapter, I've clarified a potentially bewildering array of products and terms. At this point, you should be ready to move on to the next level of detail.

CHAPTER 2

Hard Disk Technology

IN THIS CHAPTER, I'll get into the guts of any storage network—the disk drive itself. In 2002 and 2003, there was a quiet revolution going on in drive technology (pun intended). The move from parallel Small Computer Systems Interface (SCSI) drives and faster Advanced Technology Attachment (ATA) drives to serial ATA and serial SCSI was well underway. However, the myriad factors to be balanced in order to arrive at an intelligent design for a useful storage network increased rather than decreased over that period. In this chapter, I'll attempt to build an understanding of the fundamental disk components. You should also see physical implementations of the concepts introduced in Chapter 1—specifically the role of standards, interoperability, and examples of how logic is ever being pushed from the CPU to the device over an increasing distance at higher speeds.

In any case, as I drill down into the drive itself, you'll see the relationship between the hardware, software, standards, and performance limitations that have been identified and will be overcome as the storage business matures. I'll also try to demonstrate how to look beyond a snapshot of the vendor products on the market in any given period. By the end of the chapter, you should be comfortable considering the various makes of drives and interfaces and how they might be assessed for any given networked storage solution.

To accomplish this, we'll start with one key question and ferret through the technological considerations that affect the answer. Because enterprises and users generally consider storage to be a forgettable commodity and thereby overlook its complexities, I thought the best way to approach this component was from the standpoint of what could go wrong with it, and why.

Dissecting a Drive

As the primary remaining electromechanical component in a computing solution, the disk drive has one very appalling drawback—it wears out, breaks down, and quits. Given the second law of thermodynamics, we can hardly expect anything else. But the mean time between failures (mtbf) for a disk drive is *way* shorter than that for any of the other components in a storage network, or a desktop computer for that matter (see Figure 2-1).

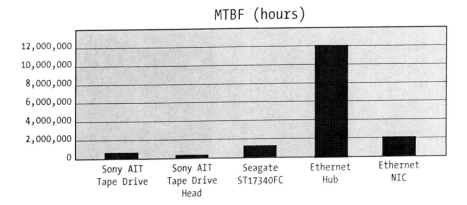

Figure 2-1. The mtbf rates for key computing components

Common sense will explain that the underlying reason for this is the "mechanical" nature of a disk drive. Electronic components, properly cooled and provided with an uninterrupted supply of power, should have a lifespan measured in years, not months. A disk drive has tremendous demands placed on it, all of which contribute to the profile of characteristics that make selecting them kind of interesting.

Mechanical Components

Disk drives are made up of platters that spin on a spindle and read/write heads that move to precise locations on the platter by way of arms (see Figure 2-2). The platter spins quietly at rates between 3600 and 15,000 revolutions per minute. The heads are positioned by the arms at a specific sector, and this movement is measured by the seek time, typically between 9 milliseconds and 4 milliseconds. The entire assembly resides in a hermetically sealed (airtight) unit called the *housing*. The instructions directing the location to access are provided to the drive by the on-board controller. This is a logic board solidly mounted to the housing and interfaced to the internal drive components via a ribbon cable. The external connectors for power and integration with the hard disk controller is typically guided by way of a plastic snap-in interface.

This generic description of a hard disk is actually a pretty fair way to depict the disk technology itself: interchangeable commodities that are differentiated on the basis of speed, price, and lifetime expectations. If you put a bunch of them together, you have Just a Bunch of Disks, or JBOD, and this can form the basis for your storage network.

The hard disk technology itself is generally identical. The differences in the competing offerings are in the controller technology that interfaces to the hard drive and the built-in support for that standard by the drive mechanism itself. Of course, there are significant differences between IDE and SCSI drives—specifically, the cabling, command set, and transfer modes.

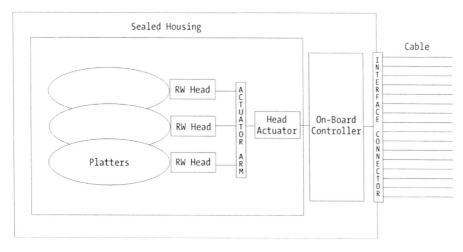

Figure 2-2. A representative hard disk

What Could Go Wrong?

I think one of the best ways to approach hard drive technology is to consider first the effect of things going wrong and second what specific things could go wrong. By and large, the impact of a hard disk failure is the same—a loss of access to data. In some cases the data is "lost" for good, and in others it may be recoverable from the doomed drive. Because the "storage" part of storage networks implies being able to retrieve your data, this is a very poor outcome indeed. So that begs two questions: What could go wrong, and what can be done to protect against it?

More than 60 percent of hard drive failures are mechanical in nature. Given the often continuous rotation of platters around the spindle at between 3600 and 15,000 revolutions per minute, it shouldn't come as a surprise that bearings crack or motors give out. These are probably the most easily imagined failures.

My Head on a Platter

The read/write head positioned just above the media surface on the platter has a clearance that is known as the *flying height*. Again, it's easy to imagine this gadget hovering just above the platter, zipping along the arm to find the right location to write or read data. What is pretty impressive is the lack of distance between the rotating platter and the read/write heads—in 2003 around 5 microinches, or five 1 millionths of an inch. The read/write heads are positioned on both sides of the platter, so rather than relying on a physical device like a spring to keep the head from making contact with the platter, an air bearing, or cushion of air, is used to separate the platter and head. In the event that the head makes contact with the platter, say due to a shock like a drop off an airplane seat tray, a head crash can occur. This is the "Russian roulette" of the hard disk world, as the drive might shrug off the event or become completely unusable. It depends on exactly what operation was occurring, on what sector of the disk, and the importance of the data located there.

From a ground up perspective, it's worthwhile to note that the platter is made up of a substrate or rigid base material, which could be aluminum or glass. That substrate is then coated with an ultrathin media layer. This layer is capable of storing magnetic charges polarized in one direction or another.

As the head, which contains an electromagnet, passes over the media, the electric current moves from one side of the head to another at that location; the direction of the movement or "flux" provides the basis for determining whether the bit is considered off or on.

Visualize the platter spinning under the head positioned at a specific position. For a particular segment of the concentric circle known as the *track,* if something has been written to the disk, it will be detectable to the read/write head as a pattern of polarity: up, down, up, down, down, up, up, up, where up is say south-north polarity and down is north-south polarity.

Inconveniently, these flux patterns don't translate directly to bits and bytes. To interpret these signals, an encoding method is defined to translate the magnetic pattern or flux transitions written on the media layer. Whereas an optical drive used pits on the drive to reflect the laser and represent an off or on bit, magnetic drives detect changes in the polarity known as *flux reversals.* These are read as voltage spikes and picked up by the read/write head for subsequent translation.

To avoid having an aggregation of polarity in one direction, which would tend to make for one larger magnetic field, some flux reversals are added to support field separation. The mechanism for determining which field represents what bit is called *clock synchronization.* By reducing the number of flux reversals needed for synchronization, and packing more reversals per linear inch of track, the density of the disk is increased. It's through these mechanisms that the same number of platters, heads, tracks, and sectors have allowed tremendous increases in storage capacity.

Improvements in detection of flux reversals have allowed exponential increases in the amount of data that can be stored in the same size physical drive.

A floppy drive uses the Modified Frequency Modulation (MFM) encoding scheme as did early PC hard drives. Run Length Limited (RLL) encoding or variations on this encoding scheme are used in IDE and SCSI drives. These are typically not features that differentiate drives from a buyer's perspective, but to help gain an appreciation for why disks fail, I thought to include this treatment of how hard disks work.

What is more frequently experienced than a mechanical failure or catastrophic head crash is the aggregation of bad sectors. *Bad sectors* refer to the areas of the disk that can't be successfully written to or read. The existence of bad sectors on a disk isn't a sign of poor manufacturing quality—drives are shipped with defect lists on the drive, which tell the system which areas aren't to be used. Like any electro-mechanical device, weaker areas of the disk that might have been okay when shipped from the factory over time can fail and become unusable. It's then necessary to update the defect list so that sector or area of the media layer is avoided. Bad sectors are frequently referred to by the operating system or disk management utilities as *bad blocks*.

Unfortunately, blocks tend to go bad in batches, which can look like the drive is failing right in front of you. When you operate a server farm or networked storage facility, you'll have blocks going bad every day. Like potholes in a busy street, they need to be avoided or filled in to avoid problems or delays.

Fitness to Task

From the discussion of how a hard disk works (or fails), you should now be able to see how the various characteristics of a hard drive might affect your choice of which to use. SCSI devices are engineered for higher temperatures and to allow management of more devices on a single chain. ATA/IDE devices are cheaper and may be more appropriate in a scratch disk scenario. SCSI connectors themselves better support hot swapping, in which an IDE array would require powering off the drive before swapping it out. Like most things in the computing world, there is no one right answer.

Not So Fast

As I discussed in Chapter 1, data transfer rate is a pretty significant metric when it comes to benchmarking computing performance. If you treat all disks as being equal, you would be forced to assume that their transfer rates are very similar as well. This is hardly the case.

In the same way that specifications (classes) dictate the rules governing the production of particular products (instances), you need to understand the various specifications that govern the construction of hard disk drives. And there are quite a few to be addressed.

In 2004, the following specifications existed for manufacturers of hard disks who wanted to create products for the mass market:

- ATA/IDE

- Serial ATA

- SCSI

- Serial SCSI

- EIDE/ULTRA-ATA

Programmed I/O, or PIO, is the most widely supported interface for PC technology. There are five PIO modes, with increasing data transfer rates, as listed in Table 2-1.

Table 2-1. Programmed I/O Modes and Transfer Rates

PIO Mode	Maximum Transfer Rate (MBps)	Standard
Mode 0	3.3	All
Mode 1	5.2	All
Mode 2	8.3	All
Mode 3	11.1	ATA-2, Fast ATA, Fast ATA-2, ATA-3, ATAPI, Ultra ATA, EIDE
Mode 4	16.6	ATA-2, Fast ATA-2, ATA-3, Ultra ATA, EIDE

The Programmed I/O modes all use the CPU to handle disk read/write operations. A bus mastering approach to ATA/IDE drives was introduced with the Direct Memory Access (DMA) modes first made available in DMA mode 0.

Scuzzy

Within the parallel SCSI definition there are a variety of offerings, based on different versions of standards and with quite different performance characteristics. The initial SCSI narrow bus channel, familiar to Mac users in the 1980s, consisted of an 8-bit-wide cable capable of moving bits at 5 MHz of up to speeds of 5MBps. Further refinements in the SCSI specification increased throughput accordingly. For instance, fast SCSI (SCSI-2) involved an increase in the standard to support 10 MHz transfer rates. Wide SCSI referred to a change in standard that allowed 16-bit instead of 8-bit bus width in the parallel transfer of bits from one device to the next. It also increased the number of devices to be supported on a single SCSI chain to 16. Compared to the 8-bit-wide, 8-device maximum, 5 MHz top clock speed enabled by the SCSI-1 standard, this was fast and wide indeed. Now, 32-bit SCSI drives can achieve 160 and 320 MBps and 64-bit SCSI yields as much as 532MBps.

SCSI-2 also introduced extensions to the command set that ran over the SCSI bus. Enhancements to the command set included tag queuing to allow multiple requests to remain outstanding for all the devices on the bus. With SCSI-2, up to 256 commands on each LUN can be backed up, like airplanes waiting to land at O'Hare.

Serial vs. Parallel Interfaces

The ribbon cables used to connect traditional drives are a very accessible model for describing parallel connectors. Older ATA/IDE drives had 40 pins; UltraDMA drives had the same 40-pin connectors but required 80-pin cables to support the back channel error correcting code to indicate that data had been received or sent with the correct checksum. Interestingly, although parallel paths were originally far more capable of higher throughputs a few years ago, serialization has caught up and surpassed the data transfer rates supported by their parallel counterparts.

For ATA/IDE and S/ATA drives, one key difference in the interface is the size of the cable. The distinctions between the two are shown in Table 2-2.

Table 2-2. Cable Comparisons Between Serial and Parallel ATA Drive Interfaces

SPEC Channel	Devices per Drive Interface	Pins per Drive Interface	Cable Diameter	Max Length
ATA/133	2	70	2"	18"
Serial/ATA	1	7	.3"	40"

As you can see from the max cable length, external enclosures under the ATA/IDE standard were greatly constrained. And although 40 inches is hardly the maximum 25 meter length you could get with SCSI (HVD), it at least allows for the interconnection of dedicated disk enclosures.

Parallel movement of bits across multiple wires is a long-established method for increasing data transfer rates. Each clock cycle the bits move across the entire parallel band in unison. In the case of a 16-bit SCSI bus, 16 bits move down the wire at a time. Unfortunately, a couple of characteristics of having all those electrical impulses line up affect the clock rate at which they can be transferred. For instance, the ATA/100 standard supports clocking speeds of up to 50 MHz. When this cycle count is exceeded, the impulses get jumbled and unreadable when they hit the end of the bus.

Similar to the problems underlying the detection of flux reversals on hard drive media, detection of the electromagnetic signals is really the work performed by the drive controller and the on-board controller for the disk. However, given the exponential increases in clock speeds (does anyone remember the Pentium 90?), it's faster and more economical to change the data transfer standards from parallel to serial in order to take advantage of the higher clock speeds.

As an analogy that will help you visualize this phenomenon, imagine a football team positioned at the top of a flight of stairs. The stairs are wide enough to support 16 players, and the coach has instructed them to jump down one stair each time he blows the whistle. The rate at which the whistle blows is the clock speed, the width of the stairs is the bus width, and the length of the stairway equates to the length of the bus.

For a SCSI chain, the terminator at each end is like having a landing at the beginning and end of the stairwell. If the bus is unterminated, the effect is roughly like coming to the end of the stairs and jumping into a big hole. Not good. The other consideration is how much energy it takes to jump along the stairs. At some point, the players will become too tired to move. This is similar to the maximum length specified for a cable. With ATA/IDE, the maximum length is 18 inches and various flavors of SCSI extend that length from 1 meter to 25 meters.

Now, let's assume that you want to move as many players as you can down the stairs in the shortest period of time. If the whistle can be blown 50 times a second (or 50 million times a second as implied by MHz), 900 players can be moved along the 16-player-wide stairway. On the other hand, if players can take each stair at 1500 times a second, even going in single file allows 66 percent more players to be moved in the same time period.

By taking full advantage of the faster clock speeds supported by today's technology, the Serial/ATA and SCSI standards allow faster throughput rates than those generated by using the traditional parallel approach.

As well as moving faster along the bus, the on-board controllers are capturing intelligence that is useful for monitoring drive health and performance.

That's SMART

The Self-Monitoring Analysis and Reporting Tool (SMART) is built into both IDE and SCSI drives. In the case of SCSI, SMART reports impending failure as a state—okay or ready to fail. IDE drives, on the other hand, provide a significant number of features that can be monitored directly.

In the interests of providing information rather than promoting products, drive manufacturers also offer SMART utilities. Seagate, for instance, offers SeaTools, online, desktop, and enterprise versions, for a range of disks such as ATA, SCSI, and S/ATA drive types. The online version of SeaTools allows you to download a plug-in to your browser and test the drive and file systems for your Windows clients and servers.

As you can see in Figure 2-3, the utility queries the SMART status of the drive and in this case returns a no thresholds exceeded message.

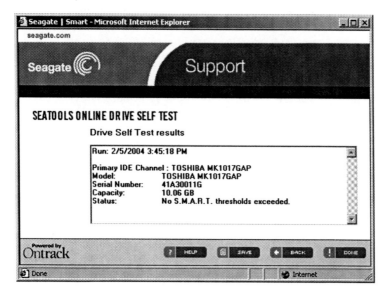

Figure 2-3. Result screen from the Seagate online version of SeaTools

In this case, the drive tested was a Fujitsu 20GB drive; as an ANSI standard, SMART utilities are expected to work on all SMART-compliant drives.

One third-party utility that is readily available on the Web for evaluation is called Active SMART. Although it isn't freeware, a downloadable trial version is available from http://www.ariolic.com/activesmart. I have no idea who these folks are, so this isn't really a plug; I just happen to like their utility, and for purposes of explaining SMART, I'll profile Active SMART in this section.

SMART provides reporting hard disk factors as described in Table 2-3.

Table 2-3. SMART Attributes Monitored by Active SMART

Factor	Description
Current pending sector count	The drive nominates sectors to be replaced where errors have been detected. This count indicates the number of sectors potentially to be marked as bad.
Off-line scan uncorrectable sector count	Number of bad sectors during previous offline scan.
Power cycle count	Displays the number of times the drive has been turned on.
Power on hours count	Drive life is measured in mean time between failure (mtbf). This metric tells you how many hours the particular drive has been on.
Raw read error rate	The higher number, the better. Points to problems with read heads or media layer.
Seek error rate	The read/write head must be positioned correctly to operate. This value should be high for a properly working slider and arm.
Seek time performance	Actual seek times for the drive.
Spin retry count	If the drive fails to spin on the first attempt, retries are counted here.
Spin up time	Averages the time it takes for the drive to go from off to full rpm.
Start/Stop count	Another good indication of wear, this tells you the number of times the drive has been spun up. This value is different from power cycle for drives that "sleep" when inactive.
Throughput performance	The metric for actual drive performance in moving bits on and off the disk.
Write error count	Shows the number of write errors encountered by the drive.

This can be reported in text form, as shown here:

S.M.A.R.T. status

Date: 14 October 2003 11:00:46

Drive model: IC25N010ATDA04-0

Serial number: 170173X4884

Capacity: 10.1GB

Drive interface: IDE

Drive temperature: 30° C

Attribute Name	Threshold	Value	Worst	Raw Value
1 (01) Raw Read Error Rate	62	100	100	0
2 (02) Throughput Performance	40	100	100	0
3 (03) Spin Up Time	33	129	129	47244640257
4 (04) Start/Stop Count	0	100	100	523
5 (05) Reallocated Sector Count	5	100	100	0
7 (07) Seek Error Rate	67	100	100	0
8 (08) Seek Time Performance	40	100	100	0
9 (09) Power-on Hours Count	0	98	98	1096
10 (0A) Spin Up Retry Count	60	100	100	0
12 (0C) Power Cycle Count	0	100	100	185
191 (BF) G-Sense Error Rate	0	99	99	2
192 (C0) Power-Off Retract Count	0	100	100	8
193 (C1) Load/Unload Cycle Count	0	98	98	22136
194 (C2) Temperature	0	183	183	257698562078
196 (C4) Reallocation Event Count	0	100	100	0
197 (C5) Current Pending Sector Count	0	100	100	0
198 (C6) Off-Line ScanUncorrect.Sector Count	0	100	100	0
199 (C7) Ultra ATA CRC Error Count	0	200	200	0

When administering the SMART reporting utility, you can set specific configuration values that you wish monitored and the threshold at which they will be reported. In Active SMART, this is done by double-clicking the blue information symbol to pop up the configuration setting as shown in Figure 2-4. Figure 2-5 demonstrates how you set a reporting threshold.

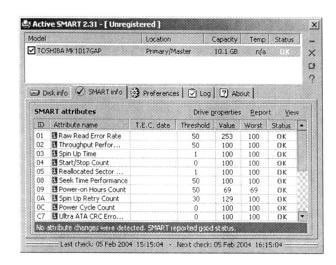

Figure 2-4. Quick view screen of SMART attributes

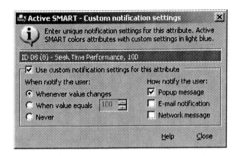

Figure 2-5. Setting a user-configurable seek error rate reporting level in Active SMART

Although it's always nice to be able to take the time to browse the status of the devices you administer, one real value of the SMART utilities is the auto-notification process. In Active SMART, for example, you can set up e-mail, pop-up, or network communication to a specified user to flag that a device is having trouble. This is shown in Figure 2-6.

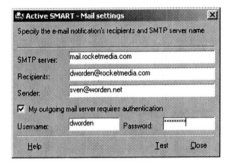

Figure 2-6. E-mail and messaging options for Active SMART–monitored devices

Of course, there are other SMART reporting tools on the market. From this brief description of how one of them works, you should be able to gain an appreciation for how much your SMART-enabled drive would like you to know about its health.

Addressing the Disk

Certainly you should be able to see that there is quite a bit of engineering under the hood of a hermetically sealed hard disk unit—which, as I've said, translates to things that can go wrong. In any case, it's necessary to look at how the disk is made available to the system.

ATA/IDE Drives

In the old days, say the 1980s, PC disks were addressed by their CHS factors—the number of cylinders, heads, and sectors contained within the drive. These factors taken together were known as the *geometry* of the disk. The number of sectors were identical on each track, which meant the sectors on the outer tracks were longer than the sectors on the inner tracks.

The original designers of the 80x86 architecture decided, quite reasonably given the technology of their day and that Moore's Law hadn't demonstrated its amazing staying power, to restrict the number of sectors to 64, heads to 256, and cylinders to 1024. With sector sizes of 512 bytes and numbering from head one (not counted as head zero), this puts the maximum disk size supported by that BIOS at 504 megabytes, which is to say smaller than a file recording a 22-minute DVD. Clearly ways had to be developed to get around this and take advantage of the increased storage capacities hard disk manufacturers were putting into their products. The point I want to make here is not one of history, but of the role played in translation software to support new drive capacities and capabilities. In the same way that 16-bit software introduced restrictions in file sizes and numbers that could only be alleviated by a 32-bit architecture, and those limitations overcome by the increased addressing size supported by 64-bit architectures, management of disk resources and file systems is affected by the operating system or service to which it is dedicated.

The traditional means of accessing a hard disk resource by sending it a command for read, write, and so on was through the Interrupt 13h (Int 13h) call to the BIOS. Inherent in this approach is a restriction to 24 bits for passing through the location of data, even when using logical geometry translation and large block addressing. These include 10 bits for the cylinder number (max 1024), 8 bits for the head number (max 256), 6 bits for the sector (63 discrete numbers, 1 through 63 with the first track [0] reserved for label information). This resulted in the 8.46 gigabyte restriction for hard disk addressing. To get beyond this, Int 13h extensions were defined.

In the 1990s an innovation called *Zoned Bit Recording* (ZBR) was introduced as a means of increasing the amount of data that could be written to the same disk. ZBR takes advantage of the increased length of the outer tracks to add more sectors. ZBR also handles removing bad sectors from the available sector list. The net effect of Zoned Bit Recording is that the physical number of heads, cylinders, and sectors is no longer supported by the BIOS of most systems, especially Wintel PCs. Instead a logical geometry is used to describe the hard disk to the system.

The hard disk controller logic is required to handle the translation of the logical geometry into the true physical geometry of the disk.

Hard Disk Performance

While I'm on the topic of the physical characteristics of general hard disk technology, it's useful to consider the role of the key metrics that marketing types put on the outside of a hard disk box to vie for a buyer's attention. These are described in Table 2-4.

Table 2-4. Key Drive Metrics Defined

Attribute	Definition
rpm	Revolutions per minute—a floppy drive goes 300 rpm, whereas high-speed hard disks go 15,000 rpm.
Seek time	The time required to position the actuator arm and read/write head to a specific sector, typically less than 9 milliseconds.
Cache	The onboard memory store that allows the host bus adapter to store more data from the drive than has been physically read or written.
Throughput	The amount of data that can be read from or written to the drive in a specified time period. Generally this is a function of the interface (ATA, SCSI, Fibre Channel) and the theoretical rate of that transfer will be higher than the speed at which the drive can physically read and write data.

The rpm and seek time form the mechanical latency factor of the disk. That is the amount of time required to position the head and for data to pass under the head so it can be written to or read from the cache.

Another refinement developed to support larger drives is Logical Block Access (LBA) support, commonly supported by BIOS chips manufactured after the mid 1990s. This is the typical auto-detected hard disk option in which the logical block and sector number are used to address data on the drive. However, this poses another limitation, also as a result of the number of potential bits that can be used to calculate an address—specifically the ATA 137.4 gigabyte limitation.

The ATA interface specifies 28 bits for the sector number when communicating between the disk and the host system. As a result, a hard disk can't exceed 2^{28} or 268,435,456 sectors of 512 bytes each—hence the 137.4 gigabyte limitation.

The T13 technical committee responsible for the ATA/IDE specification is reviewing proposals to expand the addressing to 48 bits or more. This would allow access to petabytes of storage, which is to say 1024 terabytes or a million gigabytes, more or less.

SCSI Addressing

The physical and logical disk geometry for SCSI disks is the same as for IDE drives. Other than conforming to the higher specifications for wear and tear on the arms and spindles, SCSI disk internals are identical to ATA/IDE and Fibre Channel disks. In fact, it isn't the inside of the disk that is much different at all, it's the drive controller and interface that make the disk different. This isn't to be confused with the host bus adapter, which often gets referred to as the controller.

Physical cylinders, heads, and sectors also play a part in the operation of SCSI drives, as does the translation from physical to logical, although not for the same reason as with an ATA/IDE drive. With SCSI-based disk subsystems, three additional factors need to be added into the mix: the physical and logical device numbering, cabling and termination, as well as the command set.

The Small Computer Systems Interface is more than just an interface to a disk subsystem. The SCSI specifications support a richer command set for instructing devices for any given operation. Combined with their ability to support up to 16 devices per channel, compared to ATA/IDE's two, and better machined internals, SCSI drives have long enjoyed a reputation as being superior to their ATA/IDE counterparts.

Each device on a SCSI chain must be uniquely identified. The SCSI host bus adapter is usually device zero and is internally terminated. This means to add four disks to a SCSI chain, each one must be given a unique number from 1 to 16, and the end of the SCSI chain must be terminated within 4 inches of the last device. Typically this looks like a cap-on interface as shown in Figure 2-7.

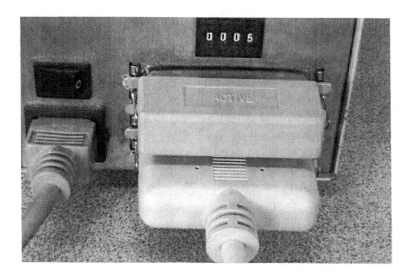

Figure 2-7. An external SCSI enclosure with a terminator

SCSI Devices

The Logical Unit Number (LUN) on a SCSI bus is a unique physical device address for each SCSI device. This is very straightforward in a direct-attached storage topology in which the SCSI device is accessed by only the one host to which it's physically attached. SCSI tape and CD jukeboxes can also be part of the storage subsystem. In some cases, these LUNs are used to identify different media or partitions within the hardware device itself. This process of allocating multiple LUNs within a discrete storage device can be applied to networked storage as well.

When you move across the storage devices on a network, a new requirement emerges. One is the ability to potentially share the device with more than one host. The other is to break the storage device into smaller logical units and to assign those smaller units discretely to any one of a number of hosts. This is accomplished through a technique known as *LUN masking*.

LUN Masking

This capability supports the exclusive assignment of a given LUN to access by an authorized list of hosts. Put another way, it ensures that only authorized hosts can attach to a given LUN by hiding unassigned devices from discovery or attachment. LUN masking may be implemented on the storage device, the hosts, or a consolidation device like a SAN server. Different methods are offered by various vendors of network storage offerings.

Implementation of LUN masking on host devices means that either the operating system or the host bus adapter queries and reveals only LUNs that have been configured for that server. This is most appropriate in an environment where you have common access and administration control of a small number of servers.

LUN masking can also be done at the storage device level. Where dozens of servers connect to a single network appliance, this would consolidate the LUN masking administration to the storage device, and no action would be taken at the host level. The servers would query and reveal all of the LUNs available to them, which would be restricted at the storage level.

A consolidated storage administration tool that supports storage virtualization would be the most efficient approach when many servers need to attach to multiple storage subsystems. Because one of the key benefits of networked storage is reduced administration, the selection of where to do the LUN masking depends on the topology of your servers and storage devices. This will be covered in greater detail when I address SAN fabrics and their administration in Chapter 9.

SCSI Command Set

As I mentioned earlier in this chapter, one key difference between SCSI and ATA/IDE is the capabilities represented by the command set inherent in the specifications themselves. The SCSI command set can be used over bus technologies other than SCSI itself. Fibre Channel, USB, and IEEE1394 disk devices have also taken advantage of the utility of the SCSI command set. One key difference between the SCSI command set and the original ATA command set is in the support for synchronous or clocked data transfers. With the ATA-2 specification, synchronous data transfers were supported by ATA/IDE drives.

Asynchronous data transfers in the context of a read/write operation to a hard disk device refers to the process of sending bits across the bus and awaiting handshaking confirmation to indicate they were properly received. Synchronous data transfers involve the allocation of a specific time for the transfer to occur before the next operation is initiated. The clocking rate must be identical for all devices in the process, but the effective throughput is increased with synchronous transfers as bits are pushed down the bus like parachutists in an old war movie. One gets pushed out in set increments of time, rather than after checking that the last guy out was successfully on the ground before letting the next guy out the door.

The SCSI command set can be used independently of the physical connection scheme used to transfer the commands. As a result, USB, IEEE1394, and Fibre Channel all have offerings that incorporate the SCSI command set.

Summary

At the heart of any storage network is a platter spinning at high speed, with a read/write head ready to be positioned over a specific spot on the disk to detect very faint electromagnetic signals. As network storage capacity grows, the number of these platters and heads increase, and with it the complexity for things to be managed, and things to go wrong, increases exponentially.

After reading this chapter, you should have gained a sense for how hard drive technology leverages increases in CPU speeds as a reflection of Moore's Law. You now have some insight into how the compromises and constraints imposed in a technical standard may have to be revisited to avoid capping another technology at an arbitrary level. Levels that one year seem far off into the future a short time later are causing congestion on the network.

After considering the similarities rather than the differences between SCSI and ATA/IDE disks, you should realize that one technology is not actually superior to the other. Everything revolves around its suitability for the task to which it is put, in the same way that direct-attached, network-attached, and fibre-attached storage are all neither good nor bad. The yardstick is how well it does its job and, just as importantly, for how long.

Perhaps the most difficult thing for technically oriented people to do is to let go of hard-won lessons and experiences gained from time. From this chapter, you now have a sense of the principles that underlie storage networks and an appreciation for just how quickly one "superior" technology can replace another, only to be back on the statistical top a short time later.

For the future, there are several "articles of faith" for you to heed. Capacities will grow. Prices will drop. Standards will be extended and/or replaced. New configurations will make the impossible practical. And distance will become less and less relevant.

The key message of this chapter is that the technology itself contributes to change. An increase in CPU clock speed gives rise to a more effective scheme for moving bits between a controller and a drive. Larger storage capacities stress transfer rates and mechanisms. Newer cabling techniques lead to faster transfer rates. By understanding the lowest level bottlenecks in each of the components, and becoming aware of developments that affect those choke points, you can design, implement, and administer an effective storage network.

CHAPTER 3

Networks

IN THE SAME WAY that we went deep inside the hard disk in the previous chapter in order to build from the ground up, we'll now get into networking technology with the same objective. Whereas the disk has the host bus adapter to control it, and the packets must be handled along the bus and then read and written from memory, networks perform the same functions over a longer distance than an 18" IDE ribbon cable. That said, there are still tremendous conceptual similarities, which is why I wanted to approach the material in this fashion.

By the end of this chapter, you should have a sense of the prevailing standards governing each aspect of a network, including the host bus adapter (aka network card), the cabling or physical medium, protocol definition and its role in handling traffic, as well as addressing and routing considerations.

By all means this is a lot to cover, but after we've sorted out the components, relevant standards, and their implications, I believe you'll be much more comfortable with how networks are constructed and the implications for networked storage. In the same way that you've come to know the differences between SCSI and IDE/ATA, by the end of this chapter you'll be familiar with the cornerstone differences between the various flavors of Ethernet and be prepared for how they compare and contrast with Fibre Channel.

IEEE 802

In the beginning there was Ethernet. If I remember correctly from the late 1970s and early 1980s, the good folks at the University of Hawaii, Bob Metcalfe (the founder of 3Com), and all those involved in the DIX (Digital, Intel, and Xerox) initiative worked in parallel (and sometimes at cross purposes) to arrive at a solid basis for networking computers—including the physical implementation in the form of network cards, wiring, and drivers.

As you've already seen, it isn't enough in this area to have one vendor decide to establish a viable way to get the job done and publish it (arguments about NFS and VHS aside). Our industry benefits from the collaboration of engineers and experts in the form of industry committees and the creation of standards that may then compete for attention, adoption, and compliance. The body responsible for defining much of the relevant standards regarding computer networks is the Institute of Electrical and Electronic Engineers (IEEE). And when it comes to Ethernet, those standards fall under the 802.x series of specifications.

Let's have a brief look at the standards and what each covers. It may strike you as odd to begin with the cable that links two network cards, but this relates to layer 1 of the ISO model for networking, and in the interests of consistency I think it makes sense to begin at the port. Because the port must match to the wires in the physical cabling, which in turn drives a set of constraints, I think you'll find it interesting to work up the stack from that foundation.

For more detail, you can download the IEEE document "802-2001 IEEE Standard for Local and Metropolitan Area Networks Overview and Architecture" (`http://standards.ieee.org/getieee802/`). Quoting from that document, the following is their definition of the scope of the 802 standard as it relates to data networks:

> *An IEEE 802 LAN is a peer-to-peer communication network that enables stations to communicate directly on a point-to-point, point-to-multipoint basis without requiring them to communicate with any intermediate switching nodes. LAN communication takes place at moderate-to-high data rates with short transit delays, on the order of a few milliseconds or less.*

Now that's good technical writing! It specifies the topologies that are in scope—namely peer-to-peer as opposed to, say, host-slave—and extends that topology to support either one-to-one or one-to-many communications. It then goes on to use adjectives that can withstand the test of time as in "moderate-to-high" data rates. As you'll remember from the discussion on disk transfer rates—what is now considered moderate was unimaginably high a few short years ago. In any case, I offer the foregoing as a truly inspiring example of how standards can survive and adapt without becoming so vague and general as to be unimplementable.

To quickly delineate the areas of concern within the 802 set of standards, and then pull out the ones relevant to this discussion, I've assembled Table 3-1.

Table 3-1. IEEE 802 Standard Family

Number	Description
802.1	Higher Layer Protocol Working Group Overview and Architecture, Internetworks, Bridging, and Management
802.2	Logical Link Control Working Group
802.3	Media Access Control and Physical Signaling for CSMA/CD
802.4	Media Access Control and Physical Signaling for Token Ring (MAP)
802.5	Media Access Control and Physical Signaling for Token Ring (IBM)
802.6	Media Access Control and Physical Signaling for MANs
802.7	Broadband Technology Advisory Group

(continued)

Table 3-1. IEEE 802 Standard Family (continued)

Number	Description
802.8	Fiber-optic TAG
802.9	Media Access Control and Physical Signaling Isochronous LANs
802.10	Security
802.11	Medium Access/Physical Layer—Wireless
802.12	Medium Access/Physical Layer—100VG—Voice/Video over 10BT
802.13	No one wanted this one—go figure
802.14	Cable Modem Working Group
802.15	Bluetooth Personal Area Networking
802.16	Broadband Wireless Access Study Group

The wireless standards covered by 802.11 have followed their own parallel path of increasing throughput by refining the standards, whether the 2/11 Mbps standard that a great many folks now have installed in their homes or the higher speed 802.11g with 50+ Mbps burst transfer rates. What is more applicable from a storage networks standpoint is the role of the cable or physical medium used to interconnect the devices.

Premise Wiring

As anyone possessed of a certain level of critical self-awareness will tell you, it's impossible to spend a decade, let alone two, in a particular profession without making some regrettably bad decisions. One of these for me was a decision taken in 1988 to not install Category 5 cable in my employer's head office building.

Being responsible for the introduction of PC workstations and the first Local Area Network file systems for this company, I decided on Novell and Compaq 386s interconnected by Ethernet for the PCs and Token Ring for connecting to the mainframe. As part of this process, we went to a competitive bid for the network installation and provision of cable. One of the low-cost bidders recommended Category 3 over Category 5 cable. It was more than sufficient for the Ethernet installation of 1988. Alas, it had to be pulled out a few years later in order to support the 10/100 transfer rates supported by copper some 10 years later.

The moral to this story is that infrastructure investments can last a long time, or more precisely that they should and will if you evaluate the technology with an eye to the future. What we didn't see in the late 1980s was, of course, the practical impact of Moore's Law in a larger setting (I know this isn't the first time I've brought this up, but it is a major theme of this book). Each of the components leveraging off advances in the others makes the entire chain faster over time.

Cat 5 cable is an example of one investment that has and can continue to provide significant value.

Category 5 and More Cable

The two most influential standards affecting cabling are the EIA/TIA 568 and ISO/IEC 11801 specifications. Based on the combined work of the Electronics Industry Association (EIA) and the Telecommunications Industry Association (TIA), the second edition of ISO/IEC 11801 was published in 2000 and provides for the specifications and design criteria used by cable manufacturers, suppliers, network architects, building designers, and pretty much anybody else who has an interest in physical wiring.

Cat 5 has been supplanted by Cat 5e and Cat 6. Work has begun on Categories 7 and 8. Let's take a look at your basic cable, how it's made and how it works.

100-ohm data cable is your vanilla-flavored patch cable, consisting of four pairs of 24 American Wire Gauge (AWG) copper wires, each wrapped in a plastic coating and twisted together, then as a group sheathed in a polyvinyl chloride (PVC) or halogen-free flame retardant (HFFR) jacket.

Although installers care about bending radius and other physical attributes of cable, from a storage network standpoint, you care more about the constraints the inherent physical medium places on you. Cable is designed to carry electrical transmissions from sender to receiver. The realities of building wiring means wires cross each other, traveling tortuous routes around elevators, lighting fixtures, and AC outlets. Basically, data cable has to deal with myriad sources of electromagnetic interference.

Similar to the problems overcome in hard disks by the "squeezing" of flux reversals into ever-smaller configurations, data cable has to support increasing transmission speeds. The original Category 3 cable I bought for my corporate Ethernet was rated for up to 16 MHz. Category 5 cable in contrast is rated at 100 MHz. Category 6 cable is rated for up to 250 MHz. Specifications being developed for Category 7 cable are at transmission frequencies up to 600 MHz.

The rated MHz rate equates to the number of bits that can be moved per second down the wire. Of course, as you've seen in the system bus and disk connectors, there are considerations other than the raw bandwidth supported by the physical medium; however, it's nonetheless a limiting factor.

I don't want to take a single metric for cable performance and jump to an unsupportable conclusion. Instead, given that copper wire, Ethernet, and their associated technologies are likely to form a part of at least some Storage Area Networks, let's take a minute to examine the characteristics of the physical transmission medium.

Wire is a conductor and is used to move electrical impulses from a sending device to a receiver. It serves as a passive pathway for electricity. That's its job. However, even the most passive transmission medium has some properties that affect electrical current. When evaluating wire, you need to keep these characteristics in mind:

- *Impedance:* The passive resistance of the medium to the current measured as a ratio in ohms.

- *Attenuation (signal loss):* The reduction of magnitude of a signal as it travels through the medium, expressed in decibels (dB).

- *Diameter:* Measure of the outer diameter of the wire, expressed in millimeters (mm).

- *Weight:* Measure of the amount of weight for a given distance.

- *Gauge:* In North America, AWG is used to describe copper conductors. The higher the number, the thinner the wire.

- *Construction:* Factors such as shielded or unshielded, dielectric or jacket properties to prevent current leakage, and of course the conductor itself, which might be copper, a copper alloy, aluminum, aluminum alloys, and aluminum- or copper-clad steel.

  Copper wiring is by far the most commonly used in data networks. Typical cable found in any building wired for a network in the past 10 years is likely to be Category 5 unshielded twisted pair, with four pairs of wire under a polyvinyl chloride jacket. This jacket is nonplenum grade, which refers to its propensity for giving off toxic fumes when aflame. Plenum-grade jackets are required by certain fire codes and have Teflon added to reduce smoke generated if the cable catches fire.

- *Unshielded twisted pair (UTP):* Plain old copper wire consisting of insulated conductors wired in pairs and twisted to reduce electromagnetic leakage and corresponding signal loss. This generic cable is useful for all voice and data device connectivity where limited ambient electronic noise is generated from the site.

- *Shielded twisted pair (STP):* The Cadillac of copper wire, shielded twisted pair has the same insulated copper wire pairs twisted together, but cladding the pairs under the jacket is a shielding (typically braided wire) to prevent or reduce electromagnetic interference.

Gigabit vs. 100Base-T Wiring

It's always fascinating to me to see the level to which marketing folks will go to promote products. For example, on a recent visit to Microcenter, I spied a flamboyant yellow package containing a fluorescent Gigabit Ethernet patch cable. Sure enough, the package was described as designed to support Gigabit Ethernet connections. Right across the aisle was a box containing a Gigabit Ethernet card that guaranteed compatibility with 10/100 network devices.

Gigabit Ethernet cards require all eight wires to be present in the end-to-end linkages between devices to achieve their optimum speeds. Some few Cat 5 patch cables for example have four wires—two pairs of twisted cable. If this cable is used, the network card will only support throughput speeds equivalent to 100Base-T.

Once again, you should be able to see how there is no part of a storage network that can simply be taken for granted. Although you may not have been in a position to purchase the specific cabling used in your premise wiring, you must become acquainted with both the resources you have to work with and their behavioral characteristics.

Connectors

The typical end to a Cat 5 cable is known as the *RJ-45 connector.* Incorporating the eight wires of four twisted pairs, the RJ-45 has been standard issue on Ethernet cards for many years. Larger than the RJ-11 telephone connector, it's only remarkable in that an improperly attached or a slightly detached connector (perhaps as a result of a strain on the connection from pulling) can result in signal loss. It's important to remember that the physical connection from one device to the other is affected by electromagnetic interference, and on a more basic level to retries due to less-than-optimum electrical transmission.

Patch panels, cables, and connectors must all be in top condition for the first layer of the ISO stack to function. When evaluating your local area for a storage network, be sure to inventory the physical medium and satisfy yourself that you won't be building on "feet of clay."

Ethernet Network Cards

Now that you've been introduced to the most basic element in the networked storage world, it's time to move up a layer—to the data link. This work is handled by the Ethernet card, and in the same way that copper wire deals with electricity instead of bits and bytes, the data link layer handles the interpretation of physically transferred signals. It's at this layer that the electrical traffic management of the card ensures that the transmission was successful and that the received signals can be interpreted into data. First, however, it's important to understand how a generic Ethernet card handles the physical signals prior to their interpretation as bits, bytes, and datagrams.

Media Access Control

Once upon a time, Ethernet cards were produced by a bunch of uncoordinated manufacturers, and it was possible to acquire two controllers that couldn't work together because they had the same address. To fix that, a 48-bit Media Access Control (MAC) address was developed, and now every Ethernet card manufactured is assigned a unique address. In the same way that a 48-bit address for hard disk sectors gives you a tremendous amount of storage, this addressing strategy for MAC addresses means that you can have a tremendous proliferation of Ethernet-enabled devices.

On a physical to data link level, the MAC protocol is where the real work of networking gets done. Not only does the network card have to reliably send and receive signals, it must also detect when the coast is clear using Carrier Sense Multiple Access/Collision Detection (CSMA/CD) and throw away bad datagrams when it receives them.

Although bits may be zero or one, the electrical impulses that travel down a network wire aren't off or on. Instead they are high and low voltages, more akin to Morse code dots and dashes. If you visualize an Old West telegraph operator, feverishly translating each set of long and short sounds coming down the wire, you can appreciate the role your Ethernet card plays at the data link layer.

Perhaps an even better metaphor is shown in Figure 3-1. Here you see two people chatting at the same time. As they talk, sound waves are created, transmitted, and received through the air. The sound waves are translated into phonemes, alphabetic and punctuating sounds that are ultimately transcribed by the brain into language and words. In this way, information and commands such as "Hey!" or queries like "Huh?" are communicated. All this requires protocols and ways to work up the stack from the transmitted energy to some kind of message that can be understood.

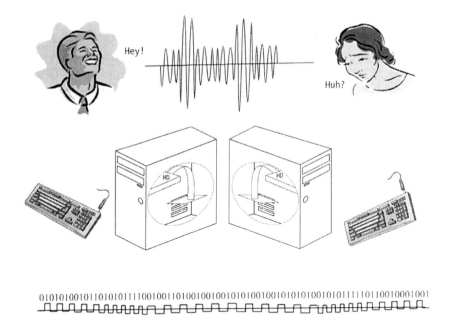

0101010010110101011110010011010010010010101001001010101001010111110110010001001

Figure 3-1. People and machines communicate using interpreted waves.

People share the air when they talk, and they can interrupt, override, and request a retransmit with conventions such as "I beg your pardon?" This isn't at all dissimilar to the way data communications networks function.

As they type, characters creating words and sentences of information and instruction must be translated into codes and ultimately electrical impulses that travel through the transmission medium to their destination.

Whereas the sound waves that can be processed by people fall within a range of about 20 hertz to 20 kilohertz, simple networks transmit over wires at 1 to 100 megahertz, wireless networks operate at 2.4 gigahertz, and visible light shows up at between 430 and 760 trillion hertz. As you probably remember, *hertz* is a measurement of wavelength from crest to crest per unit of time. 1 hertz is one complete wave each second. As you progress through this chapter, you should become pretty comfortable with the characteristics of wavelengths as they affect communication of all types.

Getting back to the Morse code metaphor, not only does each specific dot or dash have to be captured, but it must be transcribed and interpreted as part of a stream of impulses that become letters, translated into words and finally a coherent message.

The data link layer does all this and more, and unlike the Morse code operator, your Ethernet card must also be able to request retransmission of garbled or misunderstood dots and dashes. To make matters worse, other devices are transmitting at much the same time, and allowances have to be made for the possibility that a good set of dots and dashes were intended for another address. These have to be discarded.

The 802.3 ISO specifications define exactly how the electrical signals conveyed over an Ethernet are to be interpreted as data.

The MAC protocol calls for the encapsulation of an SDU with a 14-byte header and a 4-byte cyclical redundancy check (CRC) after the data. This is known as a *frame, packet,* or *datagram,* and is depicted in Figure 3-2.

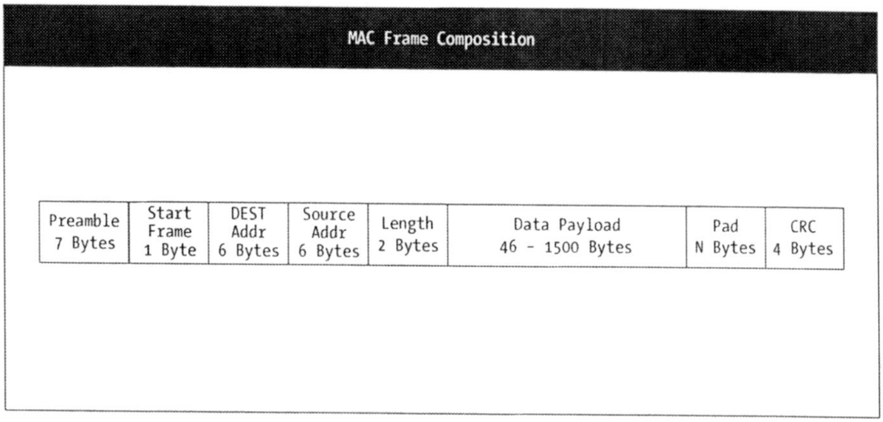

MAC Frame Composition							
Preamble 7 Bytes	Start Frame 1 Byte	DEST Addr 6 Bytes	Source Addr 6 Bytes	Length 2 Bytes	Data Payload 46 – 1500 Bytes	Pad N Bytes	CRC 4 Bytes

Figure 3-2. Breakdown of a MAC datagram

The header contains the destination address, source address, and type of datagram. The data may contain between 46 and 1500 bytes of data. The implications of this maximum transmission unit, or MTU, becomes quite significant when looking at the performance characteristics of GbE. The 4-byte CRC is used to determine that the packet hasn't become corrupted in transit.

In terms of handling the communication along the network, the card first must sense whether any other traffic is on the wire. This is the Carrier Sense part of CSMA/CD. For the purposes of this discussion, it also addresses the Multiple Access (MA) part of the equation, as without contention from multiple sources, there would be no need to sense for traffic or provide Collision Detection (CD).

To ensure the coast is clear, a minimum gap of 9.6 microseconds must occur between transmission of frames. This allows the receivers to settle after other frames have been handled. Prior to sending the new frame, an 8-byte preamble is transmitted. This allows the receiver to achieve a digital phase lock loop. This is the mechanism by which the data clocks are synchronized between the transmitting and receiving devices. During the processing of the preamble, the receiver detects the correct phase but may also not have properly handled all of the bits in the preamble. This is fine, because until the preamble ends with its last byte, no actual data is being sent. On receipt of the last byte of the preamble, known as *pattern 11,* the receiver begins to process the datagram, turning signals into bits and bytes.

Header Construction

The header consists of a 6-byte destination address, a 6-byte source address, and a 2-byte type field that identifies the IP protocol used to frame the data, including the MTU size. The destination addresses may be in unicast, multicast, or broadcast modes, depending on whether the target is a single recipient, group, or all nodes. Source addresses are used by bridges to create filter tables.

Bridges and Switches

The practice of broadcasting packets as implemented in Ethernet LANs results in a great deal of contention as nodes are added to the network. Although only the station addressed analyzes the packet addressed to it, a station must evaluate the addresses of all packets it receives. There are several mechanisms to reduce the number of stations on a given LAN segment while still allowing interconnection of segments as appropriate. At the MAC layer, this device is a *bridge.*

The net effect of a bridge is to reduce the number of packet collisions by breaking the network into smaller segments, evaluating packet addresses and only forwarding those that are intended for another segment. Bridges are less common in networks these days than routers, which perform the same function at a higher layer; however, switches are commonplace.

Layer 2 switches generally move packets from one address to another on the basis of the MAC addresses; however, unlike a hub, a switch associates a port with that address and forwards packets between the two, rather than over the network as a whole. These port switches are the most common implementation of an Ethernet switch. However, switches can be uplinked or interconnected to create segment links.

Datagrams

The minimum size of an Ethernet data payload is 46 bytes. If the actual packet is less than that, it's padded with nulls to round it up to the minimum size. The maximum size is 1500 bytes. It should be remembered that Ethernet as a standard was defined prior to 10Base-T, let alone 100Base-T or Gigabit Ethernet. Similarly to the geometry translation of hard drives and the addressing schemes to incorporate previously unimaginable hard disk sizes, this is another example of where a specification lasts longer than the technological constraints in force at its inception.

802.1Q and 802.1P

In keeping with the traditional approach of working around unforeseen limitations in the standard, an extension known as IEEE 802.1p supports the tagging of frames. The P tag value adds a 3-bit tag to the 12-bit Q tag, allowing devices to interpret both the quality of service for such a tagged packet and its priority.

By 2003, vendors had jumped on these tags to accomplish various things, including larger packet size definitions; however, they weren't implemented in a structured top-down way. As a result, enabling Q and P features on any given card might generate unexpected (read undesirable) results.

As you can see, TCP/IP and Ethernet aren't actually synonymous. In fact, the TCP/IP protocol suite is often used to refer to a great deal more than the protocol used to encapsulate bits and move them between devices.

TCP/IP Routing

Routers are layer 3 devices responsible for moving packets from one logical network segment to another based on their protocol. Through TCP/IP, a router may be used to move packets from a local Ethernet segment to xDSL WAN and back. Within a storage network, it's highly likely that you'll want to segregate traffic between servers while offering access to a large number of client workstations.

Physical network design and logical addressing has a significant impact on the performance of any storage network. Although the key to good network design is an understanding of your data traffic, effective segmentation is achieved through routing and addressing.

Using TCP/IP routing means that devices on fiber-optic and copper data networks can be linked, as well as interconnect with other WAN devices. There are three kinds of routing when using TCP/IP:

- *Static:* The path for each network is entered into a table defining routes, hops, and router addresses. The tables are maintained on both routers and connected computers.

- *Default:* The default gateway receives all packets that aren't addressed to participating devices on the local network.

- *Dynamic:* The Routing Information Protocol (RIP) is a dynamic way of creating and updating routing tables.

Even the most straightforward home network uses a combination of these routing and addressing schemes. A Linksys router for high-speed Internet connections, for example, provides a default gateway to the Internet for all participating workstations. The built-in switch handles traffic between the workstations, without being routed externally. Connections between external hosts and local stations are typically routed dynamically, but static tables can be defined for a particular host—at, say, the office or university.

Nonroutable Protocols and Addresses

A nonroutable protocol, such as NetBEUI, doesn't include a mechanism for handling logical addresses at the network layer. Originally designed for very small, contained LANs, NetBEUI was most commonly used in Windows-based peer-to-peer networks.

Additionally, TCP/IP allows for the creation of addresses that aren't routable, meaning they can't be forwarded from one network segment to another via a router. These networks beginning with 192.168, 172.16 to 172.31 and 10 are typically used to assign DHCP addresses to requesting workstations. For example, a DHCP client may be granted the address 10.0.0.2. It can only connect to a workstation with a different address, such as 200.1.1.200, via a Network Address Translation (NAT).

To avoid having to provide a unique IP address to every workstation on a network, while allowing them to connect to hosts outside their local segment, a router supporting NAT will append a port number to their IP addresses when forwarding the packets between the external and internal devices. NAT services require the client IP address (say 10.0.0.2) to be recorded in a mapping table containing both original source and destination addresses as well as the source and destination TCP/UDP port numbers. The combined activities of all these network components, as well as the review of datagram addresses and review of lookup tables, is shown in Figure 3-3.

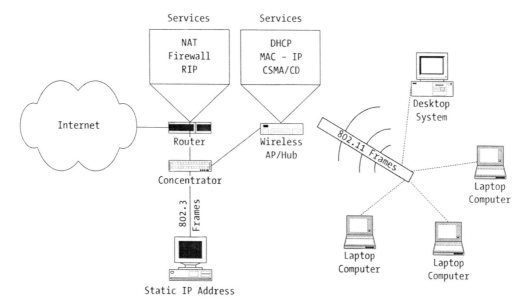

Figure 3-3. A typical client-server router topology

These lookup operations require the router to operate a store-and-forward service. Packets are written to a buffer, evaluated, and handled as appropriate. This introduces a delay in the propagation of signals between client and server. This delay is referred to as *latency*. In Chapter 6, you'll get a chance to explore the effect of latency and timeout on access to disk resources.

Firewalls

One method of protecting access to data resources at layer 3 is through a firewall supporting packet filtering. Packet filtering allows the specific identification of port numbers and IP addresses to be allowed to connect or to be blocked from connection. The tables identifying the specific addresses to be connected or blocked are referred to as *access control lists* (ACLs), and connections can be bidirectional, unidirectional, or disallowed altogether

In the context of a storage network, this service is identified only as yet another packet inspector contributing to the latency between sender and receiver and therefore the performance of your storage network overall.

ISO Layer 1 and Layer 2

The physical and data link layers of the OSI model are the unsung heroes of a copper wire Ethernet network. The relationship between the hardware and the process of converting electricity into logical data is one that people frequently take for granted—until something goes wrong. It's at these two layers that performance tuning can make or break scalability, robustness, or usability of a storage network.

The issues introduced in this chapter should be carefully considered by anyone evaluating Gigabit Ethernet as the potential solution for their networked storage. Additionally, you should have an appreciation for the work performed at the foundation level of the network. This will become more significant when fiber networking characteristics are compared to those inherent in copper-based technologies.

The interconnection of fiber and copper networks, the linkage of storage clients with servers, and the behavioral characteristics of distributed file systems all have their roots in TCP/IP and Ethernet. From this chapter, you should have a better appreciation for the physical underpinnings of a basic storage network, and be prepared to build on that understanding as I introduce components that move up the OSI stack.

Where the OSI model deals with physical media, signal handling, and data links in two layers of specification, Fibre Channel encapsulates these concerns in five discrete layers. Although storage media is the primary notion defined in the term *storage networks*, the interconnection of devices is far from trivial. The purpose of the next section is to review the underlying capabilities of Fibre Channel, its roots, and its components.

Fibre Channel from the Ground Up

The first fiber optics–based communications networks were developed in the 1970s. These featured (then) blistering transmission rates of 10s of megabits per second. The next exponential increase in speed was achieved in the 1980s by moving to single-mode optical fiber technology.

One of the most interesting things about researching storage network technologies is the lack of clear, comprehensible introductory material for laser-based communications. Adding to the confusion is the proliferation of support for other network technologies, such as copper cable and multiple protocol support for such things as IP and SCSI, and the net effect is one of alphabet soup. More acronyms (and bad metaphors) than you can shake a stick at.

I have dedicated this book to the premise that you can't effectively design and deploy virtualized storage services without understanding the principles of the contributing components. The approach, as you've no doubt picked up on by now, is one of laying a foundation and building from the ground up.

In the case of Fibre Channel, I want to approach this from the standpoint of the origin of the technology, and then move to the most prevalent implemented standards. From there I'll discuss the various options and implications of the technology. The main objective is to provide sufficient background so that you can weigh the complexity and potential contribution of any given solution set against the others, allowing you to decide the correct one for a given situation.

Let There Be Light at the End of the Tunnel

Fibre Channel was originally an all-fiber-optic technology. The ISO committee that decided such things determined that when support for copper media was added to the feature set, a new name shouldn't be adopted. Instead, the spelling was changed to the French *Fibre* to differentiate the new Fibre Channel specification from the older, fiber optics–only version.

That's enough of the marketing spin on things. At the heart of how Fibre Channel operates are the types of lasers and their application to communication. I found it difficult to grasp the implications of various Fibre Channel offerings without first gaining an appreciation for the underlying componentry, so I'll introduce you to those concepts here.

Point-to-Point Essentials

The most simplistic Fibre Channel communications occur between two dedicated devices. Point-to-point topologies allow these two devices to be directly connected. One example might be the case of a server and a storage array. As well as the issues specific to fiber-optic networking, you have the additional considerations of converting the electronic signals to pulses of light and back again.

On the server-side you need a host bus adapter to provide the translation of digital signals into light pulses. Each HBA contains within it a laser capable of generating light pulses in a specific frequency of light. The pulses are carried along the fiber-optic cable and detected by the receiving device. Detection and translation of the pulses back into digital signals is achieved using an optical modulator.

It was interesting to me to note that during my research for this book there seemed to be a consistent theme in the materials regarding Fibre Channel. Generally speaking, there is a presumption of a background in physics and technology in treating either product in marketing materials or whitepapers. My assumption is that you, as a reader of this book, aren't in a position to design or construct Fibre Channel components. I'm going to go one step further and assume that although you likely have a solid grasp of networking and direct server administration, you aren't already "up to speed" with the elements that make up a hybrid SAN/NAS storage solution.

Extrapolating from those assumptions, I think it's worthwhile to spend a bit of time setting the context for fiber optics generally, and then relate them to the specific product options available to a networked storage administrator, manager, or designer.

If the treatment of the science is too rudimentary for you, feel free to skip ahead.

Lasers One Oh One

Lasers, light amplification by stimulated emission of radiation, are now found in virtually every business and home. The intricacies of designing and building these products are even more formidable than those involved in fabricating semiconductors. However, in the same way that it's necessary to understand the process by which bits move from the CPU, through memory, along a network, and into a disk drive, it's also necessary to understand how light is used to convey data.

In a laser, electrons are stimulated by radiation. Electrons in a particular atom, left to their own existence (wherever that may be), have a specified ground-level state of energy. Their orbit around the nucleus of an atom occurs at a particular level of energy. H_2O, for example, has a lower level of energy as ice, and it gets excited if you put an ice cube in a microwave and warm it to water or boil it until it becomes vapor. As the stimulation is reduced or stops, the electrons revert back to their ground-level state and in doing so shed the extra energy in the form of photons. Imagine invisible photons being given off as the proverbial snowball melts in hell, for example. These photons are always one specific color, meaning they are at a uniform wavelength and they are emitted coherently, or in lock step with one another. With a burst of radiation, stimulating a sufficient number of electrons that are then allowed to revert back to their ground-level state, a pulse of laser light is generated.

The kinds of lasers used in Fibre Channel environments are semiconductor lasers, designed to use very low power and take up very little space. There are essentially two kinds of lasers used as part of optical Fibre Channel networks—shortwave and longwave lasers. In this case, shortwave can be specified as between 800 and 900 nanometers (nm). That is to say, the wavelength of the photons released from a shortwave laser is less than a millionth of a meter in length. Longwave lasers generate between either 1260–1360 nm or 1430–1580 nm wavelengths.

As the power and type of laser pulse used directly affects the distance and performance characteristics of the Fibre Channel network, I'll identify the various alternatives here.

There are three kinds of lasers used to generate fiber-optic pulses:

• Distributed Feedback (DFB)

• Fabry-Perot (FP)

• Vertical Cavity (VCSEL, pronounced "Vixel")

DFB lasers are used for longer haul distances such as Metropolitan Area Networks or cross-country telecommunications. Fabry-Perot lasers were the first solid-state lasers used by Fibre Channel. They are typically limited to 10 km maximum distances. VCSEL lasers are used in Local Area Networks and SAN implementations.

There are also OFC (short for Optical Fiber Control) and Non-OFC lasers to consider. OFC circuitry incorporates high-power lasers, and where a disconnection of the path occurs, such as a disconnected cable, the transmitter is disabled to avoid inadvertent damage from, say, someone looking into the network cable. Non-OFC lasers are lower powered and less likely to cause damage. Shortwave lasers are of the type typically found in CD-ROM devices. These are Class 1 lasers, which, by definition, are low powered and not dangerous.

Photodiodes

The job of the photodiode is to convert light energy to electricity. A photodiode is at heart simply a diode. Semiconducting materials, such as silicon, become conductive when they are treated with impurities, a process known as *doping*. When silicon is doped with a tiny amount of arsenic, it creates a conductor for negative charges. Silicon doped with gallium or boron creates a positive conductor. A gallium arsenide–doped silicon semiconductor can be used to create a p-n junction diode. The positive and negative conductive qualities allow current to flow or be stopped depending on the direction of current applied to it. This is the function of a diode, to allow current to flow in one direction but not the other. A photodiode has a very thin p layer on top of the doped semiconductor. The thickness of the layer is a function of the wavelength of light to be detected.

The construction of an avalanche photodiode and its components is shown in Figure 3-4.

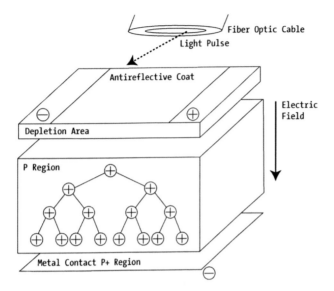

Figure 3-4. A photodiode

As the light pulse strikes the p active area, the photodiode generates an electric current. In this way, light signals are converted to the long/short, off/on, one/zero combinations representing digital data for processing by the electronic components of the system.

Propagation over Distance

As the distance between the sender and receiver grows, you can see how the signal will tend to degrade. Naturally, there are ways to boost the signal in order to propagate it over longer distances as required. For instance, to link point-to-point gigabit or faster fiber devices over distances longer than 550 meters, regeneration is required.

The refractive index of a medium is the ratio of the velocity of the propagation of an electromagnetic wave compared to a vacuum. In the case of fiber-optic cable, particular attention is paid to the refractive index of the silica or glass that makes up the core of the cable. This is the relationship of the ability of the cable medium to support the transmission of light and is analogous to the conductivity of copper for electricity.

As a pulse of light enters the cable, depending on the angle at which it enters, it's either refracted into the cladding or reflected at the core/cladding boundary. It's the reflection that allows the propagation of the pulse down the cable. This is depicted in Figure 3-5.

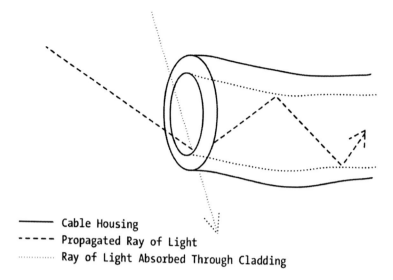

Cable Housing
Propagated Ray of Light
Ray of Light Absorbed Through Cladding

Figure 3-5. Path of light at the entrance of a fiber-optic cable

Although the loss of energy as the photon travels along fiber is nowhere nearly as great as occurs with an electrical signal through copper wire, there is still some loss or attenuation with fiber optics. In the case of shortwave fiber, the maximum distance that a Fibre Channel can reach is 500 meters. The longer wavelengths can support 10 km distances and beyond using signal regeneration and amplification techniques (which I'll discuss a bit later).

In the shorter wavelengths, attenuation in fiber optics is about 2.5 dB/km with a wavelength of about 850 nm. Contrast this to the .25 dB/km of a 1550 nm fiber-optic connection, and the reasons for the shorter maximum cable length becomes apparent. The contributors to fiber signal attenuation include the following:

- *Absorption loss:* Photons may be absorbed or converted to heat by molecular vibrations.

- *Scattering:* Interactions of photons within the glass.

- *Bending:* Physical stress on the cable, for example, weight suspended between two points, can cause a previously acceptable curve to begin contributing to cladding absorption.

Intrinsic absorption is caused when photons interact with one or more components of the fiber itself. This is a very low contributor to attenuation at wavelengths between 800 and 1600 nm. Extrinsic absorption is caused by impurities such as dissolved water in the form of hydroxyl or OH ions. At one part per million, an impurity causes 1 dB/km of attenuation at 950 nm. 1.3 and 1.550 micrometer wavelengths aren't affected by this type of absorption. Other types of impurities include metallic impurities in the silica fiber. Fabrication quality control can reduce these levels to below 1 part in 10^{10}.

Scattering occurs when some or all of the optical power in one mode is transferred to another. The principles of reflection and refraction govern all light and obviously affect the way in which fiber optics have been implemented. The loss of signal strength due to refraction of the light as the fiber cable curves and bends is an exact science.

Bending occurs as stress is applied on the cable over time. Although fiber cable is significantly lighter than copper, it isn't weightless; and as a tensile load is applied to the fiber, it's possible for cable to "kink" past the minimum bend radius specified by the manufacturer, resulting in sudden attenuation.

Loss Through Dispersion

Unique to fiber-optic cable is a form of signal loss known as *chromatic dispersion*. A number of key concepts must be explained before you can understand the factors that govern the performance of a fiber optics–based network.

The signal or pulse of light that travels down the fiber-optic cable is considered to be of a particular wavelength or color, as I've already discussed. Unfortunately for us, the real world isn't quite as convenient as the theoretical, so in practice the pulse will actually be spread out across the wavelength. This is represented in Figure 3-6.

As you can see, the bulk of the signal is centered at the designated wavelength, but the edges move out past what is called the *finite spectral width.* Each wavelength has an associated spectral width.

Because I've already introduced the notion of packets earlier in this chapter, you should be able to see how this pulse represents a specific bit of information. The pulse is directly analogous to an off or on bit in a data stream. Since it's an optical bit, rather than an electrical signal, it behaves differently than a bit moving along a bus or copper wire. In this case, the pulse moving down the cable will tend to broaden, and may even get so wide that the bit is rendered undecipherable at the other end. This makes the bit unreadable, and requires a reject/resend or NAK interaction between the receiver and the sender. I get into this process later in the chapter. At this point, however, let's stay focused on the loss of coherence in the laser signal that is known as chromatic dispersion.

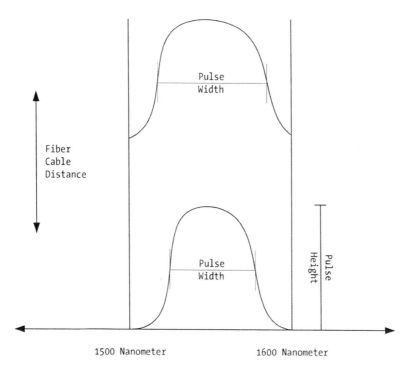

Figure 3-6. A representative 1550-nanometer pulse

The important concept to grasp at this stage is that although light and fiber provide considerable advantages over electronic signaling, there is an increased cost in complexity. The relative merits of the two networking technologies as they contribute to both NAS and SAN implementations will become apparent when I compare the pros and cons of the two at the end of this chapter.

The considerations you face when evaluating a fiber-optic network are very different from those you weigh for one based on high-speed copper technologies. There are good reasons why the telecommunications industry elected in the 1990s to deploy fiber technologies for the long distance trunk lines for voice and data.

At this point, let's resume our review of fiber-optic components and how they work.

The 3 Rs

In fact, regeneration of optical signals involves more than just catching the signal, interpreting it, and retransmitting it with renewed energy. Media converters can be used that provide regeneration, reshaping, and retiming of the optical pulse.

Regeneration in the classic sense involved converting the optical signals to electrical impulses, amplifying them, and converting them once again to optical pulses. More recently, optical amplification has allowed for all optical signal boosting.

EDFA

By doping fiber with erbium, optical signals can be amplified without opto-electric conversion. The term used to describe this is *Erbium Doped Fiber Amplification* (EFDA). Erbium is a rare earth element that excites the light when it passes through the section of the fiber cable that has been treated with it. This replaces the need for expensive converters and repeaters for long-haul fiber networks. As the light passes through the EDFA-doped section of fiber, external power is applied, and the net result is a pumping up or excitement of the atoms in the fiber. The energy from the atoms is transferred to the photons representing the digital signal, effectively amplifying them without distortion.

EDFA was developed for telecommunications networks to avoid the expense and performance hit of translating signals from light to electricity, boosting their power and transforming them back into optical signals. As storage networks consolidate data stores beyond the campus or metropolitan area, as is increasingly feasible with fiber-optic technology, EDFA devices are being incorporated into enterprise storage designs. I only introduce the term here to indicate the extended reach that is possible using fiber optics and convey a sense of the complexity and corresponding expense of devices necessary to achieve it.

Modes in Fiber-Optic Cable

One of the other common terms used when evaluating host bus adapters and Fibre Channel configurations is the mode of the cable. Two types of cable are available: single mode and multimode. Single-mode fiber has a core diameter of 8 to 10 microns and has been fabricated to optimize the transmission of a particular wavelength. Multimode fiber allows multiple wavelengths to be transmitted concurrently.

Referring back to Figure 3-5, you can see the angles of incidence or certain transmission paths along which the light travels. Each of these paths is called a *mode* and the number of modes supported in a particular cable is determined by its construction.

The characteristics of single and multimode cable contribute to specific application requirements. Multimode cable is thicker and, as mentioned, already supports multiple concurrent wavelengths. However, single-mode cable, being thinner, provides for higher bandwidth than multimode. Single-mode bandwidth can be several thousand MHz per km, whereas multimode bandwidth typically tops out at 500 MHz per km or lower depending on the distance between the points.

For the purposes of this discussion, bandwidth and capacity are the two key considerations for a fiber-based storage network. Bandwidth affects the transmission speed between the two points and will be most important for applications such as digital video streaming. The higher the bandwidth, the faster the point-to-point transfer of data. Conversely, *capacity* means the amount of traffic that can be supported on a particular fiber link. Think of the number of lanes on the highway rather than the speed limit.

Multiplexing Signals

In both copper- and fiber optics–based networks, multiplexing is used to increase the amount of traffic that can be carried on a particular cable.

Time Division Multiplexing

One method for carrying multiple signals over a single mode channel is through time division multiplexing (TDM). In this case, each input is given a slot, and the different signals are combined in a sequence. This is shown in Figure 3-7.

Figure 3-7. Multiple inputs multiplexed into a single channel by time slot

Clearly, synchronization of both senders and receivers must be achieved for TDM to function effectively. This method becomes less efficient in the event of intermittent traffic from stations, as the time slot is made available to the connection, whether used or not.

Wavelength Division Multiplexing

It's cheaper to put more wavelengths on an existing fiber-optic network than it is to add a new cable. With this axiom in mind, Fibre Channel manufacturers have turned to using wave division multiplexing (WDM). In this way, higher bandwidth is achieved on an existing fiber-optic cable by increasing the number of wavelengths concurrently transmitted along the fiber. The number of multiplexed wavelengths ranges from typically 8 to as many as 16 in the case of coarse wave division multiplexing (CWDM) to vastly more using dense wave division multiplexors. Because the wavelengths are comparatively spaced more widely than when using dense wave division multiplexing (DWDM), CWDM muxes are frequently less expensive. An example of how CWDM and DWDM occupy bands of wavelength is shown in Figure 3-8.

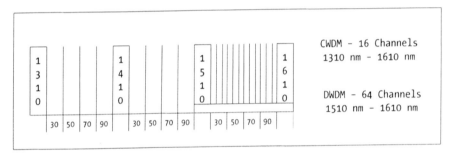

Figure 3-8. Increased bandwidth of a single-mode fiber with coarse and dense wavelength multiplexing

CWDM: Coarse Wave Division Multiplexing

By segregating the fiber-optic signals into 20 nanometer widths, multiple channels are created under the coarse wave division multiplexing scheme. CWDM multiplexors on the market support 4, 8, or 16 channels in the 1270 or 1310 to 1610 nm range.

Because colors, as perceived by the human eye, are reflections of a range of wavelengths, this analogy is often used when describing multiple channels handled concurrently along a fiber-optic cable. CWDM allows for the multiplexing of up to 16 "colors" along the same cable.

DWDM: Dense Wave Division Multiplexing

By using temperature-controlled lasers to create the signals, DWDM-capable transceivers can isolate wavelengths more finely than the 20 nanometers called out in the CWDM specification. In fact, DWDM as specified supports channels that are .8 nm apart.

The density in this case is proportionate to the number of wavelengths crammed into the fiber. A typical DWDM multiplexor can accommodate as many as 100 channels.

Protocol Independence

It should be noted that the techniques for sharing channels, interpreting multiplexed signals, or amplification are completely independent of the protocols used to translate the signals into bits. At this layer, the equipment and standards are entirely about signal handling where the electric or photonic pulse isn't representative of data but instead handled according to its physical properties.

Connectors

From the discussion on dispersion and attenuation, it should be apparent to you that light loss is an important issue when dealing with a fiber-optic network. One of the most significant opportunities for loss is at the connectors between the HBA and the fiber cable or at the switch port. To minimize signal loss, lensed fiber-optic connectors were traditionally used. More recently, butt joint connector options with different performance capabilities and characteristics have been developed by vendors. The key point is that connectors play an important role in calculating your signal loss budget.

Topologies

The detailed discussion of how fiber-optic networking operates was set in the context of a point-to-point link between a sending and receiving device. Fibre Channel has some additional characteristics that make it well suited for communications and storage networking applications.

FC-AL

The original topology for fiber-optic networks was Fibre Channel–Arbitrated Loops (FC-AL). The Fibre Channel specification supports a full-duplex channel for simultaneously sending and receiving at full bandwidth. This means that a 1GB channel both sending and receiving is actually accommodating 2GB of throughput. An example of a Fibre Channel–Arbitrated Loop is shown in Figure 3-9.

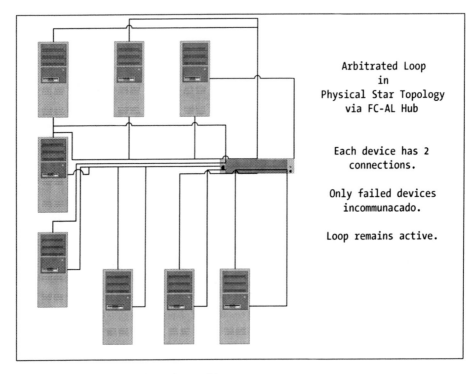

Figure 3-9. An 8-node Fibre Channel loop

Fibre Channel

Up to this point, I've discussed fiber-optic network components in a point-to-point topology. However, Fibre Channel (again, note the spelling) is more than that, and in this section, I hope to clarify some of the interconnected options that Fibre Channel enables.

First, Fibre Channel "fixes" some of the problems posed by the SCSI command set. That is, Fibre Channel allows SCSI commands to be executed over a much longer length of cable than defined earlier. Of course, part of this is due to the nature of fiber optics, but more important, it also applies to Fibre Channel over copper. Here you'll see how Fibre Channel as a standard subsumes both the capabilities of the SCSI command set, which will be defined in detail, and the transmission media used in any network. In short, Fibre Channel combines the best of both bus and network characteristics. It accomplishes this by using five layers of specification that map directly to the lower three layers of the ISO networking model.

As a protocol, Fibre Channel is block oriented and serial. That is, it doesn't require synchronization or clocking between sender and receiver. Its block orientation means that rather than handling complete files, Fibre Channel can efficiently handle data in discrete chunks, effectively supporting database and transaction operations.

At this point, let's go into how the various layers of the Fibre Channel specification support that.

FC-0 Fibre Channel Defined

The physical media specification for Fibre Channel encompasses two media types—optical and copper. The implications of single-mode and multimode fiber-optic cable are discussed under the section "Modes in Fiber-Optic Cable." Fibre Channel over copper supports both twisted-pair and coaxial cable. Although it doesn't run over a string connecting two tin cans, Fibre Channel supports pretty much any cabling you can find between the sender and receiver. Of course, there are transmission and throughput characteristics for each connectivity scheme, and part of the FC-0 level of the Fibre Channel specification defines port interconnection, transmission lengths, and allowable noise limits.

FC-1

For all of the complications in the media, connectors, and transmission capabilities for Fibre Channel nodes as specified in FC-0, there are still a number of remaining tasks to be managed in order to make the network capable of sending intelligible data. FC-1 defines schemes for the encoding and decoding of bits into bytes and includes special characters and techniques for error handling. Unlike Ethernet, Fibre Channel handles a great deal of this work at the hardware level.

Similar to the problem of ensuring a differentiation of flux polarities at ever increasing speeds in a disk drive is the problem of interpreting a flow of high and low impulses successfully as bits, and the aggregation of those bits into bytes. This is a necessary precondition for turning bytes into frames or datagrams, and it's complicated by the move to gigabit per second speeds. There are two factors that affect network performance: data speed, which I've discussed already, and the bit error ratio (BER). The bit error rate refers to the number of "wrong" bits divided by the number of bits sent.

The high and low voltage of an electrical current to signify a one or zero data value is directly analogous to the on or off pulse of light to represent data over a fiber-optic connection. Both of these interconnection schemes require the relationship of the changes in voltage or presence or absence of a pulse to a clock signal in order to make sense of the stream of impulses.

In Figure 3-10, you can see a clock signal represented as the steadily spaced rising and falling edges of the clock called out. The clock frequency determines the number of edges in a given interval. A 1 gigahertz clock allows for 1 billion intervals or one rising and one falling edge per second.

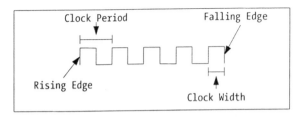

Figure 3-10. Anatomy of a clock signal

Streams of data are interpreted by overlaying the pattern of zeros and ones according to the clock. This is shown in Figure 3-11.

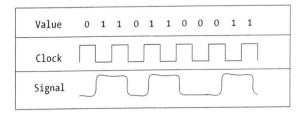

Figure 3-11. A representative bit pattern overlaid on a clock signal

The data speed is necessarily constrained by the clock rate.

Fibre Channel is an asynchronous channel for transferring data from point to point. Accordingly, in order to send the stream of impulses, whether optical over glass or electrical over copper, it's necessary to serialize then deserialize the data stream. In Fibre Channel, this is accommodated at the PHY level of the FC-1 specification by the SerDes—Serializers/Deserializers built into the semiconductor componentry of host bus adapters, switches, hubs, routers, and disk arrays.

Because the two devices separated by the Fibre Channel aren't synchronized to a clock, another means is used to set the drum beat to which the bits march. This is known as *clock recovery*.

Fibre channel devices encode a single byte as 8 bits with an additional 2 bits to establish byte type, resulting in 10-bit transmission sets. This 8b/10b technique has been designed to optimize the transmission of information across the channel.

InterSymbol Interference

Because bits are represented by high and low electrical voltages, something interesting occurs when a long string of either is sent. The copper wire over which the signals are sent can jump to a higher voltage state than the level that represents high from a bit handling perspective. Think of an electric fence pulsing regularly, then instead of an intermittent charge coming regularly down the wire, a steady current is applied for a few seconds or a minute. If you measure the jolt you receive from touching the cable while in that state, it will be higher than if you measured the voltage of the pulse during regular operation. The voltage accumulates after a certain period of time, and the wire becomes fully charged.

This also occurs with copper wire in the form of Ethernet (and SCSI) cable. When a long string of high and low voltages are transmitted, the amount of time required to change to the alternate voltage increases somewhat. This skews the clocking between the sender and receiver and can result in missed bits, which in turn results in corrupted data.

To accommodate this, Ethernet 802.3 defines a form of encoding called *Manchester Phase Encoding*. The purpose of this scheme is to ensure that an even number of high and low voltages is continuously being sent down the cable. Manchester encoding establishes the value of one as a high, and then a low combination of pulses and zero as low then high. In this way, any combination of bits will always be an even number of high and low voltages. This is known as *DC balance*.

The problem with using two signals to represent a single bit is that although it's reliable, it's inefficient. Storage networks have traditionally pushed both the speed of data being transferred and the distances over which the sender and receiver communicated. As is the case with wave division multiplexing, electrical engineers are always looking for ways to squeeze inefficiencies out of the existing equipment. In the case of Fibre Channel, the overhead allocated to coding was reduced from 50 percent to 20 percent by the introduction of the 8b/10b encoding scheme.

8b/10b

The other problem with sending a long, unchanging string of signals representing either ones or zeros is the degree of difficulty in recovering the clock by the receiver. As I indicated earlier, transitions are used in the clock recovery process, and it's a real challenge for chip designers to write the logic to recover this when there are an insufficient number of transitions. For those who like analogies, think of the number of times you've found yourself asking someone on the other end of the telephone if they were still there, just because they had taken a pause for thought.

One of the ways to ensure that the stream of signals varies is to create a coding scheme for the bits that will vary the pattern being transmitted. In the case of Fibre Channel, the 8b/10b encoding scheme is used.

This method was developed and patented by IBM. It converts 8-bit bytes into 10-bit transmission characters. There are several advantages to adding the extra 2 bits to each byte, including the following:

- Designation of the byte as data or a special control character

- Improved error handling

- Limitation of repeating high and low to a maximum sequence of 5 bits

These features in turn make it easier for transceiver designers to count on certain behavioral characteristics (e.g., a sufficient number of transitions), which allows them to more cost effectively create the circuits. Performance is optimized by eliminating the need to inspect every transmission sequence for handling instructions, instead limiting the sampling to the first 2 bits and subsequently processing only the special bytes. It's the combination of these special characters that allow the definition of frames and the subsequent assembly of bytes handled by the Fibre Channel level 2 specification.

FC-2

This is the transport mechanism of Fibre Channel, and the signaling services allow the aggregation of bytes into packets that can be directed, checked, and validated before being passed through to the intended destination.

There are five elements defined in the specification:

1. *Ordered set:* These 4-byte transmission words define boundaries using special characters, such as frame delimiters or port identifiers and status indicators.

2. *Frame:* Ordered sets are used to define start-of-frame and end-of-frame delimiters. Frames include the data payload, as well as link control data and the send/receive port addresses.

3. *Sequence:* Related frames are given sequence numbers for error control and reassembly at destination.

4. *Exchange:* Defines a set of sequences between two ports as part of a single operation.

5. *Protocol:* Services for connecting ports, logging in or out of a fabric, and describing data for upper-layer protocols such as SCSI or TCP.

FC-2 also defines classes of service to manage the transmission of data between ports. There are three classes of service under the Fibre Channel FC-2 specification:

- *Class 1:* Creates a dedicated connection between two FC ports. This allows the maximum bandwidth utilization while the connection is established, as there is no sharing or contention.

- *Class 2:* Multiple sources share a channel. Delivery of frames is acknowledged or retransmitted if the receiver is too busy to accept the frame sent.

- *Class 3:* Multiple sources share a channel, but delivery isn't acknowledged. Appropriate for broadcast information, such as a webcast or streaming video.

The transport mechanism within Fibre Channel defines, independent of the physical media, the connection between two ports, the identification of bytes and composition of frames, as well as the ordering of the frames as they are exchanged between sender and receiver.

The FC-3 definition handles the behavior of Fibre Channel when dealing with multiple ports.

FC-3

A dedicated connection between multiple ports can be created, allowing the channels to be used to aggregate the data transferred, resulting in an increase of bandwidth used and a corresponding increase in data throughput. The FC-3 layer of the Fibre Channel specification handles this process.

Additionally, FC-3 defines the aliasing scheme that allows an address to listen on more than one port. This ensures port availability for a varying number of senders. Last, FC-3 defines the multicast process for transmitting a single message to multiple ports.

FC-4

Support for multiple Upper-Layer Protocols (ULPs) is a strength of Fibre Channel and is defined by the FC-4 specification. Although there are actually many different protocols supported, note that FC-4 defines the precise ways in which Fibre Channel supports both SCSI and IP protocols.

It is this support on which I'll focus for the next two chapters, allowing you to see the relationship of Fibre Channel to SCSI and GbE Storage Area Network solutions.

Parallel SCSI, Ethernet, and Fibre Channel

Think of the traditional thick SCSI cable and its direct-attached storage heritage when you read parallel SCSI. It seems to me appropriate to have a brief treatment of the comparison between the differing interconnect models: SCSI (as a cabling scheme), Ethernet (layers 1 and 2 only, thank you), and Fibre Channel (as implemented on copper or optical cable up to and including the transport mechanism).

A good part of the difficulty posed by the convergence of protocols, cabling, and linkages involving these three technologies is the confusion that arises over the options presented to you. As I'll discuss in the next chapter, you can have SCSI commands running over Fibre Channel and fiber-optic cable. You can have Ethernet links over fiber-optic cable, and you can have Fibre Channel commands running over copper cable. It's Alice's Restaurant, where you can get anything you like. The question then becomes, "What's good here?" And to be fair, that always translates to "What do you like?" More applicably from a Storage Area Networks perspective, what is it exactly that you wanted to accomplish and within what set of constraints?

Fibre Channel over Copper Cable vs. Parallel SCSI

Whereas Fibre Channel over copper can run as far as 40 meters (30 meters traditionally), parallel SCSI cabling supports 25 meters maximum cable length. This is perhaps not a significant difference; however, when you consider the maximum number of devices supported by SCSI (15) and Fibre Channel nodes (126), the advantages become more apparent. Additionally, the maximum throughput supported by SCSI 320 is 320 megabytes per second, whereas the throughput of a 2GB FC port is 200 megabytes per second. However, because FC is specified as fully duplex, the two channels on a given host bus adapter can support concurrent throughput at 400 megabytes per second, 200 in and 200 out simultaneously.

Copper connectors for Fibre Channel come in two flavors—HSSDC (short for High Speed Serial Data Connector) and DB9. The DB9 serial connector uses four pins to mate to the twisted-pair cable used as the physical medium. Newer HSSDC2 connectors are designed to support transfer rates as high as 5 Gbps and occupy a smaller form factor, making it easier to fit more connectors into a blade or switch.

Parallel SCSI connectors require mating 80, 68, or 50 pins, resulting in a larger connector and necessarily limiting the number of connections supported for a small footprint switch or blade. Real estate then becomes one of the considerations in selecting a protocol. How many channels will you need to attach? It's only after taking these questions into account that you can select the right technology for the task at hand.

SCSI Commands over Fiber-Optic Cable

As I noted earlier, I intend to treat the SCSI command set as it runs over various media in Chapter 4. At this point, you should appreciate that the handling of bits at high speed is hardly child's play and that clearly fiber-optic components will likely maintain for the foreseeable future the performance and throughput advantage.

At the same time, the data transfer rates of Fibre Channel, from only a year past, is now possible over reasonable lengths of copper wire under Ethernet. I think for most storage network designers it makes sense to look to fiber optics for what is possible and to Ethernet for what is practical. In either case, there is a role for the SCSI command set to play.

Summary

This short tutorial on lasers and fiber optics is intended only to provide you with a basic appreciation for the components that make up the physical layer of a fiber-based storage network. Clearly, to understand the technology beyond a superficial level, you must approach it on an electrical engineering basis. That stated, you should at this point have a grasp of the fundamentals of a fiber optics–based storage network to understand where the limits of distance and data rate are encountered, and make note of the technologies that are constantly pushing these limits out.

As a rule of thumb, for any given generation of networking, if copper offers kilohertz, fiber optics delivers megahertz. The parallel synchronous bus handles a gigabit per second down the backplane; lasers encode and decode a terabit asynchronously and reliably over fiber channel. At the same time, manufacturing economies of scale can't be ignored, any more than the sheer numbers of available IP-savvy technologists. The net result is that fiber optics–based networking is a ground-breaking technology, and a groundswell of capability called Ethernet follows in its wake. (As always, the best technology can only be defined in the context of the work to be performed and the cost to get it done.)

From the standpoint of a buyer, designer, or administrator of storage networks, this chapter is intended to give you only an overview of the issues. At the same time, you should now be in a better position to understand why the expensive and complicated fiber optics–based Storage Area Network has remained the province of highly trained technical staff. This stuff is complex. Still, although you might have to be a rocket scientist to invent a microwave oven, you don't have to be to use one. The objective of this chapter was to introduce you to some of the concepts behind the buttons. I hope that at least has been achieved.

CHAPTER 4

SCSI:
The Specification, Architecture, and Command Set

IN THE PREVIOUS CHAPTERS, you've seen many of the physical media options for transporting data and commands across a storage network. The electronic and photonic properties of copper and fiber optics provide a set of capabilities appropriate to a wide range of purposes. At this point, you should be quite clear on the differences between Ethernet and Fibre Channel (FC) at the lower two layers of the ISO stack.

As you move to the third and fourth layers of that stack, the network and transport layers, SCSI technology becomes of increasing importance. SCSI cabling is a valid and common means of handling direct-attached storage requirements. Beyond this, the SCSI model for handling commands, irrespective of the media for their transmission, provides value to virtually all storage network topologies.

This chapter covers the SCSI architecture and identifies the various flavors of the command set for specific technologies such as Fibre Channel or tape devices. I'll introduce the specific capabilities of iSCSI and compare them to Ethernet and Fibre Channel implementations.

The level of detail of what I introduce to you here is insufficient to put to work directly, particularly for writing device drivers. However, after completing this chapter, you should have a sense of how the various SCSI specifications structure the coding of device drivers and administrative utilities. Even if you aren't someone who is going to face that Herculean task, it's still necessary to understand how the constituent parts interact in order to choose between the various options and implications of the different network and transportation offerings.

This chapter sets the stage for understanding how the SCSI specifications drive development of communications options, and how they interrelate to promote interoperability across multiple vendors and product offerings.

Common Command Set

In the mid 1980s, when the original SCSI specification was developed, it included provision for common commands. Early versions of the spec called for standards in the electrical signaling and elements of the middle layers for messaging and framing packets. As the specification has evolved, the architectural model has segregated physical signaling from the command layer. Within the physical layer, specific definitions supporting parallel, Fibre Channel, and serial SCSI communications have been developed, whereas the command layer is now cleanly separated from the underlying layers.

The overall architecture for the SCSI model is now considered firmly established, and revisions will be made to the specific areas of concern within the model.

SAM: The SCSI Architecture Model

The T10 Technical Committee administers all aspects of the SCSI specification. This group operates under the auspices of INCITS (pronounced insight), which is the International Committee on Information Technology Standards. INCITS is accredited by the American National Standards Institute (ANSI). The rules for defining standards as set by ANSI are followed to ensure that SCSI standards conform to ANSI standards for standards. This may sound ridiculous when read aloud, but it works.

If you had a little trouble following the who's who of standards when it comes to SCSI, you might find the SCSI Architecture Models even more circuitous. SCSI-3 (Ultra Wide) is a version of SCSI that gave rise to the SCSI Architecture Model (SAM). This was a result of the desire to differentiate the third generation of standards from SCSI-2. Over time, the set of standards governing SCSI as a whole became known as the *SCSI Architecture Model*. Naturally, the next generation of the SCSI Architecture Model became known as SAM-2, which dealt with the evolution of SCSI beyond version 3. As a result, SAM represented SCSI-3, SAM-2 represented SCSI-3+, and SAM-3 is the most recent SCSI architecture model. No one envisions a SAM-4 at this time.

SAM deals with two sets of considerations, specifically the SCSI primary commands and the signaling and interconnection of devices on which those commands may run. The relationship of SAM to the commands and interconnections is broken out in Figure 4-1.

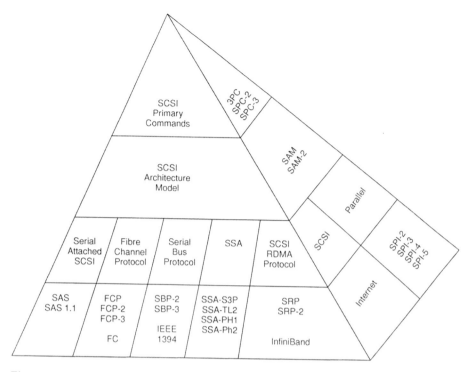

Figure 4-1. The SCSI Architecture Model layers and components

As you can see, the various SAM standards incorporate an impressive range of interconnect schemes. FireWire (IEEE 1394) incorporates SCSI commands, as do parallel SCSI, serial attached SCSI, and iSCSI, which is to be expected from their names. Perhaps more surprising is the encapsulation of SCSI into SSA, InfiniBand, Serial Bus, and Fibre Channel.

Before delving into how SCSI is implemented over these various signaling media, I'd like you to consider the range of both the primary SCSI commands and the distinct flavors of SCSI commands. The INCITS group has done a highly effective job of ensuring that compatibility and interoperability is enabled by rigorously defining standards. This is reflected in the specificity of the families into which the SCSI command sets are defined as shown in Figure 4-2.

From the figure you should be able to appreciate how the primary commands are shared across all devices supporting some sort of SCSI interface and that they can be run over a wide variety of connections.

Given the centrality of SCSI primary commands to the linking of SCSI devices over SCSI capable links, I think we're ready to look first at the primary commands for establishing a link and then at some of the different command set options available to network storage product designers. First, let me put the commands in the context of an exchange between two SCSI devices.

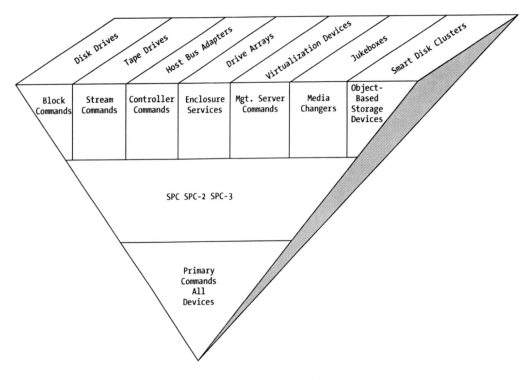

Figure 4-2. The standards architecture for SCSI commands

SCSI Communications

Here are a few basic SCSI definitions you need to know for the discussion that follows:

- *Initiator:* This SCSI device requests operations to be performed by another SCSI device. In a client/server model, the initiator is the client; but from a host/slave perspective, the initiator would generally be the host.

- *Host adapter:* The on-board controller or card that translates requests for I/O into SCSI requests.

- *Target:* A physical or virtual device accessible via a target SCSI device.

- *Logical Unit Number (LUN):* A logical identifier consisting of 3 bits.

Let's look at the best-case scenario in a connection between two SCSI devices—for the purposes of this example, a controller and a disk.

The most straightforward link between two SCSI devices involves the sending of a request consisting of a command, status return, and message interchange. This allows a contiguous set of logical data blocks to be moved across the interface. However, prior to sending a command, the link between the two devices must be established. In order to send the command from the initiator to the target, the bus must be secured for the communication. This is accomplished by detecting the bus state—specifically whether it's free or in use.

Once the bus is free, the controller first sends an inquiry to the target device. The device, the drive in this case, responds with a description of its physical characteristics so the initiator (the controller) can construct the command appropriately for the target (the disk). The number of blocks is defined within the command.

A single command can transfer one or more data blocks, and when the command is completed, the target returns a single status byte. When this status byte doesn't represent a successful operation, a Check Condition status can be sent that indicates more information on the command result is available by the target. This information may then be requested by the initiator, which then takes action as appropriate. The data may be re-sent, for example.

A simple, successful SCSI disk read operation involves the following steps:

1. The initiator identifies the target.

2. The initiator arbitrates for control of the SCSI bus.

3. The initiator selects the target.

4. The initiator sends the read command to the target.

5. The target takes control of the SCSI bus.

6. The target interprets and executes the command.

7. The target reads the data from the media and sends it to the initiator.

8. The target sends the status byte to the initiator.

9. The initiator sends a command complete status message.

10. The target relinquishes control of the SCSI bus.

The life cycle of a single SCSI command between initiator and target is shown in Figure 4-3.

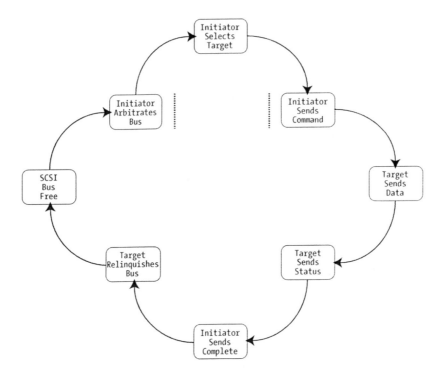

Figure 4-3. The life cycle of a command

The SCSI bus illustrated in Figure 4-3 shows the roles played by the eight distinct phases of a SCSI exchange as listed here:

- Bus Free

- Arbitration

- Selection

- Reselection

- Command

- Data

- Status

- Message

Unlike Ethernet, which shares the communication medium on the basis of detecting traffic and collisions, the SCSI model provides for multiple access over the bus by establishing its state. As defined by the original SCSI communications model, nine control signals are used to establish the state of the bus and allow devices to communicate with each other over it. These are defined in Table 4-1.

Table 4-1. SCSI Control Signals

Signal	Status	Definition
BSY	Busy	Indicates the bus is in use
SEL	Select	Indicates a target is being selected by an initiator, or a target is being reselected by an initiator
C/D	Control/Data	Indicates data or control info is being sent down the bus
I/O	Input/Output	Sent by the target to indicate the to or from direction of data
MSG	Message	Sent by target device in the Message phase
REQ	Request	Sent by target to request a data transfer handshake (REQ/ACK)
ACK	Acknowledge	Sent by initiator to acknowledge data transfer handshake
ATN	Attention	Sent by initiator to indicate message for target
RST	Reset	Indicates hard reset signal
DB	Data Bus	Identifies 8 data bits plus 1 parity bit signals

The C/D, I/O, and MSG signals are sometimes referred to as the *Bus phase*.

SCSI Messaging

The major functions performed by messaging within the SCSI protocol include the following:

- Identification and selection of target

- Control of bus operations

- Data checkpoint and error recovery

- Command termination by either target or initiator

- Multiple command handling

Each communications session must have an I_T_L nexus established. This initiator (I), target (T), LUN (L) forms the name of the link, which is used to identify the particular initiator target set for which messages or data are being transferred. Where multiple connections are supported, each instance of a connection between a target and initiator represents an I_T_L_x.

Because it was intended from the outset to support disk devices, the SCSI protocol includes built-in support for asynchronous operation. That is to say, even though the physical work of a read/write operation is taking place, the bus can be freed for use by other links. Initiators use pointers to keep track of the devices, status, and data for multiple activities. The I_T_L is the mechanism used to ensure the communication can be resumed after, say, the disk completes a long read or write operation and is ready to take control over the bus to send a message back to the initiator.

You should be able to see how this model supports multiple initiators and multiple targets on the same bus.

SCSI Commands

Now that you've seen the role commands play in the exchange of data between two devices, let's look at some of the primary SCSI commands.

Commands are contained within a *command descriptor block*. In this block, the first byte in every SCSI command includes an operation code. The next byte in each SCSI command specifies the logical unit with the exception of logic unit zero, which uses the identity message. The command and parameters follow, and the last byte serves as a control byte for the command block.

SCSI commands must be 6, 10, or 12 bytes in length. During the request operation, the initiator obtains the type of device, its physical characteristics, and any modifiable parameters that the device supports.

Commands may be mandatory, optional, specific to a particular vendor, or reserved. To support the differentiation of the type of command, the operation status code (first byte) is defined as M, O, V, and R respectively.

The mandatory commands establish the minimum commands that must be supported to meet the requirements of the standard. Optional commands may be implemented and, if they are, must be done in accordance with the standard. Vendor-specific commands allow provision for compatibility or extensions as desired by the manufacturer. Reserved operation codes are set aside for future use.

Figure 4-4 shows the construction of a typical command descriptor block for a 6-byte command.

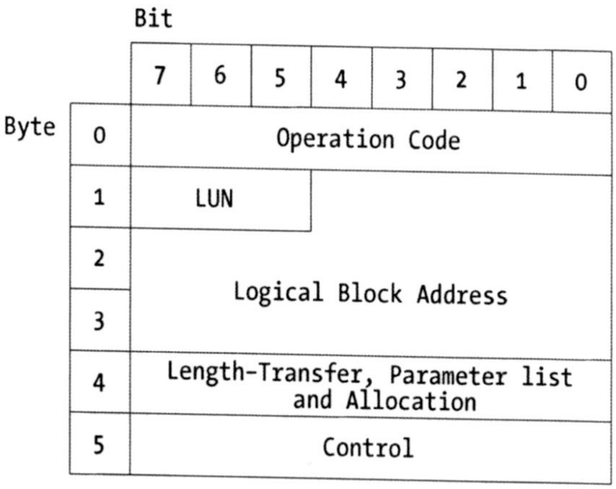

Figure 4-4. 6-byte command descriptor block

The LUN ID preserves compatibility with devices under the original SCSI-1 specification. The 10- and 12-byte command descriptors are similarly constructed, with the main difference lying in the length of the logical address block and transfer length. This effectively increases the amount of data that can be transferred via the command. The logical block specified here is an 8-, 16-, or 32-bit value depending on whether the command length is 6, 10 or 12 bytes. Blocks themselves may range in size from 1K to 64K, as set by the format options selected when the media was formatted.

Processing Multiple Commands

As I mentioned earlier in this chapter, SCSI incorporates some features that are especially useful for disk and other data device operations. There are three ways in which multiple commands can be sent from an initiator to a target, which then processes the commands and sends back a status:

- *Tagged command queuing:* This approach eliminates the need for arbitration and reselection during the execution of multiple commands by the target. This results in the bus remaining busy. This capability was introduced as part of the SCSI-2 specification.

- *Untagged command queuing:* This option allows a target to accept a new command from a different initiator even though the device is still busy executing previous commands.

- *Ordered commands:* Devices such as tape drives rely on an ordered sequence of bytes to maintain integrity. To ensure this, ordered commands require that the target execute the commands in the precise order in which they were sent by the initiator.

The SCSI command set itself cleanly addresses both NAS and SAN topologies within the operations defined by the specification. Multiple hosts can share a single physical enclosure (albeit generally with multiple or masked LUNs), or a host-to-device link can be established and maintained for the duration of a given operation. Streaming of data to devices such as tape, with its reliance on a set sequence, is supported, as are logical block addresses used by disk drives to read and write data to disks.

As you'll see a little later in this chapter, the SCSI set of specifications goes beyond disk, tape, and controllers and provides a great deal of in-depth definition for many other kinds of devices. It's interesting to note that in many cases, vendors have elected to adapt the SCSI specification to other communications protocols, as it was deemed unnecessary or redundant to go through the definition process again. With SCSI, it has often been easier to join them than to beat them.

Encapsulating Protocols Within SCSI Communications

In the same way that the SCSI commands don't depend on knowledge about the signaling of the underlying physical communications links, SCSI provides transport services through the SEND MESSAGE and GET MESSAGE commands. It's here that the data needed by the session layer is encapsulated. It's worth noting that because TCP/IP consists of TCP at layer 4 over IP at layer 3, you can easily see how SCSI over IP (iSCSI) can be handled by using commands over Ethernet communications networks. Additionally, as indicated in the protocol pyramid, SCSI standards have been derived for a multiplicity of devices.

SCSI Enclosure Services

One of the best illustrations to me of the usefulness of this segregation is when considering how the command set applies to specific sets of devices. Within the SCSI model a target contains LUNs that represent physical or virtual devices. In the context of disk drives, think of an enclosure containing several disk drives. Enclosures have unique characteristics, including sensors and alarms. The enclosure itself can monitor conditions as basic as whether or not the door has been left open.

A sample initiator/target topology incorporating SCSI Enclosure Services is shown in Figure 4-5.

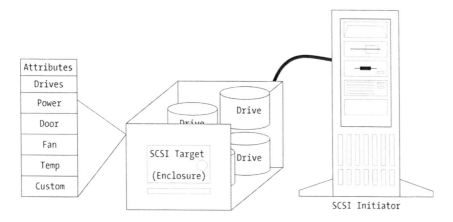

Figure 4-5. A SCSI Enclosure Services environment

The SCSI Enclosure Services specification also defines commands and parameters for addressing the operational state of power supplies, fans and other cooling devices, displays, and other instrumentation as well as the SCSI drives themselves. This is achieved by using the SCSI `SEND DIAGNOSTIC` and `RECEIVE DIAGNOSTIC RESULTS` commands, which process standard bits for the predetermined elements of the enclosure. The commands operate on elements, including but not limited to power supply, cooling element, temperature sensors, door lock, audible alarm, voltage sensor, SCSI port, and vendor-specific codes.

To establish the elements of an enclosure that are available for reporting and manipulation, a configuration page has been defined by the SES spec. The layout of this page is described in Table 4-2.

Table 4-2. SES Configuration Page Layout

Component Name	Component Description
Diagnostic page header	Describes the diagnostic page
Generation code	Identifies generation
Enclosure descriptor header	Describes the enclosure descriptor
Enclosure descriptor	Identifies the enclosure
Type descriptor header list for device elements	Holds the type descriptor headers of device elements
Type descriptor header list for other elements	Identifies remaining element types in the enclosure
Type descriptor text	Holds text descriptions of each element type in the enclosure (optional)

Although interesting, from a programmers perspective this isn't enough detail. The specification further documents the configuration page structure as shown in Table 4-3.

Table 4-3. SES Configuration Page Construction Details

Component Name	Byte Position	Component Description
Diagnostic Page Header	0	Page Code (0 1 H)
	1	Number of subenclosures
	2–3	Page length (n–3)
Generation code	4–7	Generation code
Enclosure descriptor header	8	Reserved
	9	Subenclosure identifier
	10	Number of element types supported
	11	Enclosure descriptor length
Enclosure descriptor	12–19	Enclosure logical identifier
	20–27	Enclosure vendor identification
	28–43	Production identification
	43–47	Product revision level
	48–(11+m)	Vendor-specific enclosure info
Type descriptor header list for device elements	4 bytes	Type descriptor header for each element (4 bytes each)
Type descriptor text	Variable	Type descriptor header for each element (4 bytes each)

From the specification, a coder of a device driver, or a monitoring and reporting tool for administration, now has a solid grasp of the construction of a configuration page to be provided by an SES-compliant enclosure when queried by an initiator.

Diagnostic results are returned in the form of a configuration or status page depending on the parameter sent with the RECEIVE DIAGNOSTICS command sent from the initiator. The specification allows for the diagnostic types shown in Table 4-4.

Table 4-4. SES Diagnostic Page Codes

Page Code	Description	Control or Status
00h	Supported diagnostics	Status
01h	Configuration	Status
02h	Enclosure control	Control
02h	Enclosure status	Status
03h	Help text	Status
04h	String out	Control
04h	String in	Status
05h	Threshold out	Control
05h	Threshold in	Status
06h	Array control	Control
06h	Array status	Status
07h	Element descriptor	Status
08h	Short enclosure status	Status
09h–0Fh	Reserved for SES	NA
10h–3Fh	Reserved	NA
40h–7Fh	Device-specific definition	NA
80h–FFh	Vendor-specific pages	NA

Control pages are sent by the initiator via the SEND DIAGNOSTIC command to the target enclosure to perform a particular task. Status pages are sent from the target enclosure to the initiator with the RECEIVE DIAGNOSTIC command. Note the range of vendor-specific pages that are made available by the specification.

A RAID array can be considered a common example of a SCSI enclosure. More detailed information on the SES specification is available through the SES SCSI-3 Enclosure Services Command Set documentation from ANSI.

An example of how these commands and configuration specifications are used in a device driver can be seen at http://openbsd.secsup.org/src/sys/scsi/ses.c.

Fibre Channel SCSI

When Fibre Channel was first released, the SCSI command set ran exclusively over parallel SCSI cables. However, the separation of the commands and their specification from the physical medium meant that those commands could be adopted by the Fibre Channel developers—and they were.

SCSI bus arbitration through commands became FC primitives such as ARB, which should strike you as suspiciously similar to ARBITRATE. SCSI SELECTION became the FC OPEN primitive, the R_RDY primitive indicating the ready status of the receiving port was substituted for the COMMAND phase, and so on.

This is an important example of coding specification reuse. There was no need to reinvent the wheel, so SCSI expanded well beyond the scope of its original design. The process of industry standards, discussed and developed by stakeholders, flourished beyond the Small Computer Systems of SCSI's origins and became the foundation for significantly larger computing platforms.

SCSI-FCP

This is a serial CSI protocol that supports the mapping of FC devices to logical drives accessed by a host via the operating system. The protocol allows SCSI-enabled applications to access the Fibre Channel HBA and disk devices without modification. Through this protocol, the SCSI upper-layer protocol substitutes Fibre Channel for the SCSI bus, using frame transfers instead of sending and receiving data in blocks.

The four command execution functions specified by SAM—command service request, data delivery request, data delivery action, and command service response—are mapped to frames. The initial command service request becomes a FC frame containing the SCSI command descriptor block, LUN, data transfer length, and control field. Similarly, data requests and responses are packaged as FC frames, decoded and passed up to the SCSI driver for processing.

By opening up the world of SCSI devices to the Fibre Channel network, SCSI devices gained a tremendous increase in throughput, and FC network designers gained access to a wide range of devices for processing data. This was enabled by the SCSI specification, which allowed network and device designers to understand how to interface at a finely grained level of detail.

iSCSI

In the same way that the SCSI command set migrated from running over parallel copper wires to a fiber-optic network, SCSI standards have been developed to allow commands to be executed over IP.

However, unlike the SCSI Fibre Channel protocol, the iSCSI protocol falls under the auspices of the Internet Engineering Task Force (IETF). The documentation developed as part of the iSCSI specification identifies SCSI as consisting of a standard architecture and specialized commands for classes of devices such as disk and tape drives. The iSCSI standard proposes a transport layer specification that allows SCSI commands to be executed on top of TCP as the network layer.

It's the introduction of high-speed Ethernet that makes the adaptation possible. Ethernet LAN technology is now capable of performing at rates that were the province of Fibre Channel and ATM networks only a few short years ago. Of course, as I've pointed out earlier, Fibre Channel continues to break performance records. However, the net effect and main attraction of iSCSI isn't that it appeals to the most demanding requirements, rather iSCSI offers the ability to extend storage network capabilities to a large number of new sites, without requiring migration of existing IP network technologies or skills.

iSCSI Protocol

The protocol definition revolves around the creation of iSCSI Process Data Units (PDUs) that encapsulate control messages, SCSI commands, parameters, and data. iSCSI incorporates the Service Delivery Specification of SAM-2 into its iSCSI Service Delivery subsystem.

SCSI initiators and targets are given iSCSI names and form the start and end points of an iSCSI connection. This connection is a TCP link between the requestor and responding device. The I_T_L nexus is replaced by the I_T nexus, which is a conjunction of the iSCSI port names along with other iSCSI entity names such as the network portal identifiers.

This is where iSCSI departs from the bus communications definitions on which SCSI was founded. To support the longer distances and vastly larger number of connections possible with a TCP/IP network, iSCSI has introduced several new entities:

- *Network entity:* A device or gateway accessible through an IP address

- *Network portal:* A network entity that may be accessed by a participating iSCSI node and session

- *Portal group:* Multiple iSCSI connections within a single session across multiple portals

iSCSI also takes advantage of capabilities introduced by other protocol definition efforts, such as the following:

- *Worldwide unique name:* This is a 64-bit address based on a manufacturer's IEEE identifier and a 32-bit unique serial number generated by the vendor.

These iSCSI communications components might collaborate as depicted in Figure 4-6.

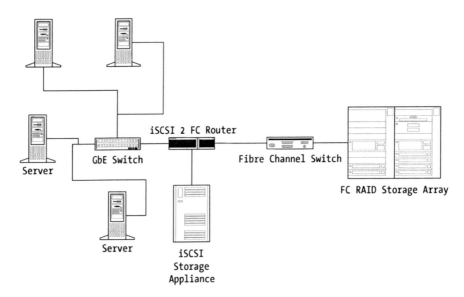

Figure 4-6. iSCSI network components

One of the major differences between communication over TCP/IP and via a SCSI bus is the delivery of packets for the former can't be assured to arrive in sequence. Given that TCP/IP traffic may be routed along various paths, the arriving packets must then be reassembled at their destination. This has implications for ordered commands and the applications that rely on them, such as streaming applications.

Summary

The SCSI specification is venerable, valuable, and viable for the future. The 1600-plus pages of the complete spec may make for daunting reading, but the provisions for implementation detail for storage network devices is all there.

I hope that this chapter gave you a sense of how to organize and segregate the SCSI models into their relevant components. I also hope you gained a sense of how the layers of the OSI, FC, and SCSI specifications allow the separation of concerns into specializations. These in turn allow a large and diverse group of engineers, programmers, vendors, and customers to collaborate with interoperable products.

An excellent example of how these specifications are implemented in code can be found at http://openbsd.secsup.org/src/sys/scsi/ses.c. Most people will be more interested in how device drivers are configured and used, but I believe the example, put in the public domain by M. Jacobs of NASA, is a first-class illustration of how open standards and shared efforts can promote interoperability.

You should be able to see how you move up the stack from the physical products, generally the province of engineers, through to the network, transportation, and session layers, where low-level programming takes place. These are the prerequisites on which systems administrators depend.

It's at these layers that the configurable options included with various products from different sources have the greatest impact on performance. As you move into the session, presentation, and application services, it's the foundation of the network and transport layers that affect you most.

As you complete this chapter on storage network technologies, you should now have a coherent framework into which new products can be cleanly placed. As the discussion increasingly moves into software and virtual services, you should keep coming back to the SCSI model time and again.

SCSI has proven to be a robust and reusable specification that has evolved over time to run on ever-faster hardware. It's an elegant and functional set of standards that is as relevant on the Internet as it is on fiber-optic cable. It might have grown far beyond its lowly beginnings of a 50-wire, 12-foot cable, but those SCSI-1 devices are still compatible today.

CHAPTER 5

RAID Levels
and Logical Volumes

DIRECT-ATTACHED STORAGE and Network Attached Storage have a great many components that work exactly alike. At this point in the discussion, I want to move to the storage stack itself and leave the implications of moving data across a network. In this chapter, you'll see the options that are available to a Storage Area Network for protecting and preserving data, as well as strategies for minimizing the performance penalty paid for that protection.

Specifically, I'll cover RAID levels from the perspectives of how they work and where you would use them. Then moving beyond the management of physical disks, we'll look at the role of the file system, and some of the options that are available.

This chapter will introduce some of the performance penalties to be paid for ensuring access to disk resources. The relative impact of these penalties will be illustrated in Chapter 10, where I review the performance of a specific 1GB file set and the performance metrics that various storage configurations yield.

I'll introduce logical volumes as supported in both Linux and Windows. The relationship of logical volumes to the hard disk devices and the file system is also explained in this chapter.

RAID Levels and What They Mean

The definition of RAID levels was introduced in Chapter 1. Given the review you've had for disk and networking technology, let's take a closer look at RAID levels.

Several terms are frequently used either interchangeably with RAID levels or in place of them. As they are descriptive and relevant, I thought it best we start with those concepts and then evaluate how they are implemented in various settings.

Striping–aka RAID Level 0

In Figure 5-1, you can see a representation of several hard disk drives with a physical volume cut away in each. *Striping* refers to the strategy of writing a given file to blocks on different volumes in a parallel fashion. The benefit results from minimizing the amount of time the heads are required to move over the platters and to put as many of the disk resources as possible to work concurrently.

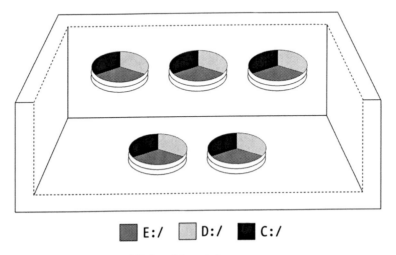

E:/   D:/   C:/

Figure 5-1. An array of disks with striping

Although read/write performance is enhanced with striping enabled, the cost is increased exposure to a head crash. Losing one of the disks of a stripe set results in the loss of the striped drive as a whole.

Spanning: When Only the Very Biggest Will Do

Figure 5-2 depicts the same array of disks created as a single logical drive. The logical drive spans all four disks and is represented as one storage pool. The advantage is that file sets larger than any one disk can then be stored intact.

A spanned drive may not take advantage of having four sets of read/write heads to make reading and writing more efficient; instead it may write sequentially, first filling up one drive, and then "spilling over" to the next. However, the risk or cost introduced by striping is also inherent in this storage strategy. Loss of one drive results in loss of access to all of the others.

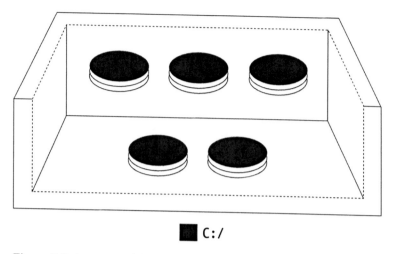

Figure 5-2. An array of disks spanned as one logical drive

Mirroring—aka RAID 1

Mirroring refers to the process of creating an exact duplicate image of a drive and providing a process to "fail over" to that mirror image in the event that the primary drive fails. Figure 5-3 shows the drive array as two drives with mirrors.

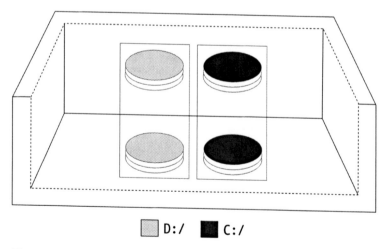

Figure 5-3. An array of two mirrored disks

Mirroring requires the completion of two sets of write activities before a transaction is completed. This necessarily increases the amount of work performed by the hardware for any write operation, which has a negative effect on its performance. Read transactions aren't affected by the mirroring process, which makes mirroring an effective strategy for any data you wish to make highly accessible for read-intensive applications.

Mirrored Stripe Set—aka RAID 0+1

To mitigate the performance hit from mirroring, you could configure your array as a combined stripe set with a mirror for that striped drive. This configuration is shown in Figure 5-4.

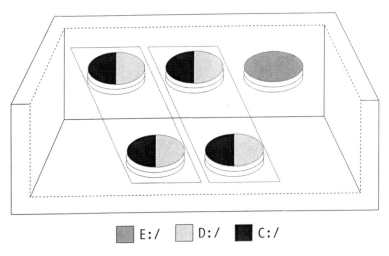

E:/ D:/ C:/

Figure 5-4. An array of striped and mirrored disks

Mirroring the stripe set mitigates the risk of data unavailability due to a disk failure. The performance penalty from the mirror is reduced to the extent possible by striping the write operations across multiple drives.

Stripe with Parity—aka RAID 3

Providing similar protection to RAID 0+1, but using a different mechanism, a stripe with parity dedicates a drive to maintaining extra information about the data that is written to the stripe set. In the event of a disk loss, the data can be re-created from the parity disk and remaining drives in the set.

Parity in this context is determined by invoking a calculation on each block of data written across the array. Using the exclusive OR operation (XOR), which says the value of the block may be odd or even but not both, the sum of the values is stored as a parity value. In the event that a disk is lost, the value of each block of data can be derived from recalculating the other values and the parity sum. Because the XOR value may only be true or false (odd or even), if all values are known plus the sum, the missing parity value can be determined. From that value, the data itself can be reconstituted on a new disk.

As shown in Figure 5-5, the key advantage to using a dedicated parity disk is the savings from not mirroring every data disk in a pair.

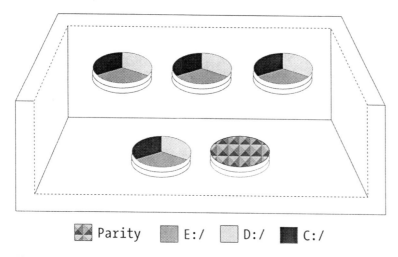

Figure 5-5. A stripe set with a dedicated parity disk

As you can see from the diagram, the cost is one disk for the entire array. This means that if you have 2 disks in a RAID array, it costs you one for parity. If you have 32 disks in the array, it costs you the same disk dedicated to parity, plus the performance hit on write operations.

RAID 5

RAID 5 operates in a similar fashion to RAID 3, with the key distinction that each drive maintains parity values as well as data. A RAID 5 array can reconstruct a data set if one or more of the disks in the array goes awry. Figure 5-6 depicts a RAID 5 array.

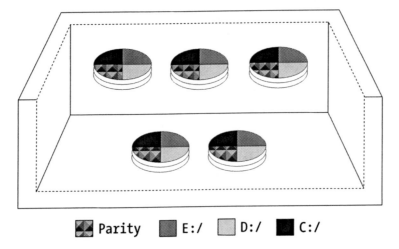

 Parity   E:/   D:/   C:/

Figure 5-6. A RAID 5 array with several disks

By distributing the parity information across multiple disks, the RAID 5 array provides a high degree of fault tolerance. As you might expect, a penalty is incurred for write transactions in terms of the time compared to writing to a stripe set.

RAID Read/Write Operations

It should become increasingly clear that the main consideration for any storage strategy is the value of the data to be stored. Archival storage for historical purposes, record retention for legal compliance purposes, and casual lookup data require a different storage and redundancy strategy from high-volume transactions. Before you can map your requirement to a particular redundancy strategy, you should first be completely familiar with the inherent characteristics of the options available.

Stripe Setting

Let's build on the read/write functions of a single hard disk. When you create a stripe set, you do more than simply distribute the operation across two or more disks: you've harnessed the disks together, and that coordination must be taken into account as part of your configuration. True, you could simply choose the defaults and mark the job done on your to-do list, but to tune your storage network, you need to know how the various components work together, as well as which options to select.

When a hard disk leaves the factory, it has been low-level formatted with pre-set block sizes, regardless of the intended operating system that will perform a higher level format on installation. At the hardware level, block sizes for data read and written to disk remain constant—typically defined by manufacturers as sectors containing 512-byte blocks. Each of the drives in the stripe set must write a block for any given record, a stripe set with four drives has a logical block size for a record set at 2048 bytes.

Mirroring

A write so nice, they performed it twice: The duplication of effort involved in mirroring is perhaps the easiest form of RAID to visualize. As you would expect, the increased overhead of duplicating drives has an effect on performance. Mirroring requires two drives: a primary drive and a mirror drive. In the event of the failure of the primary drive, the system will fail over to using the mirrored drive instead of the primary. With hot-swappable hardware, you can remove the dead drive, install a new one, and create a new mirror, which then duplicates the contents of the new primary, thereby re-creating your mirrored set. There are some issues with being able to boot servers with mirrored boot disks. These are discussed in greater detail in the section "Hardware RAID" a little later in this chapter. Additionally, lab benchmarks for software and hardware mirroring performance under Gigabit Ethernet is included in Chapter 10.

Stripe with Parity

The metadata for the parity drive requires that for every write operation, a metadata write also occurs. Retrievals also require first a lookup of the metadata to obtain the disk addresses, and then a seek operation to position the heads to read the data where located. It isn't difficult to see that contention due to multiple requests wouldn't be the ideal situation for a RAID 3 drive. However, the ability to spread the storage of files across multiple hard disks and maintain that parity information in another location is especially suited for large files to be accessed by a single application at a time. Think medical imaging files or audio/visual content to be edited. Availability and fault tolerance are critical, but it's unlikely (though not impossible) that more than one application would want the data at a time. Of course, contention can result from multiple users looking for different files, but the advantages in this case should outweigh the costs.

Distributed Parity

RAID 5 devices determine how to interleave data on the basis of logical block definitions. Logical block sizes are set by the file system when the disk is formatted and can be defined as any size as long as it's a multiple of the physical disk block. Where the logical block size is the same as the physical block size, a single disk might be accessed to handle a particular block rather than requiring data to be accessed across multiple disks.

For some of the less-expensive RAID 5 offerings, parallel reads of the disks aren't supported in order to keep costs down. Instead, data is picked off sequentially from the chain of drives. The top-of-the-line RAID 5 implementations can concurrently pull data from each disk in the set as needed to satisfy the request.

Unlike a striped array, RAID 5 can accommodate the writing of a record set that isn't as long as the block size defined by the entire stripe group. To do this, a function known as *read-modify-write* is used. As a result of this function, the old data block, old parity block, and new data block are used to create a new parity block. The significance of this is that up to two read and two write operations must be performed in order to complete the writing of a single logical block. To ensure this doesn't become a performance nightmare, most RAID 5 hardware vendors provide caching to reduce the amount of time required to look up old block and parity information.

Hardware RAID

Hardware RAID is the term used to refer to a RAID array that is managed by software built into the RAID controller, rather than through the operating system or application software such as a database server. Hardware RAID for file servers is no longer an expensive option. Readily available RAID controllers from Rocket Raid, Highpointe, and Promise Technologies—not to mention solutions available from Adaptec and others—will provide RAID levels 0, 1, and 0+1.

Generally speaking, hardware RAID isn't mix and match. An IDE RAID controller will allow you to configure up to four drives on its two channels. However, because you're looking at risk and reward at the hardware level, it bears consideration that in this setting you've introduced a single point of failure—the RAID controller itself. A mirroring strategy that allows you to compensate for not just a failed drive, but also a failed controller may be the level of insurance you want. In that event, it would be a mistake to think that you were fully protected because you had mirrored the drive and not the card.

Hardware RAID allows your system to boot regardless of whether both the mirror and primary drives spin up successfully. Obviously, at least one of them has to be available at boot time, or there would be zero boot devices available.

Software RAID

Both Linux and Windows servers provide facilities to use the operating system to manage RAID disk management. A discussion of how this is implemented and the various performance findings for an identical hardware environment are presented in Chapter 10. Like any operation that involves the CPU, handling RAID activities through software necessarily creates competition for CPU and memory resources. In small workgroup settings, this will likely be a nonissue, as the performance differences between software and hardware RAID were negligible for levels 0, 1, and 0+1. However, you can expect that scalability issues will arise when relying on software RAID under larger workloads.

RAID Strategies

A hardware mirror of your /, /boot, and /swap directories will ensure that your system stays up and running during a boot disk failure. Electing to mirror your /winnt directory in software across two IDE controllers (as opposed to two channels on the same controller) can insure you against a controller and hard disk crash. User directories and disk resources declared for application data sets such as mail or database repositories can also provide a measure of availability in the event of a hardware failure.

It should be noted that RAID is a strategy for ensuring the system resources are available, not a replacement for backups. RAID does nothing to protect against file corruption or a runaway delete due to script or operator error. The job RAID is designed for is to faithfully reproduce data contained on more than one hard disk. There are other strategies and techniques that must be applied to provide more protection and insurance against other perils.

Logical Volume Management

If RAID manages the physical volumes of more than one disk, Logical Volume Management (LVM) is an intermediate step for the administration of those volumes to be presented to the file system. For purposes of this discussion, we'll assume that a RAID array has been designed and implemented. The next step is making those disk resources available to the file system.

Logical volumes can be considered named aggregates of the physical disk volumes. They serve as a mechanism for managing partitions, including their initial configuration and installation, and subsequent changes in size and allocations. File systems aren't defined on disks themselves (RAID'd or not), but instead on volume groups, which are created and allocated using the Logical Volume Manager.

Most of the terminology I use to refer to volume groups is descended from their initial implementations in HP-UX and AIX (which is where I first worked with them) and currently available in Linux. However, for those of you who are sensitive to perceived slights against Windows Servers, be aware that the use of dynamic disks under disk management in Windows since Windows Server 2000 is very much like using LVM. In some cases, however, there are features available as part of Logical Volume Group management and services that don't have a Windows equivalent. In such cases, I'll call out the difference explicitly.

Logical Volume Capabilities

Specifically, using logical groups, you can

- Increase and decrease the amount of disk available to a particular file system.

- Add physical storage to an existing volume group.

- Create snapshots of file systems in a point in time.

- Migrate volume groups to new devices.

These capabilities aren't exactly self-explanatory. A brief description of what each capability affords and where you might use it follows.

Allocating Disk Resources

Because file systems are mounted on volume groups, you may use the Logical Volume Group Manager to handle changes in your physical disk environment without affecting your data and files. This also provides an opportunity to separate roles and responsibilities among team members, where a published schedule of volume groups can be provided to, say, DBAs who aren't allowed access to the physical server environment. In the event that a systems administrator sees a hard

disk failure predicted under a SMART monitoring tool, the change can be made
without impact on the other infrastructure components.

Unlike RAID, a volume group may have many file systems mounted on it.
Although the dynamic disk manager under Windows 2000 will allow you to put different volumes across the hardware, you assign a single drive letter to the volume
or mount it under a folder. This means that volume groups provide the additional
benefit of being able to mount multiple file systems on the same volume group.

Adding and Removing Disks

Adding and removing physical storage while the system remains operating is
something that your hardware environment must first support, of course. But with
hot-swappable drive support available in Netfinity, Dell, and HP servers among
others, the next question is how to manage that process. Using Logical Volume
Management, you would first install your new disk, and then add it to a volume
group. You might then elect to use the other interesting feature of volume groups:
the ability to migrate volume groups to new devices. This way, you can use LVM to
swap out devices without service interruption. The applicability to network storage administration should be obvious.

Snapshots

Backing up file systems and data sets that are in constant operational use is an
interesting exercise in competing interests. Naturally everyone wants the data to
be protected, and just as understandable is the desire to keep it available. Backing
up open files is problematic, given the different locking mechanisms that exist. Or
transaction dependency might exist between several databases, meaning that to
back up one and then the other sequentially would result in an inconsistent state.
One way this has been accommodated using logical volumes is the inherent ability
to take a snapshot of a file system on it without having to allocate an identical
amount of disk space for the snapshot. This is accomplished with a form of mirroring, except the only thing that is recorded in the snapshot are the changes
made to the data from the time it was taken.

In this way, a duplicate copy of static or unchanged data isn't made, and the
backup comes from the operational file system. Where changes are being made to
the underlying data, the backup is taken from the snapshot.

It should be noted that this incurs some overhead, as it records changes being
made to the system. Once the backup is completed, the snapshot file system needs
to be removed, or it will continue logging changes until it fills up and breaks.

Summary

You should now have a better appreciation for the utilities that exist for managing multiple disk resources within any given server environment. Although much of the discussion on RAID and Logical Volume Management is applicable to direct-attached storage devices, most frequently those devices would themselves be used in Network Attached Storage solutions, such as file or application servers.

In the same way there is a stack of layers in the network from physical to application, so too is there a hierarchy of services in managing disk resources. In this chapter, you've been introduced to a number of key concepts and how those services can be implemented. Whereas RAID is a way to protect against disk failure, logical volume groups and dynamic disks are a way to abstract the physical devices into a collection of resources, which can then be managed by name rather than individual physical particulars.

The value of hot-swapping drives is readily apparent to anyone who wants a server with constant up time. From this chapter, you should have a sense of how you might go about designing these features in your storage network, and additionally how you might structure your environment to ensure good backups.

By approaching storage from the standpoint of first a single drive, then a collection of drives, and ultimately a dynamically managed pool of drives, you should be gaining a sense that a seemingly monolithic storage network is actually a nested set of components. Arriving at an understanding of these interdependencies will allow you to not only effectively manage a storage network, but also design one and tune its performance over time.

CHAPTER 6

File Systems and Network Protocols

FILE SYSTEM SHARING PROTOCOLS typically operate at layer 6 and 7 of the OSI model. The presentation and management of file or data interchange is built on top of the physical, datalink, transport, network, and session services already established for a given set of servers. In this chapter, I'll discuss two of the commonly found file sharing mechanisms, Network File System (NFS) and Server Message Block (SMB)/ Common Internet File System (CIFS), as well as the way in which the two of them leverage lower layers of the networking stack.

Support for multiple communications protocols and file systems is a commonly found feature in many NAS appliances. From this chapter, you'll get a grounding in the specific behavioral characteristics and limitations of the common protocol and file system families. I'll cover this by reviewing a typical configuration from a direct-attached storage standpoint, using that straightforward example to pull out the details relevant to a storage network.

Security and administrative considerations will be identified here and covered in more detail during the chapters dedicated to those subjects. From this chapter, you should gain an appreciation for the way a given file system is associated with a family of supporting standards, protocols, and products.

The "continuum of complexity" represented by file systems and the activities they facilitate is described in this chapter. After reading it, you should be aware of the architectural differences between a dedicated OS file system and that which could support a storage network.

What Is a File System?

As you saw in Chapter 2 during the discussion of hard disk technology, the devices themselves are quite dumb. Disk drives rely on block addresses to read and write data. The format for interpreting the data and the services for relating file names, directories, encryption, and permissions is handled by the file system.

Block devices read and write data in blocks to specific locations on the disk. *Blocks* are groups of bytes in the structure determined by the file system when the device was formatted. During the read and write operation, the block addresses are used to locate, write, or retrieve data on the disk. It's the file system that converts these blocks into files and other data resources.

A character device writes streams of bytes to the disk sequentially. For the purposes of this text, the key distinction between a character device and a block device is the role of the operating system in handling the data resources. File systems using block devices will typically cache data in memory to assist in the handling process. For certain types of applications, such as transactions using a relational database, this introduces a potential risk to data integrity. In situations where an application has marked a transaction complete, but the data hasn't physically been written to disk, that transaction might be lost in the event of a systems crash. It's for this reason that databases are configured with raw or character devices rather than file system resources.

The file system used is generally a function of the operating system. Windows systems, for example, have used FAT, FAT16, FAT32, and NTFS to identify the relationship between blocks and file resources. The file allocation table (FAT) resides on the disk and is read by the operating system to determine the contents, addresses, and permissions associated with each file entry. It associates the logical file resource descriptions with the physical blocks that make up the file as stored on the hard disk. Additionally, the file system maintains lists of available blocks and allocates new blocks to files as they grow. Conversely, the blocks belonging to deleted files are marked for return to the available pool.

This is, of course, a simplistic treatment of what a file system does. As more users join the system, contention must be managed. File permissions are an attribute of the data resource, but there is a considerable amount of range in the security services provided by different file systems.

Shared File Systems

A file server is one implementation of a shared file system. In this case, only the file server has physical access to the devices. Other systems become clients of the shared file system and support updating of local copies of file resource caches. This common topology for file sharing is the heart of the NAS product architecture.

Although there are several experimental and other proprietary special-purpose file systems, in this section, I'll examine the most commonly found. From the standpoint of networked storage, your file system of choice will need certain characteristics, including the following:

- *Distributed support:* The file system must allow access to resources across the network.

- *Client support:* The protocol for accessing the file system must be readily available on a number of client/server platforms.

- *Authentication:* The ability to secure access based on established permissions.

- *Administration:* As the number of file systems and clients increases, effective administration utilities become more important.

Network File System

Developed by Sun Microsystems in the mid 1980s, the Network File System is a shared file system that allows users on the other side of the network to mount a set of file resources and access them under an authentication scheme. This is implemented through shares exposed through an application programming interface to a client. File systems belonging to one server are cross-mounted over the network. The remote host processes calls for file services to or from that resource.

In either case, the NFS services are implemented via remote procedure calls (RPCs). These calls invoke the file find, read, or write procedures on the NFS server and return the file resource to the calling client. RPCs are combined with external data representation (XDR) to isolate the programmer from the network communications specifics. Figure 6-1 depicts the stack of services for NFS.

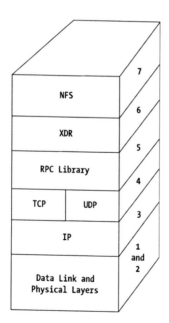

Figure 6-1. The NFS stack

The NFS API supports the following requests:

- *Read-only:* mount, getattr, lookup, readdir, read, readlink, statfs

- *Tree modifications:* mkdir, link, symlink, rename, unlink, rmdir

- *File modifications:* setattr, write

Authentication is user based, where the user ID is communicated with the RPC to the server for validation.

It's worth noting that NFS is similar to SMB in that both are a connection-oriented session layer service, requiring access to underlying network protocols in order to function. Performance is constrained in both by network configuration and the performance profiles of the network components. NFS is usually implemented over the TCP/IP communications stack.

The TCP/IP protocol suite also supports UDP. TCP is a guaranteed delivery protocol, meaning the packets are checked and re-sent if corrupted or missed. This naturally requires some processing overhead. User Datagram Protocol (UDP), on the other hand, isn't guaranteed to deliver its packets, nor are the packets sorted. They are streamed from one network device to the other.

Depending on your network topology and traffic, you may decide to opt for either UDP or TCP as the basis for your NFS network.

Network Information Services

Originally referred to as "Yellow Pages," the Network Information Services (NIS) is used as a mechanism for managing NFS mounts and user access profiles. To allow a client to connect to any machine with an NFS-mountable volume, the participating machines use NIS to synchronize the user name and password, home directory, and group information. As complex associations are built up, synchronization of NIS password files can become problematic.

Server Message Block

The most commonly found cross-system protocol for file systems and other resources is the Server Message Block protocol—SMB. Installed as part of all Microsoft-based systems since Windows 95, SMB is clearly the most prevalent file and resource-sharing protocol in terms of seats. Support for client systems includes Samba, which runs on Linux and other Unix variants and is available for Mac OS X since version 10.2.

Microsoft released a specification for SMB into the public domain called CIFS, short for Common Internet File System, which runs only over TCP/IP. SMB itself supports a wide variety of networking protocols.

SMB (and CIFS) are client/server request/response protocols in which messages are exchanged between connected systems. The resources that can be accessed under SMB include files, of course, but clients may also make requests of named pipes, APIs that support SMB, printers, and mail slots. In other words, the messages exchanged between an SMB client and server aren't limited to disk access.

As a connection-oriented protocol, SMB packets are exchanged through a virtual circuit established between the client and the server. On initiation of the SMB session, a virtual circuit is established and session user ID created along with a resource connection tree ID (tid) and file identifier. In the event that the link between the two systems is invalidated, any file handles that were previously set up are also invalidated, and the connection must be rebuilt completely.

Authentication occurs at two levels—Share and User. The Share level places a password on a shared device, and as long as the client passes the password to the SMB server, that share will be made available. This is so common as part of Windows-based networking as to be highly intuitive. User-level authentication allows the segregation of permissions for specific files on a network to specific users. The SMB client submits a UID along with requests to the server, and that UID is parsed for appropriate permission.

SMB servers broadcast their existence to clients through a browsing mechanism, and clients build up browse lists. In spite of the apparent ease of access through these browsing mechanisms, there is a performance impact on file transfers under SMB, depending on the application used to make the connection.

There are two modes available for SMB file transfers: raw and core. Raw mode typically uses 60- to 64K file blocks, whereas core mode transfers occur using a 4- to 16K block size. This makes raw mode performance higher than core mode transfers.

When connecting to a Windows-based SMB server using Explorer in order to move a file to a remote computer, the virtual circuit doesn't grant exclusive access to the command, and the transfer occurs in core mode. Conversely, when the move or copy command is issued locally, as when the file is pulled rather than pushed, raw mode is used and the transfer rate is higher. Raw mode is invoked in both directions using an MS-DOS command prompt.

SMB Protocol Stack

Samba is built on top of the NetBIOS network protocol, which in turn may be installed on TCP/IP, IPX/SPX, Token Ring, and other more obscure offerings. The behavior of SMB is greatly affected by the characteristics of the underlying network protocols that support it. Although this principle holds true for every file system potentially used to share file resources over the network, SMB/CIFS is interesting for two reasons: its modest beginnings as a very small networking protocol, and its ultimate domination as the most prevalent client/server resource-sharing service. This is due to its inclusion with all Microsoft-enabled PCs from Windows 95 onwards.

Originally, NetBIOS provided session services with network and transport services provided by NetBEUI. Given that NetBEUI is unrouteable, meaning Net-BEUI packets can't cross a bridge when they come to it, another means of providing network services was adopted. This gave rise to NetBIOS over TCP/IP (NBT). For these implementations, TCP/IP handles the addressing of SMB servers.

Standard Name Resolution

For systems where TCP/IP is the standard networking technology, such as Unix systems, SMB servers are located in the following order:

- Local hostname

- Host file lookup

- Domain Naming Services (DNS)

- NetBIOS name resolution

This is also the technique used by Windows 2000 and later systems from Microsoft.

There are three other means of resolving addresses of NBT hosts within a Windows network. The name cache contains the name to address entries for NetBIOS servers. The cache is populated from either successful name resolution requests or through preloading the LMHosts file.

Inside the LAN a broadcast is sent requesting the IP address for a server name. This NameQuery packet is sent to UDP port 137 on all computers on the local network. If the host is unavailable, there is no response, and the request is unfilled. Otherwise, the IP address is returned to the requestor, and a connection established. Broadcasting can quickly build up on a large network and is the default mechanism for Windows-based resources where a WINS server isn't configured. While the broadcast is limited to the local subnet, it does require handling of the packet by all machines on the network, not just the system providing the share.

WINS

Germane to Windows NT 4 environments, WINS uses DNS in all later environments.

LMHosts

LMHosts is similar to the hosts file on a Unix server. It's a maintained list of server names and addresses. The roots of NetBIOS in small LAN environments can be seen in these kinds of administrative artifacts. A small list of server resources, maintained in a contained geography, could use this approach, as systems and services grow; however, the administrative overhead incurred this way can become onerous.

SMB Administration

As an SMB implementation, Samba shows its roots in small networks in the lack of availability of in-depth administrative tools. In contrast, the Domain Controller model in Windows NT 4 was used similarly to NIS for the authentication of large numbers of users supporting centralized control of their access to file and print resources. With the introduction of Active Directory, this has been enhanced to include Authorization Management. This augments the access control list (ACL) editor used to set Active Directory permissions by extending permission checking to user roles and defined file system objects.

Journaling File Systems

Like many of the more advanced file system features, journaling was introduced in the mainframe data centers where bringing a system back online quickly after a reboot was a driving requirement. It's important to keep in mind that RAID protects only against disk failure. In the event that a transaction or command corrupts the file system, the RAID mirrors or parity disks will faithfully duplicate this corruption.

When the data is restored and the system restarted, large data centers found they didn't much enjoy waiting for a file systems check to be completed before the production application could be put back in business. This gave rise to journaling file systems.

Similar to the way RAID keeps a record of changes made to a disk so the image can be re-created in the event of a failure, a journaling file system keeps a journal of changes at the file system level. Examples of journaling file systems include the

Ext3 disk format found in Red Hat Linux. Other examples include JFS, XFS, and Elvis, the journaling extension to the HFS file system for the Mac OS X.

For Linux, there are several of these available, including

- ReiserFS

- XFS

- JFS

- Ext3

In each case, the file system keeps track of changes made to file system resources as a transaction. File system metadata might include inode numbers used or directory entries. Under a journaling file system, the intended changes to the file system are recorded in advance in the journal. The changes are made and the completion of the transaction duly noted in the journal. For those of you with database experience, yes, this is a log for file systems very much like a database server.

Similarly, the log or journal is applied to the file system in the event of a recovery from a crash. The state of the file system is restored to consistency by reviewing the journal and applying those changes successfully completed. The changes are effectively replayed or performed again or rolled back depending on their state.

Let's take a look at the journaling file systems supported by the Linux 2.4 kernel. I don't advocate one over another without a solid understanding of the context and requirements. They are presented here to help introduce you to some of the available alternatives.

- *ReiserFS:* ReiserFS version 3 was released as the first journaling file system for Linux. It's the default file system for SuSE, Lindows, and Gentoo. Reiser4 is based on Linux kernel 2.6 and focuses on large file system performance. It incorporates a plug-in architecture to support inclusion of third-party extensions developed for the ReiserFS environment. ReiserFS has demonstrated very high performance with smaller file systems.

- *XFS:* First developed by Silicon Graphics Inc. for their IRIX OS, XFS has been made available under a GPL for Linux developers. XFS can be installed on top of the Logical Volume Manager. It has been built into several Linux distributions including Mandrake, SuSE, Gentoo, Slackware, and JB Linux. Support for large directories and user quotas is included in XFS.

- *JFS:* Developed by IBM, the JFS is offered as open source under a GNU General Public License. Distributions that support JFS include Debian, Gentoo, Mandrake, Red Hat, Slackware, SuSE, Turbolinux, and United Linux. JFS handles reallocating bad blocks found on disk devices and provides support for SMP servers.

- *Ext3:* Developed as a journaling version of the Ext2 file system, Ext3 is provided with Red Hat Linux distributions. Resulting from identical underlying structural formats, an Ext2 file system can be mounted as Ext3, effectively converting existing file systems.

Distributed File Systems

Distributed file systems (DFSs) are more than the simple coordination of file access over multiple clients and servers. A robust DFS involves a topology known as *clusters,* and provides connection management techniques to support cluster members. These services include managing read and write activities, contention and locking, authentication, failovers, and replication.

As the services offered by distributed file systems become more complex, mechanisms for caching and synchronizing data become necessary. This introduces the idea of metadata, which is data about data. This is the point of departure for direct-attached storage, Network File Systems, and enterprise-class storage networks. Metadata managers and transformation services support advanced NAS and SAN features, such as support for concurrent access to identical data resources by heterogeneous clients. Distributed file systems development laid the groundwork for these storage network advances.

Andrew File System

One seminal development for distributed file systems was the Andrew File System (AFS), first developed at Carnegie-Mellon University. Ultimately, AFS became a product owned and sold by Transarc Corporation, a wholly owned subsidiary of IBM. AFS capabilities are relevant as a starting point in understanding the mechanisms that manage a distributed file system generally.

AFS was designed to use a persistent cache on clients for both file and directory data. This cache will survive a restart of either client or server. The AFS cell manages synchronization of cache entries. A *cell* is a centralized administrative view of a group of AFS servers, exporting file resources as volumes. These volumes can be mounted by clients, but security is handled through authentication tokens rather than on a user profile basis.

This improvement in cache management sets AFS apart from NFS and SMB.

DCE/DFS

Refinements in AFS design concepts were incorporated into the DCE/DFS file system as part of the Open Software Foundation. The reengineering effort resulted in ACLs being defined at the file level, not just directory level, extensions to support other clients (e.g., NFS), and more refined sharing through the token management.

DCE/DFS products have been offered as part of proprietary Unix variants and other hosting environments, and are available for Red Hat and SuSE Linux.

Microsoft Dfs

Through the Distributed file system (Dfs), not to be confused with DFS, Microsoft offers a single tree view for shared volumes provided by different servers on a network. Any user accessing a volume on a Dfs tree need not know the server name where the volume is actually located.

Coda

Coda has its roots in AFS version 2, but offers additional functionality to support replication, disconnection, and reintegration of volumes. While disconnected from a shared volume, Coda logs operations taken on the data when linkages are broken or slow to the point of unusability. The client modification log (CML) records changes to the data and replays those on reintegration with the server. Volume versions are stamped and validated to ensure efficient synchronization.

Intermezzo

An open source project that has its design roots in Coda, Intermezzo is a Linux implementation of a distributed file system supporting disconnection and automatic recovery from network outages. Intermezzo offers support for high availability and mobile computing scenarios.

Lustre

Lustre combines clustering, Linux, and a distributed file system in a public domain offering. Clustering technology is particularly well suited for large systems with high uptime requirements. A *cluster*, or integrated group of servers, can provide redundancy, load balancing, and high availability with optimum performance. Under Lustre, the cluster is presented as a single systems image, allowing stream-lined administration.

Lustre is a departure from traditional clustered file systems. Clusters typically share block storage across devices managed by a metadata server or distributed metadata updates. The model for Lustre is an object-based distributed file system (ODBFS), which defines storage objects that are manipulated by controllers. The command set in the object interface supports more than a mapping of names to block addresses. Depending on the implementation of the object driver, RAID, parallel write, or cryptographic encryption could be supported.

Sistina Global File System

The Global File System (GFS) shared file system for Linux is a commercial offering from Sistina for Red Hat and SuSE. Designed to support distributed database and web application servers by providing a single, common view of shared data, GFS incorporates both distributed metadata and multiple journaling techniques. Several locking mechanisms are supported, including single lock management within a dedicated lock server, or as part of a systems cluster. High availability is supported by multiple lock managers, configured to failover in the event of a failure.

Enterprise Volume Management Systems

Building on the discussion of volume management and file systems, I want to introduce you now to the Enterprise Volume Management Systems (EVMS). EVMS provides a storage management environment that includes support for bad block allocation, linear drive linking, and generic snapshots.

Perhaps the most interesting thing about EVMS is its ability to support a wide range of file systems on a number of platforms. The supported file systems are as follows:

- Ext2

- Ext3

- ReiserFS

- XFS

- Swap

The existing storage platforms on which EVMS can be operated include

- BSD

- Macintosh

- Linux MD/Software RAID

- Linux LVM volume groups

- AIX LVM volume groups

- OS/2 volume groups

- DOS (FAT) partitions

- GPT disk partitions

- S/390 disk partitions

EVMS can be operated from a command line or through a graphical user interface for use on Gnome and gtk-compliant windowing environments. Support for clustering of private and shared data containers to be administered by EVMS is provided by the Cluster Segment Manager. Through a plug-in architecture, EVMS offers membership and messaging services between cluster nodes and the EVMS engine.

With the introduction of tools like EVMS, you should be able to see the relationship between file systems management and distributed systems. Available in the open source world, these tools demonstrate the capabilities that can be found in turnkey third-party vendor NAS and SAN products.

Summary

NAS appliances offer shared file systems, typically under SMB and NFS connection strategies. From this chapter, you should have a better sense of the underlying functionality and inherent limitations of these venerable file sharing schemes.

Additionally, you should have a much stronger grasp on the relationship between network protocols and the ability for file system resources to be made available to physically separate applications. The introduction of AFS and subsequent distributed file systems should help you visualize the direction that file systems have gone in order to support the exponentially increasing demand for storage across the network.

The role of the file system in brokering data between application programs and lower level storage facilities should be much clearer to you at this point.

Some of the newly offered features in SAN products, like TotalStorage, is the ability to translate underlying file objects into the format required by a connected client. From the discussion of objects under Lustre, you should be acquainted with the levels of abstraction that must be managed to achieve this level of compatibility.

As part of the ground up approach to storage networks, the file systems described in this chapter, as well as the way they support authentication, should give you the foundation for reviewing NAS and SAN security, administration tools, and performance. These are described in the following chapters in the context of specific vendor offerings and customer infrastructure choices.

CHAPTER 7

SAN Backup and Recovery

IN THIS CHAPTER, you'll see many diverse reasons an organization would want to protect its data and information assets. I identify the ways in which this can be done in the context of Storage Area Networks and consider the implications of each method.

You'll also be introduced to the role of disk and tape devices in preserving data and ensuring that your applications have recoverability in the event of a catastrophic loss. The approach I take is to first identify the value of information generally, the specific, practical concern against which you wish to protect your data, and then to identify the general means by which that protection gain can be achieved.

I define the scope of information (as opposed to data) and its value to an organization. From this definition, you should be able to mix and match a topology for network storage to each requirement or set of requirements. The purpose of this arguably esoteric approach is to base the discussion of backup on the inherent value of the information being backed up.

Too frequently, storage networks are designed with the idea that any backup is a good backup if you can recover the data from it. Although this is consistent with a data management philosophy, it isn't consistent with an information management perspective. Return on investment (ROI), internal rate of return, and potential liabilities due to a lack of information management are tremendously relevant metrics that must be used to quantify the value of your storage network. The key concept in this chapter is relating the cost of data preservation (i.e., recoverability) to the inherent value of the data. I look at ways of determining the relative value of a data set, with the options a storage network presents for having duplicate, redundant copies as well as offsite or multisite stores and mechanisms for keeping them synchronized.

Professional administrator practices from the trenches are introduced, as well as friendly and hopefully helpful reminders for a basic, common-sense approach to data recovery that is easily overlooked.

The Fundamental Value of Data

This section serves as a context-setting discussion, before we move on to looking at the technology. First, I wanted to note some of the contributing factors underlying the attention senior executives are paying to data protection.

Everyone has heard that we're moving to an "information-based economy." On a practical level, this means that increasingly more of the value of our organizations is derived from the data it has, as opposed to the buildings it owns or the plants that it operates. Okay, so that is a mildly interesting macro-economic assertion.

The practical net effect of this is that protection of data is beginning to become as vital as the protection of monetary instruments. A store balances the till and puts the money in a safe several times a day. In a scenario where data is money, the fundamental value of the corporation is directly affected by the security of its data.

There are other equally important considerations besides the financial. Another valid example of importance is the post-production process, where, conceivably, digitally captured images could be lost and that creative asset gone forever. In a patient records context, the potential consequences of lost or misplaced data can't be overstated.

During my five years as a director of patient information at a cancer hospital, I saw several real-life examples of the need for timely intervention, not to mention the protection of personal privacy. On a lighter note, when we were digitally filming a training video in the mid 1990s, the digital camera was stolen overnight from the office and, unfortunately, it had the only copy of the previous week's shooting in it.

Professional practice is one good reason to implement solid, sensible backup and recovery procedures. As we move into how storage networks enable this, I wanted to challenge you to think first of what requirements for data protection your experience has shown necessary. Bearing these in mind as we discuss options and implications should help identify the most cost-effective route for your organization.

There are several reasons why an organization wishes to preserve its data and information. These include the following:

- *Utility value:* The information has a practical purpose on an ongoing (however frequent) basis.

- *Evidentiary value:* The information may be required to prove compliance to government regulations, proper action in response to litigation, or to document the chain of events and transactions that proves ownership or transfer of liability.

- *Archival value:* Some information (not much) is of enduring historical value. Although it's exceedingly difficult to know in the present what will become of value in the future, some information appreciates on the basis of the importance of what it documents—the flight recordings in some black boxes, for example.

- *Fiscal value:* Information might in and of itself be of actual financial worth. A client list, for example, is frequently valuated as a tangible asset of a corporation.

- *Private value:* Not all information is considered by its owners and initiators to be open for public display and consumption. Even where the information doesn't in any way connote an illegal activity, privacy has value. Individuals and corporations place a different value on privacy and have quite different notions of private and confidential.

Let me summarize this list in a different fashion. Information is power, or so they say, because it enables action or promotes a more beneficial inaction. Inherent in this is the effect of information being applied to the decision making process and the resulting actions taken as a direct function of those decisions. This is the usefulness of information.

Companies and people go to court. Information is disclosed and presented to support or detract from the claims that are made under the law. This is the value of information as evidence.

History must be recorded or memorized in order to be passed on from one generation to the next. That's what makes it a story. The proof of the story—the evidence provided to the judgment of history—is of inherent value. The details of the preparation of John and Jacqueline Kennedy's visit to Dallas in November of 1963 would have seemed trivial one day and nostalgic the next. Keeping information safe for the future is the outcome of understanding its archival value.

Money talks as we all know. Currency is inherently information. As a commodity, it's not worth the paper its printed on. Since the advent of electronic funds transfer, some money is, quite literally, information, and its value is fiscal.

Protecting Your Interests

It should immediately strike you that the ranging values of different kinds of information directly translate to a distinctly unique set of requirements for backup, security, and handling. Point-of-Sale systems that record customer transactions require different safekeeping than do the personal journals of your company's founder from 200 years ago. As a Storage Area Network professional, it's your responsibility to ensure that information is accessible to the right people in a timely manner as required and that it's protected from loss, tampering, and prying eyes.

With the unrelenting pace of change in the Information Technologies we use to build storage networks, there is a temptation to look for that "magic bullet" that will deal with all requirements at once. Unfortunately, even if that were technologically possible, it would be financially irresponsible for a company to underwrite such an investment. Little-used information doesn't have to be at your fingertips at all times, especially when that level of access comes with a high price. However, it should be noted that a more frequently felt pain is that of *not* having information at the required fingertips or even available when it's needed.

The Perils of Pauline

Whenever people talk about "disaster recovery," I'm always curious to know what kind of disaster they want protection against. Then of course, the definition of protection comes into play. Like the map that indicates *You Are Here* when you're trying to get around your local shopping mall, you need these foundational planks; otherwise it's impossible to build a backup system that actually delivers what your organization needs.

Some of the most commonly discussed disasters a data center requires protection from include

- Earthquake

- Fire

- Flood

- Act of war

Some of the most commonly experienced causes of data loss turn out to be

- Operator error

- Malicious ex-employees

- Lack of tested procedures

- Hardware failure

- Idiots with backhoes

Without being too facetious, or to minimize actual calamities that have occurred to organizations as a result of what the insurance companies call Acts of God, my point is that backup and recovery for Storage Area Networks needs to function first and foremost at a prosaic, "Oops" level, after which a more sophisticated threat protection can be layered on.

I've actually been in a data center when the lights went out as a result of an overly aggressive construction worker cutting power to the building with their Ditch Witch. The resulting unexpected shutdown unfortunately clobbered a system disk. The resulting recovery process uncovered a flawed backup procedure (which had never been tested), and many months of data warehouse information was just gone. This made for some *very* displeased vice presidents.

The Sarbanes-Oxley Act of 2002

In response to the financial fiascos and lack of corporate governance uncovered in such organizations as WorldCom, Tyco, and far too many others, the U.S. legislated a more detailed requirement of corporate behavior known as the Sarbanes-Oxley Act. This legislation sets mandatory compliance for publicly traded organizations, and for purposes of storage networks, sets retention requirements for information. It's this change in the regulatory environment that will drive the way backup and preservation of data is handled in public and private companies alike.

I indicated earlier in this chapter that there are different ways to assign value to data, and with its associated value there is a cost profile for its preservation. As a storage administrator, you should be aware that in the event your organization is bound by the Sarbanes-Oxley Act, and you don't comply with it (that is, you can't provide access to the data it indicates is required), your directors and officers can face serious penalties.

The senior partner of the consulting firm where I last worked as an employee was fond of the tongue-in-cheek expression "What interests the boss should fascinate his subordinates." How fascinated do you suppose the chief executive of your organization would be to discover that due to a slight technical hiccup, certain data couldn't be restored and as a result that person might face fines or even imprisonment?

For publicly traded organizations, and for organizations that might be valued on the basis of being acquired by a public firm, I believe this change in records retention requirements spells the death of tape backup in favor of disk-based scenarios.

The reasoning for this isn't at all technical. It's entirely around the requirement to provide security to those who will be held responsible for data being made available. Tape, and for that matter DVD, CD-ROM, or any other dismountable media (including paper records), requires indexing and location control. This isn't as trivial an issue as you might be tempted to think.

Speed Costs—How Fast Did You Want to Go?

A systems administrator I used to work with liked to tell business unit managers, "Availability 7×23.5 is way cheaper than 7×24." Of course, some data is priceless and demands the best protection that money can buy. Other data is valuable but not priceless. I've yet to meet a business user who would confess that their data was worthless. That is the continuum of data value though—priceless through worthless with varying degrees of value along the way.

Luckily, storage networks have a number of alternative ways of allowing you to protect the data assets under administration.

It's the Recovery, Not the Backup, That Counts

Certainly, everyone understands this on a commonsense level. Taking a backup is hardly the important part. Restoring the data from that backup is the litmus test for an effective backup. Unfortunately for tape-based backup solutions, the very disconnectable nature of the media means that two new levels of risk are introduced. You may not know the exact nature of the data you've backed up, and even if you know, you may not be able to find it.

The following is an excerpt from the Sarbanes-Oxley Act:

Title VIII: Corporate and Criminal Fraud Accountability Act of 2002.

It is a felony to "knowingly" destroy or create documents to "impede, obstruct, or influence" any existing or contemplated federal investigation.

Auditors are required to maintain "all audit or review work papers" for 5 years.

The statute of limitations on securities fraud claims is extended to the earlier of 5 years from the fraud, or 2 years after the fraud was discovered, from 3 years and 1 year, respectively.

Employees of issuers and accounting firms are extended "whistleblower protection" that would prohibit the employer from taking certain actions against employees who lawfully disclose private employer information to, among others, parties in a judicial proceeding involving a fraud claim. Whistle blowers are also granted a remedy of special damages and attorney's fees.

A new crime for securities fraud that has penalties of fines and up to 10 years imprisonment.

Personally, I find the use of quotation marks around the word "knowingly" to be quite fascinating. "Contemplated" also has interesting implications. Say an executive approves a system for storing records and disposing of others, such as their paper originals, and subsequently an investigation is launched into the financial practices of the company. If the system inherently allows for data to become separated from its place of origin, and during the course of the investigation it can't be retrieved, does it not seem possible that said executive might be seen to have knowingly made the documentation go away? Of course, the courts in light of specific cases must interpret legislation of this nature. For the immediate term, however, it's reasonable to assume that any risk of data loss can be mitigated by disk storage. And the mechanism of choice for this is a Storage Area Network.

Keyword Search

Perhaps the single most attractive feature, from a records retention perspective, is the ability to search through a bunch of online storage looking for files with an occurrence of a particular string. Databases and other proprietary formatted files must be mounted and searched by software that can access those formats, of course, but this too raises an interesting, nontechnical decision with technical implications. Should e-mail messages be stored as text?

In the same way that human-readable paper records can be scanned by investigators, text formatted documents can be scanned by pattern-matching software, ensuring that any key phrase or term can be used to pull up a file containing it. It's a given that you can't know in advance what documentation will be historically significant (although the guys who signed the Magna Carta probably had some clue that a copy should be kept). As a rule of thumb, I would be willing to bet that storage administrators don't really know what an SEC investigation would want to retrieve first. And if you don't work for a public company, don't be too fast to breathe a sigh of relief. A tax audit isn't a whole lot more fun from the perspective of the pressure placed on your end users and by extension on your retrieval system.

Backup Strategy by Data Type

As I've already noted, the line between Network Attached Storage and Storage Area Networks is already blurring on the basis of connectivity type. You simply can't say all Fibre Channel storage networks are SANs and all NAS implementations are Ethernet. The differentiation on the basis of file system or block I/O is still significant, however. This is especially applicable to backup and recovery strategies.

File Systems Backup

In a NAS application, a user accessing a network drive should have no idea (at least based on performance) that the network drive is across the network from the file server, as well as from their client workstation. Perhaps ideally the local workstation has no local storage of its own. As this is unlikely, let's consider a backup of a set of departmental hard drives, resident on client PCs or workstations

As storage capacity has ramped up, typical user machines are configured with more than 10GB of local storage. Although it may seem bizarre that a mere decade ago, we barely had a single gigabyte on the desktop, now users are frequently storing 4 or more gigs in their My Documents directories. How much of this data is redundantly held in e-mail folders or the folders of other users, synchronization of alterations, and other data management issues are part of the proceduralization of storage networks and data asset management. For purposes of this discussion, let's assume that it's all gold.

One hundred workstations with 10GB drives translates to a terabyte of storage required to hold drive images, assuming no compression. The classic topology for backing up data in this scenario is a dedicated SCSI tape device. In keeping with my intention of mentioning gear available from every vendor in the SAN space, let's use the EZ17 Autoloader as a representative tape device.

According to Exabyte, this device offers unattended access to over 1 terabyte of data with a compressed transfer rate of 108GB hourly. Specs for their native format are somewhat lower at 420GB of capacity and 43.2GB per hour transfer rate. Incorporating Mammoth-2 tape technology, independent reviews placed this device at more than twice the performance of obsolete digital linear tape.

But the interesting thing about this configuration is how quickly the limits are reached, and the implications of those limits for online data access.

Practical testing showed the EZ17 capable of backing up 200GB of data in a little more than 4 hours. By extension, to back up a terabyte would take a 24-hour window. The constraints in this case aren't just the attachment to the server, but also the internal limitations of the tape-writing technology. This has led to speculation that "tape is dead," but like many information technologies, rumors of this demise may be greatly exaggerated.

Let's look at some of the tape devices that came out in mid 2003 based on the Sony Super-AIT (SAIT) technology.

The Qualstar TLS-5000 family of SAIT-equipped tape libraries range in throughput capabilities from 16.5 terabytes of native capacity to 340 terabytes of compressed storage. Data transfer rates peaked at over 2.2 terabytes per hour. The company offers a Fibre Channel attachment option to support SAN and serverless backup applications.

The key point to remember is that in the same way that DLT gave way to Super DLT, Advanced Intelligent Technology (AIT) formats are giving way to Super AIT. Media improvements result in higher storage capacities, and the drive-enhanced transfer rates keep older technologies one step ahead of extinction. Tape libraries offer the characteristics listed in Table 7-1 to your backup strategy that online storage doesn't.

Table 7-1. Tape Backup Characteristics

Advantages	Disadvantages
Removable media	Media subject to loss
Expandable capacity	Highly mechanical
Lower cost	Format changes
Variety of software support	Longer reload time

Many of the characteristics of tape backup also apply to CD or DVD backup solutions. In both cases, a great deal of attention must be paid to the creation and administration of procedures. Even unattended backups require monitoring or notification of successful (or not) completion. To prevent tapes or CDs from being mislaid, they must be labeled and properly stored. This is only a function of technology in as much as the nature of removable media requires a process for its relocation. This is common sense, to be sure, but nonetheless is an integral part of a tape or removable media backup strategy.

Clearly, backing up a large number of drives, whether clients or servers to a single tape device across a network, is going to hit the limits of the system's throughput capabilities pretty quickly. On the other hand, in the same way that the introduction of a switch resolves network contention issues in a Local Area Network, it makes the same contribution in a backup setting.

Tape devices can certainly be pulled out from server-attached devices and gain the benefits of a SAN. Like storage arrays, there are tape libraries that aren't simply data devices attached to servers which then have to be administered. Instead, these backup appliances contain the necessary intelligence to manage the entire backup process without placing a processing load on a host.

Moving the tape device off the LAN and placing it on the Fibre Channel infrastructure gains two advantages. First, there is no longer contention on the network, so there is no chance that users will have their network access compromised by the large volume of bits moving from clients and servers to the tape device. Second, the throughput rate of the switch is faster than the tape device, which will reduce the overall time needed to back up the volume of data to the constraints imposed by the tape library rather than the network.

There are then three separate configurations for using tape devices as your backup strategy:

- Server and network attached

- LAN free by moving the tape server to the fabric

- LAN free and server free by adding an intelligent tape device

As noted in Table 7-1, removable media still carries with it significant pros and cons.

If one of the key ROI propositions of moving to a SAN is the increase in administrator productivity, opting for a less intervention-prone backup strategy may make more sense.

Drive-to-Drive Backup

One of the key advantages of the tape backup solution was the ability to remove and store offsite the data. With the extended geographic reach of networked storage, it's now possible to gain this advantage while maintaining data on drives. In comparison to tape, it's easier, though typically more expensive, to store the backup data online and quicker to restore it from the disk. This means the nature of the data and minimum restore time will be a factor in determining your backup strategy. Working from the ground up though, let's look at how networked storage handles file backups using disk and disk utilities.

Snapshot Copy

Disk arrays offer a snapshot copy option to support the complete copy of a file system or volume. The advantage of a snapshot is that very large datasets can be copied with only a small (seconds-long) freeze of the dataset on the array. This is accomplished by copying the pointers to the data, and recording subsequent changes made to the data in both sets of pointers.

Clone Copy

These are also managed by the disk array, and implementation specifics vary from vendor to vendor. This is a complete, physical second copy of the data, and it requires at least twice the space (some additional for the copy process), and the time to copy is a direct function of the amount of data and performance characteristics of the array. The advantage is, of course, having a complete image of the file system or volume as it was at that point in time.

Mirror Copy

This is analogous to a combination of clone and snapshot. A mirror copy of the data is created (time and space conditions apply), and changes to the mirror are made in synch with the updates, inserts, and deletes of data in the mirrored volume. Mirrors can be used for failover, in the event that the mirror is broken or inaccessible, and the changes are logged and applied when the mirror comes back online. In this way, a mirror copy can be used to synchronize data, and the file selected for backup to, say, tape is the mirror. This means use of the master data is uninterrupted during the backup process, and the mirror is brought back into synch when the backup is completed.

Remote Copy

This complete copy of the volume or file system is remote by virtue of the fact that it's copied from one array to another. However, it should be noted that interoperability of remote copy has traditionally been disappointing, and remote copies generally work from arrays offered by the same vendor. There are two variations on remote copy: synchronous and asynchronous.

Synchronous Remote Copy

When this option is selected, a transaction resulting in a change to the underlying data is only marked complete when both the primary data volume and the copy have successfully written the changes and returned that result code.

Asynchronous Remote Copy

Used when disk subsystems are quite far apart, the write transaction is completed as soon as the primary system has made the changes. Updating the copy and synchronizing the two data sets in the event the link between the two subsystems is broken is handled by the primary array.

Extended Copy

The SCSI-3 extended copy command was specified as part of the ANSI T10 committee efforts. It allows the copy of data from one set of devices to another set, whether disk or tape. This command can be executed on devices connected via SCSI cables of Fibre Channel fabrics. This "third-party copy" command allows one subsystem to directly contact another, and for the two devices to manage the move of data without intervention from a host. Naturally, there are specific implementations of this copy from different groups of vendors, and claims of interoperability should be verified based on your specific requirements and the phase of the moon.

Restore, Recover, and Fail Over

When I ran the systems administration group for the big oil company (that got eaten by an even bigger oil company), we had an annual test of the remote failover procedures. The idea was that in the event that downtown got clobbered by a catastrophic event, all essential computing processes would fail over to a site at the airport, some 15 miles away. In 5 years, we never had the failover go smoothly, and it wasn't a question of a lack of competence or commitment. Each time, there was some particular (different) hurdle that hadn't been foreseen. How much more difficult would it prove to be when recovery procedures aren't tested at all?

Arguably, data held in databases is a more valuable asset than files lying around in My Documents directories. It occurs to me that this wouldn't be true for medical imaging, video production, law firms, and myriad other organizations where the data assets are text or image oriented. However, grant me this assumption, and let's look at the considerations that govern what to back up and how often backups need to occur.

A traditional database environment has two assets that need to be backed up for a production database—the database itself and the transaction log. This is directly analogous to a full file-system backup and an incremental one. In both cases, incremental backups must be restored on top of the last full data backup.

There are two considerations involved in this, the first being the security of the incremental backups. If you want to test your backup procedures, just look at the labeling, filing, and retrievability of the incremental files. In a fire drill situation, how long does it take to locate and assemble the needed assets? The next question, and it's one that is usually only asked by management after a system outage where a recovery has become a necessity, is, How long does it take to apply the incremental backups?

A full database backup takes more time than a backup and truncation of the transaction log. Unless you're using the mirror copy strategy to perform the backup, there will be an impact on user performance as the full backup is performed. This investment in backup pays dividends when it comes time to do the restore.

The reason you should benchmark all of your key data sets from this standpoint is to help you determine the kind of backup strategy needed for each one. Chances are, even a small-to-medium organization will incorporate a combination of online and removable media backup devices. As I'll cover in Chapter 12, a dataset-by-dataset review of the importance of data is an excellent way to justify storage networks and the associated backup devices.

What Was the Question Again?

The needs of a hospital systems administrator will be quite different from someone planning a disaster recovery strategy for a multinational corporation. The available solution components are the same for everyone; however, it's the way you mix and match them that will meet your identified objectives.

The question to be asked is, What steps have been taken to safeguard the data assets of your organization? Clearly, storage networks are an excellent means to ensure and enhance recoverability. And equally clear is that not all data is equally valuable. The main vulnerability is the loss of irreplaceable data that provides an organization with some differentiation or competitive advantage. The data that makes up the phone directory is more important to your firm if you're in the business of publishing that data to subscribers.

In terms of technology, meeting backup and recovery requirements are significant examples of how storage networks provide value. Then again, speed costs, so the dilemma is how best to match the strategy to the requirement. A basic point? Perhaps, but it's amazing how many IT organizations can't remember the last time they tested their backups or can identify the data sets of most value to senior management.

78s, 45s, 33s, 8-Tracks, Cassettes, CDs and MP3s

If you were born before manned spaceflight, you may well remember the old wind-up phonograph and the extra-thick vinyl records called 78s. My grandfather had one. Beatles-era music lovers certainly played their 45s, and Peter Frampton had the single most popular LP of 1976. As the 8-track gave way to the cassette deck and CD player, which in turn gave it up to iPod and Napster, many of us ended up with collections of media that we no longer had working equipment to replay.

This isn't some kind of nostalgia tour. It's a very real problem with tape, in my opinion. Yet when you read the exchanges between administrators on the relative merits of various options, from some of the flame posts you might think someone accused the other of having an ugly baby.

I have clients who installed Digital Audio Tape (DAT) and customers who went Digital Linear Tape (DLT). Even my little boutique organization has records stored on quarter-inch streaming tape, and 8 mm tape. More recently I've been offloading to DVD.

In my book, tape is dead. Not really dead, of course, any more than we have paperless offices and microfilm; dead records and archives are things of the past. We still have buggy whips—that industry is just a little smaller than it was a hundred years ago.

I stated that the reasons for not using tape weren't technical. Offline media that evolves over compressed periods of time requires either backward compatibility or maintenance of multiple pieces of equipment. Of course, you could always elect to trust that a service bureau or the Smithsonian can be called on to recover data, provided you know where to find it. However, at least for organizations that fall under the jurisdiction of the Securities Exchange Commission, there are indeed other considerations.

Summary

The backup and recovery options introduced in this chapter ran the gamut from an example of a single server-attached tape device to asynchronous mirrored copies of databases held in offsite locations.

Even with the increases in throughput enabled in storage networks, assisted by copy capabilities built into storage devices, making online copies of data has a cost in time and resources.

From this chapter, you should have a better feel for how to segregate your data backup requirements into priorities, and match those priorities to resources that appropriately address them.

The bottom line is that you should be evaluating your backup capability from retrieval, not a storage perspective. Tape is a weaker media for retrieval than disk, which is getting cheaper all the time, and proprietary formatted files are harder to restore than text copies. If you think this just exploded the scope of what you need to store, you're probably right. I hope you found at least a couple of good justifications for increasing your storage network budget, and some solid buttons to push to get your nontechnical executives to approve it.

CHAPTER 8

Storage Security

AT VARIOUS TIMES in this book, I refer to the asset value of information. Like all assets, data needs to be protected against loss, tampering, and theft. In Chapter 7, I talk about backup and recovery options for Storage Area Networks. In this chapter, I'll introduce you to the underlying concepts and technologies that contribute to making a storage network secure from unauthorized access.

I have several colleagues who are quite qualified in the areas of security. Super Dave, for instance, got his master's degree in cryptography at Georgia Tech before joining the Air Force. I have no doubt that the treatment of the topic of security that you'll find here is inadequate. The history, scope, and depth of the efforts this technology encompasses are nothing short of staggering. There are folks who would take the position that you simply can't summarize the issues surrounding data security.

However, given my background as a systems architect and administrator, I felt it was important to pull these technologies into the discussion of SAN components and to put them into perspective. If you're truly interested in security, I would suggest that a single chapter in a technical book intended to cover a range of technologies can only be an introduction.

In this chapter, I'll show you the basic elements that contribute to a secure storage network. After learning about the elements of data security generally, you'll see how a given storage network security solution incorporates those features.

Let's take a look at the security considerations that are applicable to any networked storage environment.

Can't Read What You Can't Get

The corollary to this statement is, of course, that to protect your data you should make sure that if someone can get their hands on it, then they can't read it. That points to the two key approaches to information security: access and encryption. Let's start at the state of the art and work towards the commonly available approaches.

The prevailing opinion is that fiber-optic cabling offers the most secure network, as it's difficult to tap. It's popularly held that unlike copper wire, or wireless transmission of data packets that can be copied by eavesdropping, fiber requires that you physically intercept the signal, which is a detectable intrusion. Actually, there are commercially available clamp-on receivers that bend a fiber-optic cable and detect the photons that don't successfully bounce off the cladding. The signal leakage or loss is generally less than 2 percent or .1 Db, so it arrives at its destination without indication that it was intercepted.

This is the position taken by an Australian security firm specializing in security products for fiber networks. I have no experience, nor does anyone I know have any experience, with undetected interception of fiber signals (although I did see it in a James Bond movie once).

The main point here is that there is no security like physical security. Signal interception requires physical access to either a fiber or copper wire. Then the signal must be collected and interpreted. Because I do have experience in security issues from wireless clients, I'm going to spend most of this chapter addressing encryption rather than interception protection or detection.

It's Classified

Like most of the technologies you've read about in this book, security is very much an activity that must be evaluated for suitability to task. Put another way, there is little or no point to investing the time, effort, and money into a system for securing the collection and storage of spam e-mails. Classifying information according to its value and corresponding risk of interception is a necessary prerequisite. Contracts are more important than correspondence, financial information is more sensitive than marketing materials, and research and development can represent a huge investment or an attractive target, depending on whose perspective you take.

Industrial espionage isn't just the stuff of fiction. For any company that relies on technological advances to maintain and grow its business, there is likely a competitor in some jurisdiction who would be quite happy to be kept informed of progress. Granted, a great many organizations, especially smaller ones, have little or no need for a highly secure environment. Like data backup and disaster recovery strategies, you must start with an understanding of exactly what you're trying to protect against.

For purposes of this chapter, I'll assume that you've identified a need to take steps to protect certain data from snooping. You may work for a hospital with a legal responsibility to protect patient privacy, a law firm that negotiates and litigates cases of interest to the press, a top-secret defense research lab, or an accountancy that would lose too many clients if their financial data leaked.

Gates of the Great Wall

The Great Wall of China is the most physically imposing testament on the planet to the human desire for security. It's also interesting to consider that over the course of time since it was built, the wall hasn't actually functioned very well in keeping out invaders. In particular, the case of the Mongol invasion of China in the thirteenth century comes to mind. The Mongols didn't swarm the wall. They didn't have to. Instead they bribed someone to open the gate and let them through. Cupidity is often the greatest threat to security.

The notion of gatekeepers is a powerful metaphor for storage network security. Although software agents can't be bribed, they can be tricked. And that is the threat I'll deal with next.

Tunneling

The very feature that makes stacks of protocols so functional is the key to undermining it. Packets carry information from sender to recipient without knowing what the package contains. All it knows is whether the packet has become corrupted during its journey.

The process by which one protocol is encapsulated within another is called *tunneling*. A virtual private network (VPN) provides a way for a client to gain access to the network via a tunnel established for that purpose. Security, for purposes of this chapter, is comprised of the steps needed to ensure that only valid users are taking authorized actions in the context of network access and storage operations.

Three tunnels are required when using a VPN that is enabled with IPSec, or Internet Protocol Security, as defined by the IETF. A management tunnel must be created and communication tunnels provided to serve as lanes for bidirectional communication between the host and client. The management tunnel establishes authentication of users (whether a user is allowed to connect) and encryption protocols (what code is that message in). The other two tunnels provide actual data traffic from node A to node B and from node B back to node A.

Like the Great Wall metaphor, if unauthorized access is somehow acquired, which would then allow access to files and messages, the next level of defense is obtained by making those files and messages undecipherable. In this way, a spoof of an IP that obtains the torrent of signals from a lower layer, whether through eavesdropping on a wireless hub or tapping a cable between sender and receiver, may still not be able to make sense of the signals as captured.

Secure Socket Layers

Secure Socket Layers (SSL) are probably the most familiar means of authenticating users and encrypting communication. It was first developed by Netscape for browser-based interfaces, and it's used by some Storage Area Network products to provide secure access for web-based administration. Because SSL addresses some of the fundamental security considerations, let's take a look at it first.

First defined in 1996, the Secure Sockets Layer specification has been subsumed into the IETF Transport Layer Security specification RFC 3546. As of June 2003, it was still under review and discussion.

The SSL protocol incorporates two main protocol components—the SSL record protocol and the SSL handshake protocol. The format of data to be passed between client and server is defined using the record protocol. Once determined, the handshake protocol is used to establish a connection between the devices. An SSL connection enables

- Authentication of servers to clients and optionally clients to servers

- Negotiation of supported cryptographic algorithms or ciphers

- Select public key encryption techniques to be used in the session

With these elements in place, the SSL connection is established.

Port 443 is the default server port for SSL connections. When a client initiates an SSL connection, a ClientHello is sent to the server. Typically, this means an HTTP connection has been made between the client and server on port 80, and the client then indicates it wishes to initiate an SSL or TLS secure connection. An example of this is when you log on to your bank's web site and select Pay Bills or similar as an option, thereby indicating you as a client wish to move to a secure connection for accessing your financial data.

The initial authentication is performed using public key infrastructure (PKI) and might be one of these three major varieties: RSA, Diffie-Hellman, Fortezza. This kind of key encryption doesn't require the sender and receiver to use the same key. For this reason, it's referred to as *asymmetric encryption*. You'll get a chance to read more about how keys work after I introduce IPSec in the next section; for the meantime, let's focus on the main steps of establishing a secure connection between client and server over the Web.

Once the authentication has been established, either server to client or both, depending on the security level, SSL defines a set of security characteristics to control the integrity and confidentiality of the messages sent. There are three main ways to encrypt data—through the use of ciphers, or hashing, or a combination of both. Within these types there are several options, including the following:

- *Cipher methods:* RC2, RC4, DES 40, DES 56, Triple DES

- *Hash methods:* MD5, SHA-1

During the handshake process, the client and server agree to which set of encryption methods will be used during the session to protect the data being exchanged. A typical financial transaction over the web will involve 128-bit encryption. Data Encryption Standard (DES) 40 and DES 56 are 40-bit and 56-bit encryption algorithms originally developed by the U.S. government. According to the National Institute of Standards and Technology (NIST), the same computer dedicated to cracking a 56-bit DES encryption key and completing that task in 1 second would take 149 trillion years to break a 128-bit Advanced Encryption Standard (AES) key. Who has that kind of time? To be fair, in 1999 it took a team about 22 hours to decipher a DES 56 message at a rate of 245 billion keys per second.

As a server administrator, you elect which cipher suites and encryption strength you wish to support for access over SSL/TLS. If you intend to support web-based administration of your Storage Area Network assets, you'll likely opt for stronger rather than weaker SSL security.

IPSec

The Internet Protocol Security Working Group of the IETF handles definition of security protocol behaviors to be supported by devices communicating over the IP protocol. IPSec is an important security consideration as it may be used for iSCSI, iFCP, and FCIP. The IETF defined three approaches for supporting IPSec as part of iSCSI solutions: as part of the hardware (e.g., QLogic HBA logic), via software, or incorporated into a VPN device such as a switch. No matter what approach is used, it's worth noting that IPSec is an optional security facility for Storage Area Networks with implications for security, performance, and cost. I'll evaluate several approaches and technologies for implementing IPSec for Storage Area Networks at the end of this chapter in the section "Get a GRIP." From that discussion, you'll be able to see how these implications apply to Storage Area Networks specifically. Prior to that, however, it's important to understand the underlying security concepts.

The IPSec approach to securing data transmissions between Ethernet nodes has two modes: transport and tunnel. For security purposes, these nodes can be considered Ethernet hosts, security gateways, or a combination of both. In transport mode, the data within the packet is encrypted, but the header is not. Tunnel mode provides increased security by encrypting both. In each case, a public key is shared between the sender and the receiver. The protocol for sharing these keys is known as ISAKMP.Oakley, or the Internet Security Association and Key Management/Oakley protocol, which allows the receiver to authenticate the sender using digital certificates and public keys. ISAKMP separates the process of key exchange between parties from the details of security association and key management. It provides a common framework for agreement of format for the SA attributes as well as for negotiation, modification, and deletion of security associations.

The Keys to Enlightenment

I've touched on communications protocol–level security attempts to validate station-to-station authorization by using challenge-response authentication of users. You can take another approach to ensure that, even if received or intercepted by unintended (and by extension undesired) third parties, a message can only be understood by someone with the key to unlock it. Of course, I'm referring to encryption and the two main means of encrypting digital messages—schemes based on private and public encryption keys.

A text message sent with no attempt to scramble or obscure its content is said to be sent "in the clear." Many programs such as FTP-based ones will send user names and passwords in the clear, meaning that if the communication is indeed intercepted, it takes little or no effort for a malfeasant to determine what those values are, and subsequently to use them as if that person were the original authorized party. This naturally leads to a desire to perform an additional obfuscation of files and messages through encryption.

Coded messages have been sent between parties for millennia. The art and science of this practice is cryptography and its product is encryption. In the digital era, this involves the invocation of an algorithm to scramble the order of the message that requires a matching key to decode the contents. The assumption is that if you have the authorization and the encryption key, you're the party to whom the message was sent or you're qualified to see or modify the contents of a file. This is all very straightforward, but it quickly gets more intricate.

One of the side effects of our seemingly ever-increasing computing power is the ability to apply "brute force" to determining the encryption key used. Brute force in this case means evaluating possible keys until the right one is found. To get around this, cryptographers increase the number of possible permutations until it exceeds the computing power or the amount of time available to crack the code.

Of course, starting with the Enigma code-breaking efforts of the Allied Forces in World War II, another approach emerged: deciphering the algorithm itself based on patterns rather than trying to guess it randomly. From the development of encryption and decoding practice over the past 60 years, a number of major leaps in security algorithms have occurred.

Digital Signatures

Digital signature schemes assume the public key of the sender is available to the recipient. This can be achieved by having the sender include the public key with each message sent. Or the sender can reference a location where the key can be accessed such as an FTP or HTTP address. Additionally, the public keys can be stored in central directories accessible for key lookup.

One of the key benefits of digital signatures (yes, I meant that) is known as *nonrepudiation*. Not only does a digital signature affirm that the message hasn't been corrupted, but it also identifies the sender specifically.

Digital Certificates

To further associate digital signatures with a particular message or file, digital certificates were developed. These certify that a particular public key belongs to, is bound to, or otherwise associated with a specific individual or organization. When downloading files for updating the Windows operating environment with security patches, a certificate notification is presented unless a user has opted to always trust content from Microsoft.

A public key certification authority, such as VeriSign or Thawte, authorizes issuers of digital certificates. These authorities digitally sign certificates issued under their jurisdiction with their own private key. However, the force and effect of the authority is really simply a reference or attestation that the certification authority knows the issuer. This is why in some cases you'll receive warnings about certificates having expired. This doesn't necessarily mean that the issuer can't be trusted, rather that they have for whatever reason allowed their licensing fees with the certification authority to go unpaid. One of the main reasons for supporting certificates is to build consumer confidence for online purchases. Expired certificates don't exactly inspire such confidence.

A server certificate allows a client's browser to verify that the connected server is actually the right one. In keeping with the online banking scenario, you certainly wouldn't want your banking information rerouted to third parties. To accomplish this, your browser checks the digital signature, which is the public key of the certificate authority validating the certificate. A further validation is done against the common name of the requested URL and the dates of the certificate and the client computer. The stage is thus set for negotiation of a private connection.

How Encryption Works

Management of the exchange of keys is a critical issue dealt with by the likes of Internet Key Exchange (IKE) and Internet Protocol Security, as well as public vehicles such as certification authorities. However, it doesn't provide an explanation of how messages are actually encrypted and decrypted. Perhaps now is the appropriate time to drill down to the next layer of detail.

Because the decoding of an encrypted document or message is done with a key, as established by Enigma, the trick is to ensure that the key itself can't be guessed or deciphered. So far, so much common sense.

One method by which the representation of the key can be scrambled is called *hashing*. A hashing algorithm is a way of computing a "condensed representation" of a message or data file. It results in a fixed length output of the file called a *message digest* or fingerprint. It isn't the content of the file itself, but rather it's a 128-bit value based on the data that was hashed. Even the slightest change in the content results in a different fingerprint.

Through this mechanism, the representation can be checked to ensure the message hasn't been tampered with or faked. The algorithms are specified by standards bodies like NIST or individuals such as Rivest, Shamir, and Adleman—the venerated RSA. The algorithms are then codified, added to APIs for various programming languages, and subsequently incorporated into device drivers.

You should be able to see that hashing provides a sense of certainty that the message wasn't tampered with, but alas, who knows what evil lurks in the hearts of humans? To provide security against interception and subsequent review of the data, that data must be rendered undecipherable. This is the job of encryption.

Two of the other bright lights in cryptography, Diffie and Hellman (not the mayonnaise magnate), published a ground-breaking proposition in 1976 which basically went like this:

Classic cryptographic operations involve two functions and an object. The functions are encryption and decryption where the object is a message or data. Private key encryption, which was the only kind in history up to this point (1976), required both the encryptor and decryptor to each have identical keys. Public key cryptography provides for the creation of a key readily available to the public for purposes of encryption. Decryption of the message, however, is dependent on knowing the components of the public key. These components are private keys and are known only to the recipient of the message. In this way, a message can be encoded by a sender who could not subsequently decode his or her own message. In fact, only the creator of the public code, knowing the private key, can decrypt the message.

Of course, the tricky part was coming up with an algorithm that would allow decryption based on a subcomponent of the encrypting code, detailed discussion of which is beyond the scope of this book.

Between the two methods, hash and ciphers, messages can be identified as coming from validated senders, that they haven't been tampered with in transit, and that the contents have been scrambled so that if intercepted, the messages will be undecipherable without the right decryption key.

Techniques like SSL and TSL perform these encoding/decoding operations in software at the transport layer. IPSec can perform these operations in either hardware or software at the network layer. There is, naturally, a performance implication to having the contents of the frames encrypted and decrypted, as well as session overhead incurred in the transfer of digital signatures and exchange of validated digital certificates.

Drilling into IPSec

IPSec uses Encapsulated Security Payload (ESP) for encryption. Like the Authentication Header (AH) process for authenticating remote IPSec senders, ESP depends on defined security associations (SAs). An SA is comprised of a source and destination address, a protocol (ESP or AH), and a unique identifier. These identifiers are defined by the security parameter index (SPI), a pseudo-random number. In transport mode, the ESP header is inserted after the IP header but before the next layer protocol header. In tunnel mode, it's inserted before an encapsulated IP header.

The instructions supported by the SA establishment between the two IPSec-enabled nodes will define the levels of confidentiality, authentication of data originator, and the means of ensuring connectionless integrity among other controls for a particular exchange of data.

The Domain of Interpretation (DOI) within ISAKMP supports the grouping of supported protocols when negotiating SAs. Within a DOI, the protocol and cryptographic transforms are selected from a common namespace. The identifiers for key exchange protocols are also selected at this time, along with a mode for common interpretation of payload data. The DOI is required to supply the following security services and definitions:

- Naming scheme for DOI-specific protocol identifiers

- Interpretation of the Situation field

- Set of security policies to be applied

- Syntax for SA attributes

- Syntax for payload contents

- Additional key exchange types as required

- Additional notifier message types as required

The initiator and responders use cookies to identify the security associations established, notified, or deleted. The type of payload that next occurs in the message, major and minor versions of the ISAKMP protocols being used, type of exchange, ISAKMP exchange flags, unique message identifier, and total length of the message expressed in octets are all passed between the two nodes to establish a secure message transfer.

This process supports multiple security protocols such as IPSec (v4 and v6), TLS, TLSP, OSPF, and others. The purpose of the specification is to reduce duplication of effort in handling secure communications in higher layers, which would have a deleterious impact on performance. One of the supported protocols for key exchange is the Internet Key Exchange, or IKE. Unlike IPSec, IKE is a bidirectional security protocol.

IKE

Some of the benefits of IKE include

- Establishing a lifetime for the validity of the key exchange—this avoids the need to set up a new security association for each session.

- Changing encryption keys during an IPSec session—this increases the security of the destination/sender association and protects from IP spoofers.

- Supporting certification authority.

- Providing dynamic authentication of peers.

- Automating setting of IPSec configuration options.

Although IKE has been submitted to the IETF, it's a protocol that is proprietary to Cisco and supported on their switches. IKE v2 supports user-level authentication and an internal IP address for use in VPN tunnels. This is accomplished by a gateway downloading an IP address and configuration details to a client during the IKE negotiation. Mobile computing users who want to establish secure connections to Storage Area Network resources while working from a hotel or wireless hot spot will benefit from these services. The challenge, as always with systems security, is to allow access but not open the network up to unacceptable levels of vulnerability.

FCSec

Encapsulating FC-2 frames within an IPSec ESP protocol was proposed to the T11 committee of the IETF in mid 2002. The goal of this technology, referred to as FCSec, was to leverage the work done to date on IPSec, resulting in a common SAN security framework for those installations that don't actually use IP at the network layer.

SAN Fabric Security

Storage arrays typically use a single port to connect to the switch, yet contain multiple LUNs behind that port ID. As the number of switches on the fabric increase, additional security is required to prevent unauthorized access to fabric management or data resources. This is known as *fabric security*.

Intuitively, it should make sense that declaring a network resource available to two or more discrete servers will require either software-based management such as that found in a Microsoft or Linux cluster or hardware-based management of conflicts as in IBM's virtualized Storage Tank. One of the preeminent features of FC SANs are the management consoles and controls incorporated into the switches themselves. There are several means of establishing fabric security. I touched on LUNs and LUN masking in the discussion on SCSI and networking generally in Chapter 4.

Another method of restricting access to data resources behind switch ports is through zoning. *Zoning* defines groups of devices, as well as access pathways, to ensure appropriate segregation of storage and switch resources.

Persistent binding is used to ensure that a host obtains a predefined LUN and SCSI target ID if it requires those static identifiers to perform data-related activities such as a backup to tape.

In each of these cases, the management of switches and ports, target IDs, and HBAs vary greatly from one vendor to the next.

Brocade, for example, has developed what they term their *Secure Fabric OS* to support policy-based security for managing interconnected SANs. The elements of their security offering include

- Digital certificates and signatures

- Multilevel password protection

- Strong password encryption

- Public key infrastructure–enabled authentication

- 128-bit encryption

Let's look in more detail at what each of these security elements entails.

Digital Certificates

By combining these secure certificates and access control lists (ACLs), switch-to-switch security can be increased. In this way, security zones based on authorized switches can be established. The process of segmenting SAN devices into domains of authorization is known as zoning. Soft zoning uses software at the switch to control access to devices using worldwide names and port numbers managed by a name server database. When changes are made to the zone, a Registered State Change Notification (RSCN) is sent to devices listed in that database. Only devices that correctly handle the RSCN can communicate with other devices connected through the switch.

Hard Zoning

The worldwide name (WWN) is used within a zone as the address for a target device. The switch consults its route table to establish whether the two ports are authorized to make a connection.

Soft Zoning

Soft zoning takes advantage of the server name database stored in the switch to identify port and WWNs belonging to each zone.

LUN Masking

Whether using a RAID array on a single port, or virtual devices managed through a virtualization engine, LUN masking manages access of shared disk resources by multiple servers. It does this by presenting the logical unit number representing a subset of disk resources so those previously identified servers alone may use them. In this way, different hosts can share a storage array without being aware of other storage and other servers using the array.

CHAP: The Challenge Authentication Protocol

Under this scheme, user name/password exchanges are further validated by the transfer of a hash code value that is compared to the value expected by the server, and authentication only occurs on a match. This can be performed periodically during a session to provide further assurance that the client is indeed the correct entity authorized for access.

As each SAN component vendor strives to make their system perform better and offer more in-depth security options, the cost comes as a decrease in interoperability.

To this point, I've introduced the means by which Storage Area Networks can be secured. It might help to identify the most likely threats against which a network might be vulnerable.

Attack Types

As I've indicated earlier in this chapter, the key to security is understanding your vulnerabilities. At a high level, this can be understood in the context of the types of attacks that might be launched against your storage network.

Denial of Service (DoS)

A steady stream of ping commands against an open port on a network device is known as a *ping flood*. The idea behind this is to overload the device with handling the frequent requests for service, thereby dropping overall service levels to the point where other transactions and connections timeout.

Malformed Packets

In some cases, packets crafted in a specific fashion will invoke undesirable behavior in the router or host. An example is the SSH packet malformation that caused certain Cisco routers to reload before authentication was invoked. Like any software, handling certain exceptional cases can cause aberrant behavior, and where this is known (or experimented with), a router's services can be disabled or bypassed.

IP Packet Fragments (Frag Attack)

IP fragmentation can be used as a way to disguise TCP packets from the IP filters used by routers. Packets sent from across the Internet, such as in a VPN connection, may arrive at their destination out of order. To reduce congestion at the router, the header information contained at the beginning of each packet is inspected and filtered by the router. In some cases, such as fragments of a certain size (i.e., tiny fragments), the router filtering rules are bypassed and the packets passed through to the network. Sophisticated hackers can employ a "wolf in sheep's clothing" approach to passing their packets past the router undetected.

Inspection of packets allows properly formed data packets from authorized sources to be passed through by the router. Unfortunately, like e-mail attachments containing worms such as Welchia, this still leaves vulnerabilities at higher layers of the protocol stack. The following sections cover examples of these attacks.

Worms

Like a virus, a worm is code that copies or replicates itself from one machine to another. Unlike virus software that is typically attached to an e-mail and invoked when the attachment is activated, a worm scans a network looking for open ports. Once identified, the worm copies itself through the port to the target machine and begins the scanning process from there.

Buffer Overflows

This is the most common vulnerability by which remote, unknown attackers can hijack a program and then potentially take over control of a host. To do this, the attack code must be inserted into a program's address space, and then the program must access that code, placing certain parameters into the system's registers and memory. Vulnerabilities in some server programs mean that parameters in the form of native CPU instructions can be passed as arguments or as an input string to an existing piece of code. When that string is executed, the malicious instructions are invoked, and the system can then fall under the control of the attacker's code.

Application Attacks

Web-based applications are vulnerable to certain types of attacks. A URL with an embedded script may be posted onto a web site by an attacker. When that URL is accessed, the script can execute often for the purpose of obtaining unauthorized data. A legitimate page from a web site may be downloaded and modified by an attacker, and then reposted in order to affect variables used by the application. Debug modes, or wildcard declarations, might not be specifically excluded by a web application, creating vulnerabilities that can be exploited.

There is a range of security weaknesses up and down the ISO stack from physical tapping of wires or capture of wireless packets through to the point of manipulating the application itself. In the context of storage networks, the network is the vulnerability and the data store is the target. DoS attacks and viruses are of less concern in a Storage Area Network than, say, worms or application attacks. Obtaining data such as user names or passwords literally opens the door to theft of files and confidential data, whereby worms can delete documents indiscriminately, depriving an organization of important assets.

The Theory in Practice

A client asked for a storage network topology that I describe in greater detail in Chapter 11 in the section "What Did I Buy?" Without going into too much detail here, I wanted to pull out the security considerations so you can see how the general discussion about security elements applies to a specific case.

In this situation, a web-based application consisting of a cluster of four web servers, a database server, and its mirror was to be hosted at a colocation site. The nature of the application was financial, which necessitated a more stringent review of potential security holes. To work with the selected systems management software, the switch selected turned out to be the Dell PowerConnect 6024, the topology of which is depicted in Figure 8-1.

As shown in the figure, the security profile consisted of the elements discussed in the following sections.

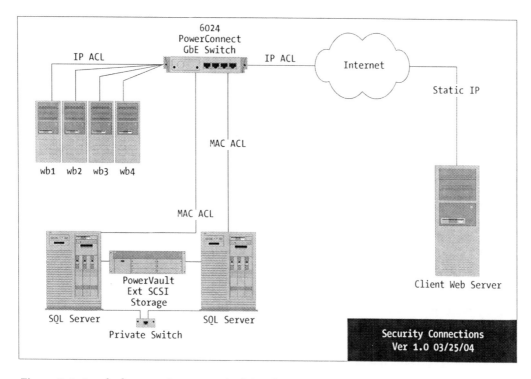

Figure 8-1. A web cluster using networked database storage

ACL Configuration

ACL configuration under the Dell PowerConnect 6024 can support access identified by IP address, UDP port, or MAC address.

For our first line of defense, I decided to protect the data from unauthorized access by configuring ACL permissions to deny all connection attempts except those from the four web application servers identified by MAC address. This ensured that IP spoofing wouldn't be sufficient to gain access to the databases. However, it didn't protect against access being gained via the application or web servers themselves.

VPN Authentication

Due to the business-to-business nature of this particular application, we had the opportunity to identify a discrete set of potential servers through which users and applications would connect. This allowed us to configure VPN tunnels on the basis of the predefined IP addresses of the servers.

Impact and Implications for Storage Networks

Fibre Channel SANs have enjoyed a reputation for higher levels of security, in no small part due to their segregation from other network assets. With the introduction of IP-based storage network technology, whether iSCSI, iFCP, or FCIP, the very strengths of IP-based communication present some disadvantages.

The aggregation of enterprise data into a SAN tends to create a single point of focus for unauthorized access. It seems more lucrative to pull one bank heist than hold up depositors one at a time in front of the automated teller. Given that, like the situation involving the Great Wall, the majority of unauthorized data access, updates, and deletes comes from internal sources, the integration of data assets from inside the firewall poses some difficulties.

Although VPN is used successfully to create relatively secure links between remote points and enterprise servers, that technology reflects its use in the context of a slower point-to-point connection than is supported with even GbE technology. And there's the rub.

As you'll see in the benchmarks for GbE in Chapter 10, server-to-server and client-to-host communication at gigabit speeds is an order of magnitude faster than a T1 line. You'll also see the effect of CPU utilization on data throughput. Applications that use the CPU as part of the data transfer process slow it down dramatically, and as I discussed in the first chapter, moving this logic closer to the hardware is the only way to get the performance back.

So now I can finally bring all this background discussion to the point. Security in the form of IPSec-compliant encryption and decryption has a staggering impact on data throughput as a result of the calculations required. As a general guideline, a 2 GHz processor can just about keep up with the calculations required to transfer IPSec data over a 100Base-T link. It isn't practical, then, to implement GbE Storage Area Networks using software-based IPSec security—which means you have to look at hardware acceleration if you're going to put storage assets on a widely accessible IP network.

Before doing that, though, let's consider the cost. As we know from the review of host bus adapters, the more specialized the logic that is built into a card, the more expensive it becomes. Complexity ain't cheap. The most readily available source for this kind of logic is on the ASICs built into VPN routers that support IPSec-compliant protocols.

The Cisco 515 PIX is one such device, and I found sites where its list price was more than $5,000, whereas the street price was as low as $1,500. For this device, various IPSec VPN encryption algorithms were supported including 56-bit DES, 168-bit Triple DES (3DES), and 256-bit AES. Although some models have hardware acceleration built in, Cisco also offers a PIX-ready VPN accelerator card (VAC), which handles the off-loaded IPSec mathematical calculations. Prices for this card ranged just under $2,000. Given that the number of 10/100 ports supported by this security appliance totaled less than six (for the models and prices discussed here), I felt this was a pretty good example of the kind of pricing and performance impact you can expect when incorporating IPSec.

However, limiting my treatment of storage network security to a snapshot of the market leader's standard issue seemed to me to provide poor support for one of the key themes of this book. Yes, specialized and expensive gear provides new capabilities and the highest levels of performance and security. But the sheer volume of mass-marketed components, and the robustness found in the IP standards and products resulting from them, creates alternatives that compete with, if not equal, the value proposition of the pioneering offerings.

Nowhere is this more evident than in the creation of security enhancements for GbE-ready IP storage network solutions.

Get a GRIP

Gigabit Rate IPSec (GRIP) is an important achievement for securing storage network implementations based on IP networks. The central approach to achieving this level of data throughput is, as I've already introduced, hardware acceleration. One of the factors that affect the design of any given secure storage network over IP is the choice of encryption algorithm. Advanced Encryption Standard lends itself effectively to incorporation into off-load processing and as such is widely expected to become the IPSec protocol of choice for IP networks.

Cryptographic acceleration puts a physical device in the stack between the network card or host bus adapter handling the Ethernet data link and the assembly of packets into intelligible data assets to be managed by the file system. In the event that the data stream was intercepted, the data would have to be decrypted; using 256-bit AES, this feat is virtually impossible without the key. That, of course, is the whole point behind encrypting point-to-point communication; the idea here is to evaluate how that can be achieved while realizing the performance potential of GbE links between systems on the inside of the firewall.

Fortunately, the folks at Hifn have been doing more than just giving the matter some thought. In February 2004, Hifn introduced their HIPP II 8155 Security Protocol Processor. In their words, "This intelligent packet processing security processor delivers optimal price and performance for IPSec and SSL applications such as routers, switches, and VPN gateways at gigabit rates." Similar in function to a TCP/IP off-loading engine, this security processor alleviates the burden on CPU and memory resources by taking on the calculations required to encrypt and decrypt data streams.

Perhaps of even more interest to those of you contemplating which storage network technology to apply in your own environment are the products announced later that incorporate this processor.

Global Technologies Group, Inc. (GTGI) of Arlington, Virginia, announced their PowerCrypt 5X Encryption Accelerator card incorporating the Hifn 7962 security processor. I spoke to a company representative who informed me that rates of 632 Mbps of IPSec AES encryption could be achieved. The list price for a single card was $595.

Similarly, the Streamwise products from Seaway Networks incorporate the Hifn security processor. Seaway built a PCI-X card to off-load layer 2 through 7 functions as a network content processor. Targeted for OEMs, the card is intended to free up system resources to allow value-added application execution while preserving the gigabit throughput rates between devices on the network.

Encrypted Storage

Implicit in any discussion about IPSec is the notion that the transfer of data is encrypted. That introduces the notion that the data isn't stored in encrypted form, which has generally been true. Storage of encrypted data has a different set of concerns, not the least of which is the management of keys.

When two devices pass encrypted data between them and a key is lost, it's necessary to renegotiate the transmission, including reauthentication. This might prove to be a nuisance from a performance or data latency standpoint, but it isn't catastrophic. However, when you consider losing the key to data that is encrypted on a storage medium, this leads to a completely different outcome: lost data. It should be especially easy to imagine how this could occur where the encrypted data is stored on tape and squirreled away in some obscure data store, only to be resurrected by some court order. Now where did I put that key?

Entirely in keeping with the dynamics of the storage networks world, developments are occurring on two fronts. The IEEE is defining a standard for encrypted storage, and vendors are offering products to manage them. In December 2002, the IEEE held their first workshop dedicated to security within storage networks;

much of the focus for their members revolves around object stores and distributed file systems.

Less esoteric are the products available from companies such as Decru, Vormetric, and NeoScale. The Decru DataFort, for example, features compartmentalized data stores they refer to as *cryptainers*. Each of these represents a CIFS share or NFS export that is encrypted with its own unique key. Contents in the file system are subsequently encrypted with their own keys. By building their own hardened operating system, and processing all keys within their appliance, Decru promotes this as a means of securing file system data against any unauthorized access. Block-level data is secured by treating the cryptainer as a distinct LUN. As well as encryption keys, the DataFort supports ACL definitions to delineate stations that can access and decrypt data within a specific cryptainer.

Vormetric's CoreGuard product can provide transparent encryption of Oracle databases, among other encrypted storage services similar to the DataFort. NeoScale's CryptoStor FC interoperates with Brocade fabrics to provide policy and rule-driven encryption for data.

Summary

There should be no question in your mind that Storage Area Network security is a topic requiring deep knowledge and background to design and implement effectively. Although vendors deliver products that support security options, they don't necessarily end up being configured in a way that provides actual security against interception or unauthorized access.

As IP-based Storage Area Networks penetrate into commercial settings, network security for controlling access to consolidated data stores will become an increasingly important consideration. From this chapter, you should have a better sense of the areas requiring attention, and some of the alternatives open to you as you design and manage your Storage Area Network assets.

You should be able to see how each layer of the network stack opens up potential security risks and how Storage Area Network vendors have reacted with a multitude of features, many of which necessarily affect interoperability.

At the very least, you should have an appreciation for how security controls and encryption can affect performance and see how solutions closer to the hardware could provide benefit. I hope that the requirement to fully understand and segregate stored data on the basis of its intrinsic value and the threat posed has also been reinforced here.

At various times in writing this book, I found it difficult to relate storage network concepts to their implementation without referring to specific vendors' products. As I'll reiterate in Chapter 11, my objective was to treat vendors as representative solutions, incorporating principles and standards into their products with varying degrees of success or value at any given time.

Mentioning one over another isn't intended as an endorsement for any given purpose, nor have I deliberately omitted any particular offering. The key point of this chapter is that the playing field changes rapidly between Fibre Channel and GbE, and you'll need to bone up on the specific state of affairs for your own purposes.

That said, I believe this discussion of the implications of security for storage network solutions serves as a case in point for my larger premise. Within the plethora of products and standards available at any given time, there is a combination that is right for your situation.

CHAPTER 9

Storage Networks Software and Content

AT THE TOP of the ISO network stack lies the application software layer. In this chapter, I'll cover a range of software applications as they relate to storage networks including design, administration, and performance. As you might expect, this accounts for almost every kind of application available—some dedicated to managing storage networks, and others that drive consumption of storage network resources. Applications generate and consume data. This chapter will also discuss the requirements that come with content and data management. This should help set the stage for discussions later on in the book on compliance and other "hot button" management issues that can be addressed by Storage Area Networks.

In Chapter 1, I delineated storage networks management as consisting of

- Storage network management

- Storage resource management

- Policy management

- Data management

- Virtualization

In this chapter, I'll describe the role of each of these and introduce products that demonstrate how this role is handled by some vendors and extract a general discussion of the issues surrounding them.

For the purposes of writing this book as an overall treatment of Storage Area Network technology and issues, I envisioned this chapter serving as the integral link between two sides of an arch: First, building up from the "ground" in storage assets as they move from physical to logical, are the components of storage networks and the technologies as they relate to the layers in the ISO stack. Then, following through with vendor offerings, performance considerations, the value of information as an asset, and building a business case, the arch continues back towards the "ground" of your specific setting.

Software and data link the general discussion of standards and components with the solutions offered by vendors for your storage network requirements.

Also, I'll introduce you to the emerging discipline of data or information life cycle management and identify some of the key areas of impact this will have on storage networks. Last of all, I'll discuss autonomic computing agents that provide adaptive software based on policies governing data.

Managing Storage Network Resources

In Chapter 8, one of the issues that I didn't really touch on were the mechanisms you can use to prevent interference with your storage network via management consoles and functions. Let's do that here, but with emphasis on the features of storage management software, not just security.

Storage Network Management

As I covered in Chapter 8, access control lists are a commonly used mechanism to ensure that connections between fabric switch ports and host bus adapters are authorized. Software tools for configuring these devices are provided by each vendor, of course, but that introduces complexity when products from multiple vendors are involved. Some vendors, such as Brocade, offer fabric management software that works with their switches as well as host bus adapters and storage arrays from other vendors. The other approach they support is to allow the Brocade fabric to be managed by third-party software applications, such as BrightStor from Computer Associates or Tivoli from IBM. This is accomplished via the application's programming interface provided by Brocade for the fabric OS as integrated by the software provider.

Typical management functions include the following:

- Creating zones to isolate SAN resources into groups of authorized interconnects

- Updating configuration information such as thresholds and connect paths

- Monitoring activity for diagnostics or troubleshooting

Initial setup for remote access and configuration of a switch is often done via a serial link as a local console port. Once this is set, the management port is enabled. This is typically a dedicated 10/100 Ethernet link and is referred to as an *out-of-band connection*. In-band connections, or connections to other fabric devices, may be made over the Fibre Channel links once the first out-of-band link is established. As indicated at the beginning of this section, vendors have built-in security to ensure only authorized access to these management ports. The security mechanisms include setting the secure shell option on the switch as well as specifying the type of encryption key you want to use.

When performing the initial Cisco switch configuration, for example, the following values are set:

- Switch name

- IP address and subnet mask for the management port

- Administrator password

- Simple Network Management Protocol (SNMP) v3 user name and password

- IP routing, DNS, and gateway addresses

After that, the switch is enabled for remote management and can be seen or accessed by other management software, as authorized.

Scripting can be used to automate the polling or update process on a device-by-device basis, but the full scope of storage networks becomes most visible at the management software application layer. Let's look at some of the offerings for managing resources.

Storage Resource Management Tools

To better demonstrate the kind of tools available today for managing storage networks overall, let's look at some of the leading providers of storage resource management tools, including Tivoli from IBM, and StorageCentral from VERITAS.

Tivoli Storage Management

The Tivoli suite of products is the brand under which IBM has solidified its storage network and infrastructure management software. One of the integral functions of this software is the *probe*, which sets up an agent to interrogate a system or subsystem and report on findings as specified when it was created. In Figure 9-1, you can see a range of Tivoli setup options, with Probes highlighted in the work pane on the left side of the screen.

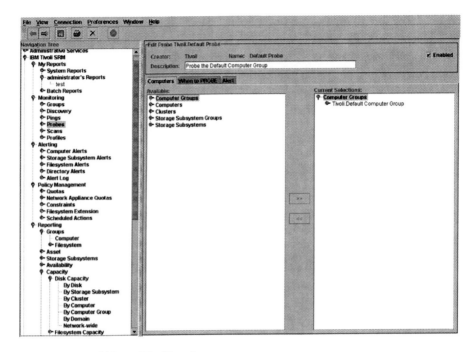

Figure 9-1. Defining a Tivoli probe

In Figure 9-1, you see the Tivoli web-based console for administering network devices. By incorporating APIs such as the one provided by Brocade, Tivoli can access devices from a number of vendors and report management information in a unified fashion. The other two tabs shown on the main pane of the Tivoli console include the When to PROBE page, which allows settings for intervals for probes. This is shown in Figure 9-2.

Information across all storage network devices can be gathered at scheduled times as shown in Figure 9-2. The results from the probe can trigger notifications. The configuration options for this are found under the Alert tab, which is shown in Figure 9-3.

Probe conditions, such as a failure to complete as indicated in Figure 9-3, can be set and responses triggered as defined. Of particular note is one of the options called the TEC Event, where TEC stands for Tivoli Event Console. This mechanism allows escalation of the event to be handled by an intelligent management console. IBM is extending this mechanism to support autonomic management through their Autonomic Management Engine, which allows adaptive systems reactions without human intervention in accordance with predefined policies governing specified events.

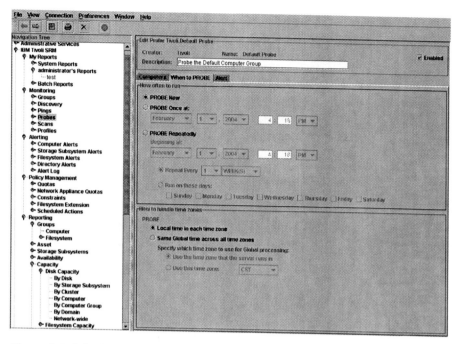

Figure 9-2. Scheduling probes

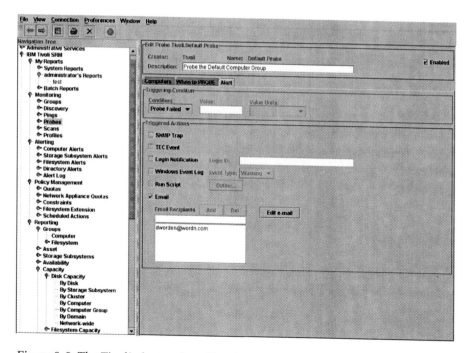

Figure 9-3. The Tivoli alert and notification options

The kinds of reports that are generated by Tivoli include device usage and capacity reporting. An enterprise summary that I generated with Tivoli is shown in Figure 9-4.

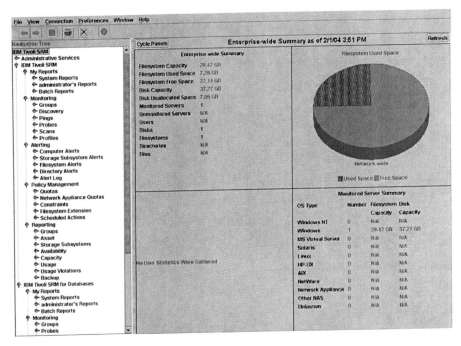

Figure 9-4. An enterprise summary report

As shown in Figure 9-4, the number of servers and disks on this particular network is not spectacular, nor would I anticipate that IBM would be eager to see Tivoli employed in a single-server environment. However, for a dashboard view of a complex set of devices within a Storage Area Network, this kind of reporting can add considerably to capacity planning and troubleshooting.

StorageCentral

There are three versions of StorageCentral available, and I'll discuss the capabilities of each briefly in the following sections.

StorageCentral Active Directory Edition

This disk management tool uses Active Directory from Microsoft to control storage devices on all versions of Windows 2000 and Windows NT 4. The product is designed to monitor storage space whether it belongs to users on their desktop or to file servers. Allocation of space can be made according to policies, and certain types of files may be blocked from being stored. In Figure 9-5, you can see how media files such as MP3 downloads are locked out from storage on a corporate server.

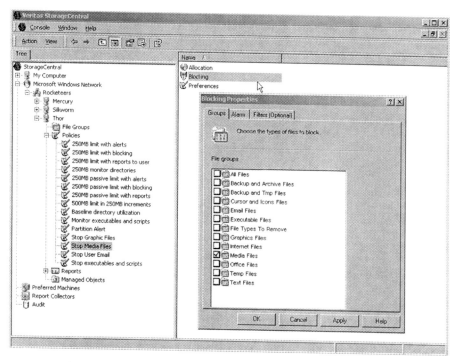

Figure 9-5. The VERITAS StorageCentral file blocking configuration screen

In Figure 9-5, you see that the transfer of many different file types can be blocked via StorageCentral. This helps enforce compliance to policies for aligning storage resources with file types to be stored.

StorageCentral Network Appliances Edition

NAS appliances running Microsoft's Server Appliance Kit (SAK) 2.0 can be managed centrally using this edition. File blocking is also supported for NAS appliances, and detailed web-based reporting of storage consumption, trends, and allocations is provided.

StorageCentral Enterprise Reporting Edition

Storage on NAS appliances or SAN devices, or directly attached to servers running AIX, HP-UX, Linux, and Solaris, as well as Windows, can be reported according to usage by user and application. Capacity utilization trends are projected to predict space requirements based on patterns of usage (see Figure 9-6).

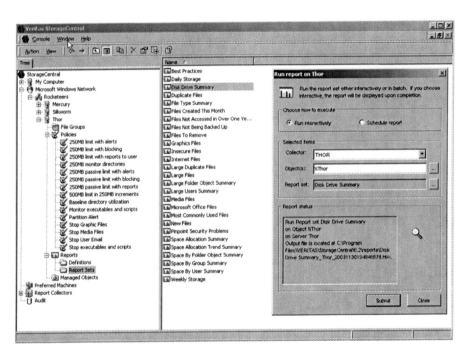

Figure 9-6. The VERITAS StorageCentral report options

VERITAS provides a suite of storage administration tools beyond managing disk storage. By incorporating server and application management tools into their offerings, VERITAS enables the management of infrastructure under the utility computing model.

There are a great many other providers of software utilities for storage resource management. The key functions provided by the software have been, I hope, suitably touched on here, including the following:

- Consolidated web-based reporting for many storage network resources

- Scheduled device queries and information gathering

- Triggers, thresholds, and notification options

- Definition and enforcement of storage policies

- At-a-glance capacity planning and predictive reporting

These are the core functions of storage resource management tools.

Virtualization

From the treatment of Tivoli and StorageCentral in the preceding sections, you should be able to see how storage resource management tools give you a single-image view of your entire Storage Area Network and its assets. The management software treats the collection of disparate resources as a virtual integrated system. Yet, this isn't quite all that virtualization tools and techniques hope to achieve.

Virtual machines have been part of the computing landscape since the 1960s. Then, as now, the idea was to have systems management software allow the segregation of resources, including processor cycles, memory, and disk, into discrete, compartmentalized execution environments.

From a storage networks perspective, virtualization extends to the goal of representing disk resources in whatever format is required by an application (such as a database or file system) at a given time. Ideally, the data contained on a particular disk would be shareable on demand, providing, say, the same work files under CIFS to a Windows user and under NFS to a Unix client. Under this arrangement, the virtualization software would also be required to manage contention as well as translation of the resources into the target format.

From a hardware perspective, the abstraction of data away from the disk on which it resides through logical volumes is also a form a virtualization. The ability to swap out a failed drive in a RAID array treats the disk as a physical component of a virtual system where the data resides on a virtual disk resource, namely the logical volume. Once the failed component is replaced, the logical volume takes advantage of the new disk by rebuilding the data image from the parity disk or mirror.

Clearly, there are degrees of virtualization. In the context of Storage Area Networks, virtualization is enabled by the systems software that supports access to content without its being bound to specific hardware resources. As these resources are allocated dynamically, policies governing security and relative priority of each consumer must be established. Mechanisms for applying these policies are then also required.

Policy-Driven Storage Management

In Chapter 1, I referred to policies as a means of aligning storage costs with data usage. A bit later in this chapter in the section "The Information Life Cycle," I'll discuss the life cycle approach to information and how policies can be derived from that life cycle. In the discussion of StorageCentral and Tivoli, I referred to the definition of policy control of storage resources for these products.

At a basic level, policies such as the containment of mailboxes at some arbitrary size (e.g., 100MB) can be considered an example of policy-driven storage management. However, I don't think we should restrict the scope of policy to device utilization. Policies are the rules and regulations that are intended to govern behavior, and this applies to people as well as to machines. Before getting into the role of policy to control the way people use their storage resources, let's look at some of the emerging tools for automating policy enforcement for storage networks.

The Autonomic Model for Storage

Recently, I've been able to work with some of the IBM autonomic computing tools prior to their release to developers and administrators. I would like to use these autonomic tools to show how IBM proposes to interrogate storage network assets and take action on them.

IBM's autonomic computing model relies on their MAPE-K concept, which is depicted in Figure 9-7.

The monitor function relies on the sensors built into autonomic software agents. Sensors rely on consistent and common descriptors across resources, similar to Resource Description Framework (RDF) or the common logging format promoted by IBM as an open standard. The K in this case is the knowledge base used by sensors and effectors to determine what action should be taken. From a Storage Area Networks standpoint, a sensor could determine that a file had passed its expiration date and had been superceded by another. The action defined for expired documents could be an archiving to an offline storage mechanism such as tape or an offsite disk-based storage facility. These policy-driven activities are enabled by the underlying autonomic infrastructure, including consistent descriptions across data resources, sensors, and effectors that determine the current state of an asset and actions to be taken depending on that value.

Like most things in IT, it's somewhat more difficult to implement these things than to imagine them. At this point, I would like to introduce you to the Integrated Solutions Console (ISC) and the framework by which IBM supports making servers autonomic. After reviewing the ISC, you should be able to envision how Storage Area Networks could incorporate policies across multiple devices and different resource management.

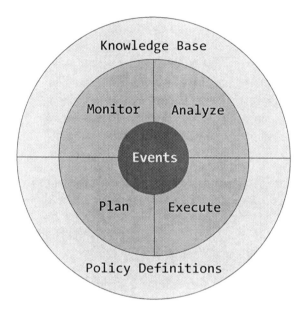

Figure 9-7. The IBM Autonomic Computing MAPE-K model

Integrated Solutions Console

The initial release of the Integrated Solutions Console is available from IBM's developerWorks web site (http://www.ibm.com/developerworks). As I write this, it's free to folks who register. I believe this tool incorporates many of the features necessary to develop and deploy increasingly autonomic systems administration functions. This extends to software for management of storage networks and aligning storage policies with data life cycle definitions.

The ISC provides a browser-based interface to a centralized management console, similar in approach to existing storage administration tools. One key difference is the use of the WebSphere Portal Server runtime as the application engine and the integration of its credential vault with ISC components.

The distinction that I want to call your attention to is the ability for any ISC component written by a developer to obtain logon and password credentials to effect changes in other systems on the network. Obviously, this is subject to an initial authorization and ongoing controls, but the major point is that ISC components can obtain the needed credentials to log on to other resources and execute a predefined action without requiring human intervention.

ISC components are simply portlet-compliant Java servlets and Java Server Pages contained within an XML wrapper. This means that any administrative function that has already been created as a Java servlet can be imported into WebSphere Studio for Application Developers (WSAD) and redeployed as an Integrated Solutions Console component. The component can operate as a status checking or sensing function and execute administrative notification or action as defined. In this way, the ISC becomes a tool for enabling autonomic computing. By automating the sensing and effecting processes, storage network administrators can predefine situations to trigger actions without relying on day-to-day human training, observation, and intervention. An example of the Integrated Solutions Console running a problem determination scenario is shown in Figure 9-8.

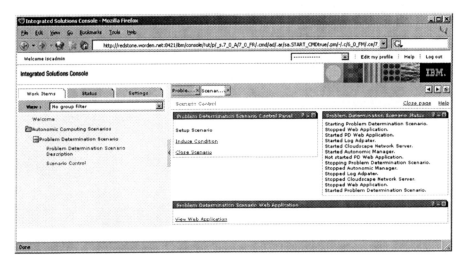

Figure 9-8. The Integrated Solutions Console

In the work pane on the right-hand side of the console, you can see the processes spawned by the problem determination component under the ISC. In this example, events are recorded in small-footprint data stores called *cloudscape databases*. These records are parsed for occurrences of events defined in the component. You should be able to see how this mechanism can be extended to report on life cycle events, such as transaction log dumps that have been succeeded by full database backups, allowing the incremental logs to be deleted.

Components can consist of many different kinds of resources. A listing of the resources available inside the ISC are shown in Figure 9-9.

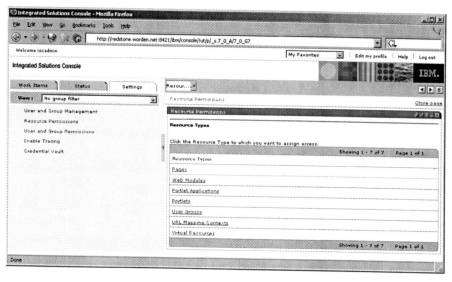

Figure 9-9. Integrated Solutions Console resources

In Figure 9-9 you can see the kinds of resources the Integrated Solutions Console can manage, among them portlet applications, web modules, and virtual resources. Individual administrative accounts, with tailored permission profiles, can be established and sets of resources assigned to account groups. The portlet applications must be written to comply with standard JSR 168 from the Java Community Process. This standard Java portlet API ensures that complying applications will work with portal products from different vendors. Portlet applications can provide any number of functions, including database queries and remote procedure calls. Using this mechanism, the console can be used for components that extend deeply into the data domain as well as monitor and execute actions based on log and trace results.

In Figure 9-8, you can see a reference to the Autonomic Manager, which is the Autonomic Management Engine (AME). The AME provides monitoring services for autonomic components and among other actions can raise notifications in the Tivoli Event Console.

Proprietary Products vs. Open Standards

All things being equal, almost everyone acknowledges that where possible you're better advised to go with an open standards–compliant product. Unfortunately, proprietary "locked-in" solutions are generally the first to market. When you really need relief, sometimes sooner is better than waiting, even if it means you forgo some flexibility or could be forced to rip-and-replace later. Within its autonomic computing initiative, IBM has introduced several new technologies that provide server and network administration services and integrate (but not exclusively) with their own monitoring platform.

If the network is the computer, and storage is a discrete service to be managed within that notional computer, interoperable, multiplatform monitoring tools will be essential to automating the sensor/effecter control loop currently performed by human administrators.

To this point in the chapter, I've introduced how standards bodies are working towards defining cross-platform application programming interfaces. These provide effective methods of tagging data so those applications can run not only on different platforms but also against heterogenous data sources. These are the underlying prerequisites to enable information or data life cycle management.

Accessing Storage Assets

To this point in discussing software for Storage Area Networks, I've put a great deal of focus on network management and security considerations for moving data from one system to another. That leaves the issue of software that uses the storage network to be addressed, specifically looking at what such software expects from the data when it arrives at the storage location.

Here I would like to call your attention to a few key ways that data is read and written, using three typical server applications as examples. These include database servers, mail servers, and shared office documents. The key points I hope you'll take away from this review are the implications for consolidated storage when interspersing data from multiple applications on the disk assets within an array.

Database Servers

For performance reasons, database management systems have long supported the creation of resources that are explicitly tied to disk segments. In a given relational database implementation, for example, you must have systems data maintained in tables, logs for tracking changes, the data itself, and indexes to speed retrieval. The type of access and the organization of the data is critical to balancing overall application performance. Indexes are frequently separated from disks containing the underlying table data and are created to avoid wherever possible that time-consuming table scan, which evaluates each data row one by one to satisfy a query.

Let's take as a given that you're dealing with a well-defined usage pattern that requires a specific database to support write transactions that change the data and concurrent, frequent queries on a number of key values. The completion of a data modification necessitates an update of the indexes. This in turn requires the database engine to manage contention between transactions.

Fair enough, but if you consider the database manager to be a traffic cop at a heavily traveled intersection with its traffic lights out, would you really want to reduce the available lanes at the same time? Of course not, and to avoid this, database administrators use named disk resources. In Oracle and DB2, these are referred to as *tablespaces;* in SQL Server, they are called *filegroups;* and in Sybase implementations, they are known as *segments.* When tuning database applications, specific disk resources are allocated to particular disk consumers with reads and writes separated as much as possible.

It should be immediately apparent why any DBA who has invested considerable time in tuning a direct-attached storage array to support a production application might be less than enthusiastic when approached about consolidating that storage with everyone else's.

I raise this point to call attention to the need to be aware of the usage patterns of all the applications using the storage network, not just in terms of network traffic, but in the requirements for disk access as well. When moving tuned database applications into a storage network, you may find it necessary to duplicate the tuning process within the new storage environment. You may choose to isolate the disks from other applications by LUN masking and segmenting them further to support tablespace definitions optimized for the access patterns.

Mail Servers

With corporate e-mail accounts deemed a business asset, and the increasing importance of e-mail as evidence, it should be no surprise that more mail administrators are moving to Internet Message Access Protocol (IMAP) implementations over the commonly found Post Office Protocol (POP) combined with Simple Mail Transfer Protocol (SMTP). IMAP allows you to store on a server an entire mail box and synchronize it with local data stores, preserving folder entries and important information such as new or read mail indicators.

Managing the proliferation of Outlook PSTs for a large number of users is a real headache for many mail administrators. Moving to IMAP for Domino or Exchange changes the nature of that pain to one of consolidated mail storage and the never-ending growth of inboxes and sent items. The main upside is centralized backup and restoration.

Unlike relational database servers, however, mail servers don't provide a way to segregate internal storage consumers like folders onto named disk resources via tablespaces. Of course, the entire mailbox file could be maintained on a storage network, but it should stand to reason that recently received or frequently accessed messages and their attachments would benefit from higher speed retrieval and loading as compared to, say, project status reports from a year earlier.

Savvy e-mail administrators might leap to the defense of their servers by bringing up the ability to create public and private folders, which could be offered to users as a means of archiving older data without their having to manage its physical disposition. However, as of Lotus Domino 6.5, although it's possible to create private IMAP folders for users, the information was still maintained centrally within the Domino database, and I wasn't aware of any means to align Notes database components with named disk resources.

I bring this up to call your attention to two factors: The first is the need for software vendors to make their products more "storage network aware," one example being mail servers capable of creating individual folders on virtual storage volumes. The other is more related to the management of personnel than technology. By this, I mean the workflow and habits of users as they relate to the way those users store and access company data assets, via a storage network or not.

Office Documents

Some people are organized by nature, and others are not. Some folks seek out structure and rely on regulations to ensure orderly access to information. Others crave an outlet for their creativity and shrug off the need for consistency as a petty-minded hobgoblin. In most organizations, both types of people are expected to work side by side. If they are members of the same unit, team, or project, they are also usually required to share work product. And therein lies the single biggest contributor to storage growth—Pack Rat Syndrome, aided and abetted by the personal computer.

Microsoft Office is undeniably one of the most, if not the most, commonly found business applications anywhere. It was designed for the personal computer and personal use. This manifests itself in many different ways, not the least of which is demonstrated if you remove a floppy disk (remember those?) from a drive to which you saved a Word document you didn't close. The Lock Manager within

Office programs expects to have sole access to the file while you have it open. And it will complain if it doesn't. In reaction to this, people sharing documents will sometimes open read-only copies and save them under a different name, thereby creating a different version of the document. Inevitably, some of these will be changed, resulting in a new document, which in turn should be consolidated with the original, creating yet another new document. Where additions and deletions are in and of themselves important in the drafting of legal positions, for example, this results in a proliferation of digital data.

Financial models based on snapshot data also can result in conflicting inter-pretations, and in no small part this is due to the disconnected nature of the underlying data sources used in their creation.

Version control and code repositories are frequently used by software develop-ment teams to overcome this problem. These kinds of solutions aren't yet commonly rolled out for controlling office documents, though it may prove to be an additional initiative to add to your storage network project. In other words, when considering how to implement your storage network solution, you should consider how the data to be stored on it will be used and, more importantly, how it will be controlled. If your current storage practices are a mess, and you apply technology to consolidate it, you may run the risk of ending up with a consolidated mess.

The main point to take away from this discussion is that the software that uses your storage network can have a tremendous effect on it, as will the users of that software. Performance considerations, especially for production web-based appli-cations, can greatly affect how you lay out and design your storage network. As part of your initial plan, you may want to budget for acquiring some performance-tuning expertise. As an ongoing process, you should be looking for storage resource management reporting that will allow you to predict where tuning may benefit your applications, rather than waiting to respond to a lack of performance as perceived by your users.

Content for Storage Networks

Storage networks represent far more than just the storage and networking technologies on which they are built. Emerging in 2003 and 2004 was a growing awareness that the content itself required management. Concurrent with this requirement was the realization that the tools to accomplish this were far from mature.

In this section, I'll take you on a tour of the issues and options facing a Storage Area Network administrator from the systems and content management perspec-tive. You'll see that the underlying components to integrating your storage assets are only one (admittedly crucial) aspect of Storage Area Networks.

From my earlier treatments of the lower layers of the communications stack, and the complexities inherent in both Fibre Channel and copper-based networks, you should appreciate the obstacles to interoperable heterogeneous storage solutions. Clearly, this is a prerequisite to achieving the grand visions expressed by virtually all of the existing vendors.

At the same time, it's important that you fully understand your requirements, and given that full data and information life cycle management isn't widely practiced, I want to start by describing how this could work. From there, I'll take you through some of the existing and evolving tools for managing both your information and your storage network assets.

The Information Life Cycle

My early training was in a discipline called *information management.* At the time (late 1970s), this referred to records management, as in paper files; micrographics, as in tiny photographs of paper files; and forms management, as in designing and printing forms for collecting data.

One of my first jobs was in an inactive records center, where I was master of my domain—in that case a warehouse full of so-called dead records, which every so often would be recalled back to life for a lawsuit or audit.

My introduction to the life cycle of information was at the end of their days. It was there I learned the absolute value of knowing exactly what information you can destroy.

I mention this to call attention to the fundamental point of a Storage Area Network. Perpetual storage of data isn't the goal. Having the right data, being able to locate it, and transmitting it to the people who require it, cost-effectively—that is the goal.

As organizations face increased penalties for either failing to keep information on hand or failing to keep it private, the value of this discipline increases dramatically. A key application for a Storage Area Network administrator is deleting data. To put it in perspective, let's look at the life cycle as a whole, as depicted in Figure 9-10.

As you can see in the figure, information is created, used, disseminated, stored, and destroyed. This makes intuitive sense if you consider a driver's license as a representative set of information. It's issued on passing a test; a copy of the information is stored with a Motor Vehicle Department branch, but the license itself is in a human-readable form (albeit usually with a bar code for scanning). If you're pulled over for speeding, that information is disseminated to an authorized party—a traffic cop. If you get pulled over too many times, your license will be suspended, meaning not only will the data values be changed at the Motor Vehicle Department, but also they (whoever they are) will hold onto your physical record until the suspension is lifted. At the end of your career as a driver, the data is kept offsite for a specified period of time, and then ultimately, when it doesn't really matter that you ever had a driver's license, that information is purged both electronically and in paper form.

The key consideration prior to disposal is the *retention period*. This term refers to the governing rules for each piece of information dictating how long it must be maintained by the issuer or holder. People generally refer to holding on to their files for 7 years. In many jurisdictions, this is actually specified in statute as 6 years plus 1 day, and that has been rounded up to 7 years. When you consider storing something unnecessarily for 364 days out of the required 2,192, an additional 16+ percent unnecessary overhead is incurred.

Costs of storing paper records can be easily calculated—the square footage cost of the warehouse plus administrative salaries, for example. For a corporation with 10,000 cubic feet of record boxes, a 16 percent savings can add up. However, storage networks change the calculation considerably.

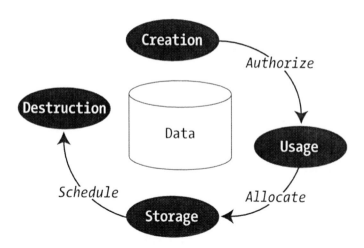

Figure 9-10. The life cycle of information

ILM Value Proposition

If a "dead record center" represents one end of the continuum of costly and awkward-to-administer data assets, how much different is a warehouse (or storage cabinet) full of data tapes? In Chapter 7, I went so far as to state that tape was dead. Under the information life cycle management (ILM) umbrella, you should be able to see that clearly it's not. It is, however, similar to dead records in as much as they are both appropriate vehicles to store static information.

The other end of the continuum would be dynamic data that changes every minute or even within seconds. Take stock prices as an example. At any given moment during the trading day, a stock price may be changing. The value of the information to a buyer or seller can be significant, as it relates to their decision to act. In terms of historical highs or lows, patterns for analysis or establishing the trading price at the end of the day, depending on the moment and the context in which the data value falls, it may have a longer term implication. But generally, the price that scrolls by at the bottom of the CNN channel is just a blip. Like the temperature outside, it may be interesting or even important, but its usefulness is fleeting.

Between these two types of information lies a significant management requirement—how best to organize and store the data for the least cost. I cover the factors you can use to establish value—historical, fiscal, utility, and legal—in Chapter 12. In this chapter, I just want to introduce the notion that data has a value that relates to its accessibility and the medium on which it will be stored. As you should be able to appreciate from Chapters 2 and 3, high availability and accessibility as enabled by high-performance storage networks can be very expensive, as can losing information that is required. The value proposition of the information life cycle is matching your requirement to the most suitable storage and network platform for its type.

Metalogical Representations

The painter Rene Magritte exhibited his work—*Ce N'est Pas Une Pipe*—in Paris in the early twentieth century. Translated, this painting of a pipe is entitled *This Is Not a Pipe*. And of course, it isn't a pipe—it's a painting. In that sense, data generally represents a noun in the real world—a person, place, or thing. Metadata, however, is data about data, and it's the key to addressing the data life cycle or information life cycle. Typical metadata attributes consist of originator, creation date, dependencies, and authorization levels for access or change. In mainframe parlance, a Create, Read, Update, and Delete (CRUD) profile is associated with each record. In the context of ILM, these descriptions change as the data moves from one stage of life to another. It should seem clear that this means that you now have a new use for the metadata that is usually found in logical data models. And that use is for purposes of storage administration.

Metadata Mechanisms

The world of data management is intricate and frequently arcane, with heated debates arising over precise classifications and key definitions. Most organizations have some level of an enterprise data model, and it's there you can look first for metadata clues to establish the value of your data and where best to house it. I think it's important to note that data life cycle and information life cycle approaches are in their infancy. Let's look at two models for acquiring data about data.

GFS—The Google File System

I think Google is a fascinating phenomenon. Beyond the macro-economic implications of what they do, there are down-and-in technical considerations, such as their 1,000+ Linux servers and the file system they created to run on it. Sanjay Ghemawat, Howard Gobioff, and Shun-Tak Leung of Google wrote a terrific treatment of their file system experience, and instructions for how to obtain it can be found on my web site, `http://storage.worden.net`.

Google, of course, is a search engine. The mechanism that Google (and other search engines) use to obtain metadata is known as a *spider* or *bot*. Spiders work by downloading pages, finding HTML links, and downloading those links. As pages are downloaded, words are parsed, and an index built with Google proprietary algorithms to match the pages to keywords entered in the search page.

The nature of the World Wide Web and its consistent format for content makes this a straightforward, albeit voluminous, approach. An inventory of data is built without human intervention. That inventory consists of hundreds of terabytes of files running on thousands of off-the-shelf commodity hardware with the Google distributed files system on top of it. Corporate intranet content could be accumulated in this fashion, and data mining tools invoked on the accumulated content. The web pages pulled onto the Google storage network can be considered an archive, and their technology addresses many of the general requirements facing any network administrator—component expense, performance, scalability, reliability, and availability. Because of the underlying assumption of frequent component failure, monitoring and mitigation are key functions, which Google has automated.

IEEE—Learning Object Metadata

This is the opposite end of the spectrum from the approach taken by Google. IEEE has chaired a working group (WG12). As part of its evolution, from its inception in 1997, the IMS project under EDUCAUSE (then EDUCOM) initiated a specification for describing learning resources available on the Web. In 1999, the group approached the W3C consortium for adoption. In its current form, the Learning

Object Meta-Data Specification describes how to represent IMS metadata in Resource Description Framework binding. An RDF is a language for representing World Wide Web resources. It uses an XML syntax and defines a lexicon and properties for describing those resources. An example of an RDF property would be creator or creation date. There are several RDF schemas defined for learning objects, including a life cycle schema. The properties in the life cycle schema include such things as version (draft, revised, or final) and contributor subproperties such as initiator, validators, and terminators.

Learning objects in this case relate not so much to objects that learn, but rather objects or resources to be used in the learning process. You should be able to see how content can be described using the RDF approach, and that retention, disposition, and accessibility attributes used by Storage Area Networks could be extended in this fashion. The core concept here is that each object, (e.g., record or data) is classified when it is created and additionally can keep an ongoing description of its state. This allows software to interrogate the object and to take action—such as moving it to a cheaper, slower storage facility as it ages (or other determinants are triggered).

Modeling Your Storage Network Content

In the rules for relational data, Dr. E. F. Codd stated that it was the key, the whole key, and nothing but the key that mattered when relating sets of data. From the discussion in the last chapter on encryption keys, you should be able to see that Dr. Codd's Rule can be more widely applied—not only to linkages of data via foreign and primary keys, but also to interpretation of data through public and private keys. The other vital aspect of managing information is the key to its location. By this, I mean how data is relegated to a type of storage and associated with an access profile, and ultimately how a key can unlock the existence of the information itself, allowing it to be destroyed.

In the 1980s and 1990s, organizations expended a great deal of time, effort, and money on enterprise data models. The outcome of these initiatives was often a map of the data assets generated by a company stored in a data warehouse. As supply chain automation, customer relationship management, and financial information systems were integrated, new ways of creating relationships among the data were developed. At the same time, workflow and business process models were also developed in some companies. These tended to express operations in terms of the products and resources (usually data) needed to support each process within the organization's mandate. It is these models that serve as a way of establishing where data can be stored most cost effectively, although that was often never considered during the development of the models originally.

One problem that emerges when attempting to align storage modes with the data life cycle is how best to capture and display that information. Granted, logical and physical data models for relational data are likely the most complete and mature, but workflow and business process models generally account for data collection in forms, as well as reports that might be generated and passed on.

Enter UML

As you may already know, the Unified Modeling Language (UML) evolved from work done by Booch, Rumbaugh, and Jacobsen at Rational Technologies during the mid 1990s. The intent was to provide a consistent and thorough set of diagramming and notational techniques for communicating all aspects of software development, with a particular emphasis on object-oriented software development.

UML is a way to describe systems rather than a methodology for building them. The key artifacts created by UML include the following:

- *Use case diagrams* describing the problem domain with business scenarios

- *Sequence diagrams* showing dependencies and scheduling

- *Collaboration diagrams* indicating interactions between components

- *State diagrams* depicting life cycle changes

- *Activity diagrams* tracing the workflow of a system

- *Class diagrams* defining the structure of classes

- *Object diagrams* specifying the structure of objects

- *Component diagrams* identifying related elements at a consistent level of granularity

- *Deployment diagrams* laying out the physical environment of the software

These core artifacts are augmented by other depiction techniques called *profiles*. These profiles allow UML to describe other areas of expertise related to systems. For example, UML profiles for business process modeling and data modeling have been developed. This approach could be extended to encompass storage-related issues as well.

Even without creating a specific UML profile to describe storage structures, the deployment diagrams can be used to relate application components to the storage network resources on which they will rely. I bring this up to stress the point that storage deployment issues are a function of the data and applications that access storage. UML-based modeling tools can allow you to collect the interrelated views of the business activity using content, the data and content itself, as well as the security, performance, and cost issues surrounding access and storage.

This is the context in which data life cycle management exists, and I believe all of these factors must be well understood for ILM to be successfully implemented within a Storage Area Networks environment.

Summary

From this chapter, you should have gained the sense that there are multiple levels of impact that software and data make on Storage Area Networks. I introduced some of the administrative functions that storage network applications feature, including device and resource management techniques.

Separation of data from dependency on the underlying hardware through virtualization was discussed. You should appreciate that this rapidly emerging software technology will have a tremendous affect on your options for constructing storage networks.

I also discussed the nature of certain applications regarding their access of disk resources. From this, you should be aware how allocations of storage network resources vary according to the behaviors of the applications that they serve.

In the treatment of autonomic computing and policy-driven storage management, I wanted to give you an insight into the emerging techniques for administering storage networks. From that discussion, you should be able to see the potential for the virtualization of some systems administrative functions.

Last of all, I covered the issues surrounding the content maintained by a storage network. Information life cycle management was introduced as well as ways to identify, classify, and model data. From this, you should recognize that not only will your storage network evolve over time, but so too will the data and applications it serves. From reading this chapter, you should have a much better sense of how your storage network hardware must integrate with the applications, data, and workflow of the rest of your organization.

CHAPTER 10

Do-It-Yourself Network Storage Components

IN THE FIRST FEW CHAPTERS, I took you through a tour of the basic technologies that are incorporated into any storage network. Hard disk technology, whether SCSI, Fibre Channel, or ATA/IDE, works under certain principles. Network communications, whether a SCSI command set or an FTP transfer over Gigabit Ethernet, handle packets using protocols and have transmission characteristics that define how fast and how far bits can move down the wire. Logical Volume Management and RAID strategies help you manage risk of failure and administer resources more or less efficiently. Add to that mix a diverse set of clients and abstract the storage away from a dedicated server, and voilá, you have yourself a Networked Attached Storage solution.

In this chapter, I want to reinforce the points made about the various components and look at how they work together in the real world. I also benchmark certain configurations and establish a baseline for how networked storage could be expected to perform. In short, I show you how I went about creating a "do-it-yourself" storage network.

The purpose of this chapter is to review how the newer file serving technologies can enable the creation of storage solutions that simply weren't available even 18 months ago. In Chapter 11, we'll look at some of the vendors who provide network storage appliances, and provide proprietary or specially tuned solutions for certain storage customers.

As part of the ground up emphasis on a more NASCAR than NASA do-it-yourself approach to networking storage, I decided I needed to do more than just browse vendor catalogs. Clearly, you may be more interested in what you can do with your own components than shelling out for a turnkey, consultant-installed, high-end Fibre Channel solution. (Not that those are bad things, but if you like to tinker with gear, this chapter is for you.)

To validate the lessons learned from earlier discussions of data throughput, mirroring, and bus bottlenecks, I'll show you how to build a representative solution using readily available components.

This chapter is for those preparing for a consolidated storage solution right now. If you happen to have a set of preferences or prejudices regarding Windows versus Linux, you may find this section challenging. Here, you'll find a head-to-head comparison, feature-by-feature, and speed-to-speed, based on my own trials. In the interests of fairness, I've set both my examples and results up to be reviewed, and I certainly hope they are repeatable.

All too often I've found that technical preferences escalate to a religious war. And I stand by the separation of church and state-of-the-art. To my way of thinking, vendor offerings aren't really an appropriate outlet for passion—certainly not when one has enough experience to realize the well-adjusted thing is to approach all of them with a high degree of skepticism.

Recognizing that by the time you read this, new releases and versions of products will be available, I didn't obsess (much) about getting the latest and the greatest for purposes of benchmarking. Instead, I looked for representative implementations on a reasonable price/performance basis. It may well be that in any given class of component there is a better, stronger, faster product than the one I used. The point of this effort was to show what could be achieved with off-the-shelf parts, rather than fight the robot wars with components.

In any case, I feel strongly that the conclusions reached are justifiable, and can be extrapolated to apply to new components under revised standards as they become available.

I have found in the past that there is occasionally someone who is displeased with a particular position taken on any given technology. The reason for providing both the method and the findings for the labs was to encourage anyone to contradict or confirm the lab results. While I'm not looking for an argument, I most certainly encourage spirited discussion. If you can question the findings based on your own tests or find fault in the method, please feel free to e-mail me at dworden@worden.net. Thanks.

Fitness to Task

I believe that even for products that don't find a market, or succeed in the long run, there is a particular use or situation to which they can be put that is better than others. With that philosophy in mind, let's approach the configuration of various servers and services to gain an appreciation for what general guidelines or rules of thumb could be derived to govern where some of the most common technologies should be applied in place of others.

The main criteria I use in evaluating a particular problem before determining potential solutions consist of the following:

- *Reliability:* This includes stability, or "up time," extent of expertise required to maintain or service the product as well as likelihood of inconvenient failure. The risk of catastrophic, nonrecoverable failure is also part of the reliability issue.

- *Performance:* Speed, speed, speed. Number crunching, network processing, data transfer. How fast does it need to go? Is that in a straight line or around corners?

- *Cost:* Time and materials, opportunity, and total cost of ownership are all factors that contribute to cost. Ask a procurement officer, and you'll find out that sometimes high operating costs and low capital costs fit the budget, other times it's quite the reverse. If you have high capital and high operating costs, hopefully you have something uniquely beneficial for an important one-off requirement. The International Space Station comes to mind.

- *Risk:* With every technical solution, there is the possibility that it won't be delivered on time, on budget, or even at all. While few managers will tell you that they will sign off on risk of 0 percent delivery, there may be cases where a make-or-break approach fits and experimentation to create something new is justified.

- *Uniqueness:* Many problems are fundamentally the same. Other problems are inherently unique and require functions that aren't reusable or recoverable from other existing solutions. Fitness to task means you can identify exactly what new wild-and-wooly thing is required in your solution and why.

Network Storage Experiment

For this chapter, I set up a test to benchmark network performance for a storage strategy using off-the-shelf components. The test was intended to review a common requirement for network storage access, to implement viable configurations to meet those requirements, and to test the configured solutions. The sometimes-surprising results are described in the context of the underlying technologies discussed in Chapters 2 through 5.

By the end of the chapter, you should be in a position to relate the many alternative technologies to a given networked storage situation and predict a level of performance. The test definition has been developed to ensure you could repeat it with similar gear and arrive at similar results.

Elements of the Test

As you've seen in previous chapters, performance is a function of a great many factors. Disk subsystems, transfer protocols, network topologies, switching capacities, file systems, and variable settings such as buffer sizes and server configuration all work together to create a storage network. The performance of any given network may not be greatly affected by a single component. Given that component costs can vary greatly, my intent was to arrive at a test to demonstrate what measure of performance could reasonably be expected from a storage network built from readily available (read cheap) components.

Of course, the real objective is first to illustrate the interrelationship of the components described in the previous section, and second to design and implement a storage network to solve my own storage problems.

As part of the lab work I did, to ensure the highest level of accuracy in my assertions, I developed a suite of copy tests. These tests showed the effects of various configuration options and provided some level of expectation that I've included in this book as rules of thumb.

To achieve a gigabit in under a minute, however, I knew it would be necessary not only to get the sustained transfer rate up past 51 percent of the theoretical max inside the server, but to ensure the network wasn't the bottleneck either. Based on the results achieved in the lab, I felt I could be more confident that any other upgrades I considered would be of practical benefit.

The key elements to be addressed in the test included the following:

- Disk configuration—RAID 0, 0+1, 5

- File system options—CIFS vs. NFS

- Linux vs. Windows

- SCSI vs. IDE/ATA vs. S/ATA

- GbE vs. 100Base-T

To ensure a like-to-like comparison, the target servers used identical hardware, specifically

- IBM xSeries e-Server

- Pentium III—1 GHz

- 1GB RAM

- Two ATA/100 Seagate Barracuda IVs (7200 rpm, 9 ms, 8MB cache)

- Two SCSI Seagate Hawks (5400 rpm, 10.4 ms, SCSI-2)

- Two Quantum Atlas II (SCSI-3 160, 10,000 rpm) drives

Three file sets of 1GB in size each were prepared consisting of 1 file name, 15 file names, and 3000 file names. This was intended to gauge not only the consistent system-to-system transfer speed, but also the impact of opening and closing file names on transfer performance.

In each case, the sending system was a Windows 2000 Server, configured with Microsoft Services for Unix. The tables and graphs that follow will allow you to consult the transfer times for both Linux and Windows 2000 Server for each configuration.

The Premise

The foundation for the design of my solution was simply that Storage Area Networks gravitate towards one end of a continuum, with high performance on one end and high availability on the other. Add in considerations such as scalability for meeting demand fluctuations and cost constraints, and you can treat the continuum as a box with four points as shown in Figure 10-1.

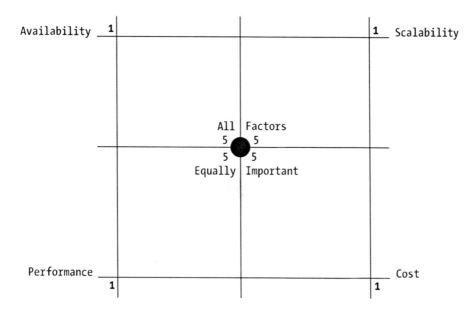

Figure 10-1. The priority box

As the old expression goes, you can have it good, cheap, or fast—pick any two. Applying that principle to Storage Area Networks and you get CAPS: Cost, Availability, Performance, Scalability.

Let's apply the constraints to my options. Striping partitions across drives is one technique for increasing disk access performance, whereas mirroring them is a way to eliminate downtime from a failed component. Still, it occurred to me that there must be a way to accommodate both, without incurring either onerous performance hits or large component costs. The question became how best to take advantage of all my existing direct-attached storage in a way that moved my environment closer to being Storage Area Network ready.

Based on this premise, I wanted to find ways of upgrading my environment but still leverage my existing investments. This led me to Fry's Electronics, where I acquired some new toys: Gigabit Ethernet adapters and some Serial ATA disk components.

Theory and Practice

In theory, the Western Digital Serial ATA drive (model WD1200JDRTL) sustained read/write activity at 150 MBps. The Ultra/ATA 100 controller and Hitachi DeskStar support disk throughput of 100 MBps. On the surface, that seemed to mean I had the potential for a significant (33 percent) increase in disk performance inside the system. Depending on the point at which the Gigabit Ethernet network became the bottleneck, I could optimize the synchronization of the two servers as well. From a design standpoint, this meant I needed to consider where in the transactions bottlenecks would occur and allocate the faster gear at that point to reduce the overall performance hit of supporting mirrored storage across a network.

The Results

Table 10-1 contains the configuration name, start times, end times, duration, and average duration for a representative set of tests.

Table 10-1. Test Results

1 GB From/To	Start Time	End Time	Duration	1 GB From/To	Start Time	End Time	Duration
From ATA 100 over 10/100 to Fat 32 simple	13:40:38.21 13:42:38.03 13:44:37.50	13:42:37.84 13:44:37.31 13:46:41.64	01:59.63 01:59.28 02:04.14 02:01.02	From ATA 100 over GbE to ATA 100 H/W Stripe	19:54:11.18 19:55:11.06 19:56:10.34	19:55:10.92 19:56:10.20 19:57:08.59	00:59.74 00:59.14 00:58.25 00:59.04
From ATA 100 over 10/100 to SCSI-2 Stripe	13:46:41.87 13:49:21.46 13:52:03.82	13:49:21.28 13:52:03.65 13:54:42.23	02:39.41 02:42.19 02:38.41 02:40.00	From ATA 100 over GbE to ATA 100 S/W Stripe	13:32:35.13 13:33:33.82 13:34:36.89	13:33:33.18 13:34:36.78 13:35:35.09	00:58.05 01:02.96 00:58.20 00:59.74
From ATA 66 over GbE to SCSI-2 Stripe	16:39:32.29 16:42:17.09 16:45:08.98	16:42:16.90 16:45:00.78 16:47:50.78	02:44.61 02:43.69 02:41.80 02:43.37	From ATA 100 over GbE to NFS H/W Mirror	11:27:55.59 11:32:20.00 11:43:25.33	11:29:32.49 11:33:56.33 11:45:02.10	01:36.90 01:36.33 01:36.77 01:36.67
From ATA 100 over GbE to SCSI-2 Stripe	12:19:58.45 12:22:41.56 12:25:21.78	12:22:41.45 12:25:21.66 12:28:02.36	02:43.00 02:40.10 02:40.58 02:41.23	From ATA 100 over GbE to SMB H/W Mirror	17:01:44.32 17:01:44.32 17:01:44.32	17:03:22.32 17:03:22.32 17:03:22.32	01:38.00 01:38.00 01:38.00 01:38.00
From ATA 100 over GbE to Spanned SCSI-2	16:47:50.85 16:52:04.87 16:56:23.46	16:52:04.68 16:56:23.37 17:00:41.25	04:13.83 04:18.50 04:17.79 04:16.71	From ATA 100 over GbE to Linux ext2 filesystem on ATA 66	17:45:38.22 17:46:56.18 17:48:11.23	17:46:55.73 17:48:11.09 17:49:26.14	01:17.51 01:14.91 01:14.91 01:15.78
From ATA 100 over 10/100 to Spanned SCSI-2	12:44:41.78 12:49:02.06 12:53:24.14	12:49:01.89 12:53:23.93 12:57:39.71	04:20.11 04:21.87 04:15.57 04:19.18	From ATA 100 over GbE to Linux ext3 filesystem on ATA 66	15:16:01.26 15:17:21.15 15:18:41.18	15:17:20.98 15:18:41.00 15:20:00.79	01:19.72 01:19.85 01:19.61 01:19.73
From ATA 66 over GbE to Fat 32 Simple	16:35:58.20 16:37:09.57 16:38:20.65	16:37:09.00 16:38:20.50 16:39:32.18	01:10.80 01:10.93 01:11.53 01:11.09	From ATA 100 over GbE to Linux ext3 H/W stripe on ATA 100	18:04:33.02 18:05:46.11 18:07:16.60	18:05:45.40 18:07:02.00 18:08:29.05	01:12.38 01:15.89 01:12.45 01:13.57
From ATA 66 over GbE to NTFS Simple	11:59:29.59 12:00:39.23 12:01:49.72	12:00:39.12 12:01:49.61 12:02:59.48	01:09.53 01:10.38 01:09.76 01:09.89	From ATA 100 over GbE to ATA 100 H/W Stripe and mirror	13:37:19.86 13:38:29.45 13:39:49.19	13:38:29.31 13:39:49.05 13:40:58.59	01:09.45 01:19.60 01:09.40 01:12.82

continud

Table 10-1. Test Results (continued)

1 GB From/To	Start Time	End Time	Duration	1 GB From/To	Start Time	End Time	Duration
From ATA 100	11:47:33.38	11:51:30.83	03:57.45	From ATA 100 over	13:52:25.77	13:53:26.27	01:00.50
over GbE to	11:51:30.95	11:55:30.86	03:59.91	GbE to ATA 100	13:53:26.27	13:54:28.20	01:01.93
SCSI Simple	11:55:30.96	11:59:29.49	03:58.53	H/W Stripe	13:54:28.20	13:55:28.56	01:00.36
			03:58.63	4 drives			01:00.93
From ATA 66	16:32:10.19	16:33:24.01	01:13.82	From ATA 100 over	13:43:50.02	13:48:48.65	04:58.63
over GbE to	16:33:24.23	16:34:36.62	01:12.39	GbE to SCSI-2	13:48:49.17	13:53:48.19	04:59.02
IDE Stripe	16:34:37.00	16:35:58.20	01:21.20	S/W Mirror	13:53:48.34	13:58:44.78	04:56.44
			01:15.80				04:58.03
From ATA 100	12:28:02.48	12:29:11.96	01:09.48	From ATA 100	14:03:55.87	14:05:04.13	01:08.26
over GbEto	12:29:12.07	12:30:23.36	01:11.29	over GbE to	14:05:04.24	14:06:10.98	01:06.74
NTFS ATA 66	12:30:23.47	12:31:34.12	01:10.65	Linux ATA 100	14:06:11.09	14:07:18.13	01:07.04
			01:10.47	S/W Mirror			01:07.35
From ATA 100	13:46:57.32	13:47:54.70	00:57.38	From ATA 100	15:05:48.51	15:07:53.31	01:36.90
over GbE to	13:47:54.70	13:48:52.12	00:57.42	over GbE to	15:08:00.43	15:09:59.76	01:36.33
NTFS ATA 100	13:48:52.25	13:49:49.67	00:57.42	Linux SCSI-2	15:10:06.62	15:12:04.03	01:36.77
			00:57.41	S/W Mirror			01:36.67

Comparisons

The combination of drive types and configuration options such as stripe and mirror are broken out in the following comparisons. From these descriptions, you should be in a better position to see the relationships reflected in the performance metrics.

SCSI vs. ATA/66

As promised, striping across drives did yield better write performance than a simple drive and considerably better performance than a spanned drive. When you look at the comparison of performance between exactly the same disk configuration on identical hardware where the only difference is the Gigabit Ethernet cards, however, an interesting point emerges. The comparison between the two configurations, using the same server and client hardware, excepting only the network cards, and transferring the same 1GB file set is depicted in Figure 10-2.

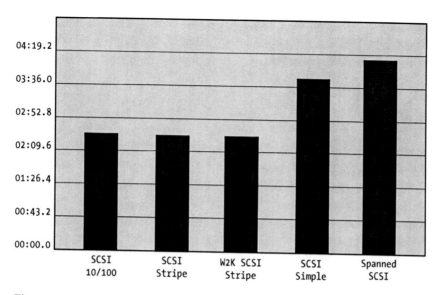

Figure 10-2. SCSI-2 disk performance under Windows Volume options—GbE vs. 10/100

Slower disk subsystems don't benefit from higher network transfer speeds.

The elapsed time for the striped drive to the SCSI disk subsystem using Gigabit Ethernet was 2 minutes and 43.4 seconds on average. The elapsed time for the same transfer with a 10/100 3Com bus master card averaged 2 minutes and 40 seconds. Given that the range for all of the transfers using those configurations was between 2 minutes and 38.4 seconds and 2 minutes and 44.6 seconds, performance is about equal.

Conclusion: Disk transfer speeds are the limiting factor—not network performance at 20 MBps disk throughput rates.

This would seem to be borne out by the comparison of the spanned drive metrics as well. An average duration of 4 minutes and 16.7 seconds was experienced for the GbE configuration and 4 minutes and 19.4 seconds using a 10/100 card. Again, essentially equal performance.

This leads to an interesting question: At what point does the disk subsystem take advantage of higher network throughput? To answer this question, I decided to compare Ultra DMA 66 transfer rates to the SCSI subsystem. During the course of this experiment, I discovered that the onboard IDE controllers in the NetFinity weren't actually providing DMA support for the Seagate Barracudas. In fact, they were falling down to PIO mode. This meant that the transfer rates of the system, using the disk controller provided with the server, was operating at about the same level of performance as the SCSI disks. Even though the drives themselves offered a higher throughput rate, the controller wasn't taking advantage of that capability, and as a result, my GbE hardware, once again, wasn't providing any measurable improvement in overall transfer speeds. I elected to add in a Promise Ultra/66 controller card as the disk controller.

10/100 vs. GbE

The benchmark transfer of the 1GB file set from the 2000 Professional client using GbE to the Windows 2000 Server, now enabled with ATA/66 and Seagate Barracuda IV drives, averaged a transfer rate of 1 minute and 11.1 seconds. The same transfer using the 3Com 10/100 card took on average 2.01.0 seconds.

Conclusions: A faster disk doesn't gain you much when constrained by the network. The 10/100 card that worked fine in the 20 MBps configuration didn't contribute a whole lot when the disk throughput was increased to 100 MBps. Arguably a 25 percent increase (120 seconds compared to 160 seconds) is pretty good. But in the context of this review, I was looking for the thresholds in limiting data transfer rates overall. The five times increase in throughput theoretically enabled by the faster disk was restricted to 25 percent overall due to the network speed. To validate this, compare the transfer times of the SCSI simple drive to the ATA/66 simple time under GbE. You can see that the same file transferred to the 20 MBps disk took 3 minutes 58 seconds. I already established the transfer completed in 71.1 seconds using Gigabit Ethernet and an Ultra/66 controller with an NTFS-formatted drive.

Corollary: A faster disk provides multiples of throughput capability when unconstrained by network performance.

NTFS vs. FAT32

So far, each of these transfers have been done using NTFS. I remember hearing background noises about the performance of various Windows file systems—and that FAT32, although not as robust or as secure as NTFS, would perform better. Because it's relevant to this review, I thought this would be an excellent opportunity to see how much, if any, the file system choices affected the performance of the system as a whole (see Figure 10-3).

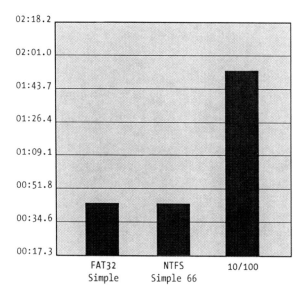

Figure 10-3. Comparison of NTFS and FAT32 target drives

The 1GB file set transferred using a copy command in a command window from one Windows 2000 system to another with the remote drive mounted through SAMBA showed no material difference in write performance. The same drive formatted under NTFS or FAT32 supported virtually identical file copy times. In fact, the NTFS drive was marginally faster, with an average throughput time of 69.9 seconds versus FAT32, with 71.1 seconds duration.

ATA/66 vs. ATA/100

Given that I was limited to only a 33 MHz PCI bus, it seemed that to benchmark drive controllers, I would be better advised to look at the difference between DMA 4 and DMA 5. In this case, the theoretical transfer difference is 33 MBps—the difference between 66 and 100 as it were. The performance comparisons between the two drive controllers (same drives, same network, same files and scripts) is shown in Figure 10-4.

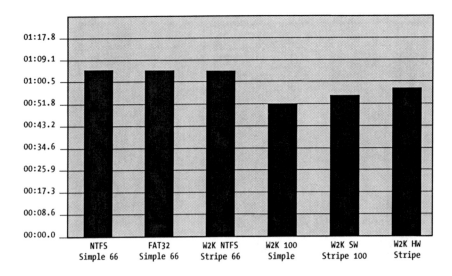

Figure 10-4. File transfer durations comparing ATA/66 and ATA/100 controllers

The simple ATA/66 NTFS drive finished writing the file in 71.1 seconds as you already saw. The ATA/100 NTFS simple drive completed the file transfer in an average of 57.4 seconds. This amounts to an average improvement in 13.7 seconds, or roughly 20 percent.

However, the performance for ATA 100 stripe drives averaged 59.0 and 59.7 seconds for software and hardware striping respectively.

Conclusions: Increased file transfer performance is still available from the network throughput provided by GbE at DMA 4 and DMA 5. The transfer rate of the hard-disk controller is the only factor that changed between the two and yielded a direct 20 percent improvement in file transfer time. Striping didn't provide any performance benefit across two drives for the 1GB file set. Both hardware and software RAID 0 provided essentially the same results.

SMB vs. NFS

In the discussion regarding the performance of various file systems, I made note of feedback from various proponents of particular file system formats. Although NFS does require a client to be configured on each station, it may or may not be a more appropriate choice given the environment in which you work. Regardless of environmental factors, I wanted to see whether, all things being equal, there was a performance difference between the two file systems.

In this case, I elected to compare the ATA 100 disk and controller with hardware RAID 1 (mirroring) enabled. Because this forces the two disks to be kept in synch, it seemed an interesting way to put the demand on the file system itself. In any case, the like-to-like comparison yielded very similar performances for both SMB and NFS running on Windows—specifically, 96.7 seconds for NFS and a slightly slower 98 seconds for SMB over the hardware mirror.

There is also file system overhead incurred when reading and writing many file names as opposed to managing a stream of blocks belonging to a single file. I changed the test data to reflect a 1GB file with 3000 file names in order to see how the results would be affected. The impact was marginal, although performance was somewhat slower as I expected.

Linux File Systems

Under Red Hat 9, I was pleased to note that my D-Link GbE, Promise, and In Land controller cards were all detected and required no intervention on my part. This is to say I used the default drivers for all the gear on the Linux platform. I wanted to see what impact there was on opting for the ext3 journaled file system over the traditional ext2 file system. With transfer times of 75.8 seconds for ext2 and 79.7 seconds for ext3, there was a measurable difference, but not significantly so. It was interesting to note that the dedicated ATA/100 controller clocked the same kind of improvement over the ATA/66 between the two file systems.

FTP

Most everyone who has spent any time working as a dedicated systems administrator knows that it's hard to beat FTP for moving large files around a network. Sure enough, the very best times for file transfers under either Linux or Windows was using command-line FTP—53 and 55 seconds to transfer the file set, respectively. However, when using a GUI-based FTP application, transfer times jumped to 4 minutes for the same file. Performance monitoring showed the application utilized more than 50 percent CPU and hogged a bunch of virtual memory. The application used for the transfer clearly does matter!

Spanned, Mirrored, and Mirrored Striped Drives

The performance hit for spanning the SCSI-2 drives was considerable—1GB transferred in 4 minutes and 16.7 seconds. Mirroring also had an impact, 4 minutes and 58 seconds on average. The ATA/100 mirrored drives completing the synchronized transfer to two disks in 67.3 seconds. To get an idea of the trade-offs between stripes and mirrors using a hardware RAID 0+1 configuration, I tied four Seagate DMA 100 drives to the RAID controller and split the RAID set into disks 0+3 (primary and secondary master drives) as the source with disks 1+2 (primary and secondary slave drives) as the mirrors. A 2GB partition was created as a simple drive under Windows 2000 Disk Manager. Under this arrangement, the file transfer of the 1GB file set I had been using for all of these tests took an average of 72.8 seconds to complete across three tries. That makes a 5-second performance penalty for mirroring over implementing a stripe set alone across the same two drives.

The SCSI-3 drives, when spanned, completed the write in 57 seconds.

If drive transfer rates are to be considered the limiting factor, I thought it stood to reason that the most efficient and therefore the best performing configuration using the collection of components I had assembled would be the following: a four-drive stripe, specified with a 2048 byte write size to work with the 512 bytes handled per operation by each drive, with a simple drive under the NTFS file system also specified to allocate in 2048 bytes.

The result was an average transfer rate of 60.9 seconds for the stripe set. In other words, a marginal speed decrease occurred over striping two drives with hardware or for that matter with the Windows 2000 Server software stripe.

Sustainable Performance

Because the premise of this exercise was to determine the optimum arrangement of components to support high availability, low cost, and good performance, I needed to get some idea of the performance profile of each component. I had decided to work with Gigabit Ethernet, and after buying three different cards, I wasn't pleased to discover that only one of them supported jumbo frames. Given that the most likely use of this platform would be to cascade bits down the wire for a successful write to disk as quickly as feasible, it seemed to me that jumbo frames could help the process. I had little network traffic with the switch dedicated to the two-node cluster and could see no source of interference. The question then became one of matching disk speed to network throughput. I decided that of the four components and five variations, a suite of tests would help me arrive at the best results.

As such, I conducted various point-to-point file transfers with the identical 1GB file and FTP approach. Table 10-2 indicates my findings.

Table 10-2. Best Results

Source Drive	Target Config	Duration
ATA/100	ATA/100 (GbE)	57.87 seconds
ATA/100	S/ATA (GbE)	50.41 seconds
SCSI/160	ATA/100 (GbE)	56.91 seconds
SCSI/160	S/ATA (GbE)	47 seconds
ATA/100	ATA/100 (jumbo frames 9K)	67.15 seconds
ATA/100	S/ATA (jumbo frames 9K)	43.26 seconds
SCSI/160	ATA/100 (jumbo frames 9K)	67.15 seconds
SCSI/160	S/ATA (jumbo frames 9K)	43.89 seconds
ATA/100	ATA/100 (internal copy)	55 seconds
ATA/100	SCSI/160 (internal copy)	60 seconds
ATA/100	S/ATA (internal copy)	36.6 seconds

If you're going to try this at home, please remember that I didn't achieve the same results when either one of the systems was a domain controller. To get under a gigabyte per minute transferred between two boxes, those boxes were each configured as Windows Advanced Server(s) 2000 as members of a workgroup.

Cat 5 vs. Cat 6

In the transfer from ATA/100 to a Serial ATA drive over GbE, there was no measurable difference in transfer times when changing out the cable from Cat 5 to Cat 6. This remained true when using the Hawking switch or the direct connection via a cross-over cable, using the default 1500 MTU size. Using jumbo frames, however, was a completely different story.

Jumbo Frames

Of the several manufacturers of GbE cards that I had acquired as part of this project, only one—D-Link—supported jumbo frames. To determine what, if any, effect this option would have on my cluster, I decided to acquire a matched set of D-Link GbE cards. As is often the case with technology, because it had been a few months from the purchase of the first D-Link card, that particular model was no longer available. I wasn't to have an exactly matched set, but instead one 500T and another 530T, both of which supported jumbo frames.

However, in setting up the cluster nodes to communicate with each other using GbE and jumbo frames, I discovered a few interesting things. First, I had to eliminate my switch, since it didn't support jumbo frames. As the Advanced Server cluster only allows two nodes, and I was using either a 10/100 or the onboard Broadcom GbE card to communicate with the WAN router, I figured I'd simply opt for the cross-over cable. The 530T card has an option of selecting jumbo frames, but not for changing their size. Its default is 9014. The 500T, on the other hand, required an explicit value. When I did that, and added each statically defined IP address for that card as the default gateway for the other, I was able to restore the connection. The transfer of my 14 files totaling 1GB took almost exactly 100 seconds to transfer from the ATA/100 drive on the xSeries to the S/ATA drive on the FIC machine. I concluded it had to be the cable.

This necessitated yet another trip to Fry's, where I acquired a Cat 6 cross-over cable. The transfer time for the 1GB file set was consistently half or less than that obtained using the Cat 5 cable. This was also the best time for a cross-network transfer, with the 1GB file completing its SMB copy operation in under 45 seconds, a sustained throughput rate of 22,755 megabytes per second.

Tuning GbE Storage Network Components

I was quite pleased with the outcome of the various tests, at least in terms of how they illustrated the practical application of the concepts discussed in Chapters 2 and 3. In the comparison between Serial ATA technology and its parallel counterpart, it proved possible to get a significant percentage improvement. As stated, the parallel ATA drive was an Ultra/100 drive and drives capable of throughput rates of 133 MBps are on the market. However, the choke point in the process then would likely have been the PCI bus at 32 bits wide and 33 MHz.

Still, the point should have been clearly made that the media can make a difference—in some cases. The controller mode, bus speed, and drive attributes will, in some cases, become bottlenecks. Jumbo frames can provide a performance increase—under the right circumstances.

In the do-it-yourself lab that I created for this chapter, I managed to get the fastest write time on my gear of 37 seconds for a drive-to-drive transfer within a box. I also tweaked the network link until it achieved a transfer of the same file in 43 seconds between two boxes. Without opting for a card and driver that supported jumbo frames, the best transfer time I could get was 50 seconds, which clearly points to the network card and switch as the bottleneck in that case, since upgrading the connecting cable from Cat 5 to Cat 6 had no effect.

From these results, I could extrapolate that if I'm writing across a vanilla-flavored GbE Ethernet link, I shouldn't expect a performance increase from striping my Serial ATA drives. In the case of the Microsoft two-node cluster, I tuned the performance by opting for a combination of one high-performance drive and optimizing my network settings and media. This was done very cost-effectively, considering that the Cat 6 cross-over cable cost $5.99. For any other straight copy or simple file transfer operation such as disk-to-disk backup, the relationship between components will likely apply to other environments. For database, web server, or application-specific environments, other allowances will have to be made.

Methodology

Before applying the findings to my specific requirements, I wanted to note how the tests were conducted. Drives were mounted using SMB. To facilitate using the same scripts in the Linux and Windows environment, Services For Unix was loaded onto both the clients and servers. All transfers were initiated and clocked through scripts, with a log maintained to show the start time, stop time, and files being transferred from drive to drive. The NFS transfer times were handled using the same files and scripts, but the SAMBA drives were removed and replaced with NFS mounts.

A sample script for transferring files from the client data directory to the server drive is shown here:

```
set startspantime=%time%
echo 100 span started %startspantime%>> volumetest.log
copy g:\data\*.* p:\
set stopspantime=%time%
echo 100 span copy ended %stopspantime%>> volumetest.log
rm p:\*
set startspantime=%time%
echo 100 span started %startspantime%>> volumetest.log
copy g:\data\*.* p:\
set stopspantime=%time%
echo 100 span copy ended %stopspantime%>> volumetest.log
rm p:\*
set startspantime=%time%
echo 100 span started %startspantime%>> volumetest.log
copy g:\data\*.* p:\
set stopspantime=%time%
echo 100 span copy ended %stopspantime%>> volumetest.log
rm p:\*
```

An example of the log entries is shown in the following log sample:

```
100 span started 17:26:12.72
100 span copy ended 17:27:12.71
100 span started 17:27:12.86
100 span copy ended 17:28:12.11
100 span started 17:28:12.26
100 span copy ended 17:29:10.53
```

The numbers were transcribed into an Excel spreadsheet, which was used to calculate the times. An average of three copies was used as the number reflecting the performance of the configuration. The two servers were attached to a Hawking Gigabit Ethernet switching hub, and there were no other stations connected or traffic on the network.

Oh, and for what it's worth, the files I transferred repeatedly from drive to drive consisted of video files. Every once in a while I would play them to make sure they hadn't become corrupted (they hadn't), and I rebooted between transfers to clear out any buffers and cache contents.

My Requirements

With a theoretical throughput capacity of 33 MBps, it seemed to me that even the venerable PCI bus should be capable of supporting sustained transfer efficiencies of 51 percent. That, at least, was the target. At 51 percent of 33 megabytes per second, a system could throw around a little more than 1GB per minute. Given that most of the workstations we used had 20GB capacities, this struck me as a practical level of performance—a full system backup in 20 to 30 minutes.

Because my environment consists of a mail server, web server, conference server (instant messaging), FTP site, and shared developer environment including code repository, most of my client connections came through the Internet. Necessarily, this limited the amount of performance gain that would be felt by my user community, including myself when accessing the services from a motel or boat. Implied in that statement is a sense of distance from my physical plant; hence the importance of availability. Scalability in my case was more a strategy for meeting planned increases in demand rather than reacting to a run on my services by a sudden swell in the number of customers.

My development environment drove a subtle, but important, requirement, which is after all my core business. As much as I like to use Linux for my production services, some of the IBM-based software we work with for autonomic computing is released first for the Windows 2000 platform. Linux versions follow, but to incorporate or evaluate beta code, that environment had to be made available first.

I decided that to secure the desired level of availability, I needed a redundant server that replicated the data and software of the primary system. This led me to design the topology shown in Figure 10-5.

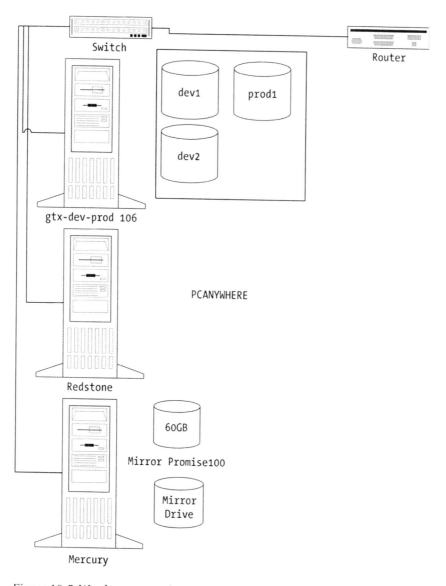

Figure 10-5. Worden.net topology

As you can see in the diagram, my first order of business was to create two Windows 2000 Advanced Servers using MS Clustering Services in order to ensure a "civilized" transition from one server to another in the event of a systems outage. Of course, I was at the mercy of Southwest Bell to maintain my connection to the outside world, but with dial-out capability for absolute emergencies, I was prepared to live with that risk.

Perhaps the most important aspect of this configuration is that it's a precursor for the introduction of shared storage. The failover of server software and hardware resources allows uninterrupted service, but the cluster can share access to data resources via SCSI or Fibre Channel storage arrays. I didn't feel ready for the full Fibre Monty, but I was impressed enough with the SCSI performance and reliability to go that route. Ideally, I could configure a Serial ATA array.

A quick note on the limitations of Microsoft Advanced Server 2000, the server configuration supported by Redmond, WA. It consists of a cluster of two nodes, which don't have to be identical but can't exceed 8GB of physical memory or 8 CPUs each. To move to a four-node cluster, or support larger servers with 32 processors or 32GB of RAM, I would have had to move to the Datacentre 2000 product. The Windows Server 2003 family scales up to as many as eight 64-bit server nodes with 64 Itanium processors and 512GB of RAM apiece.

Network load balancing, a means of distributing TCP/IP workload across up to 32 servers, is supported by Advanced Server.

However, in this case I was only looking to introduce an "auxiliary bridge" to maintain my services to the not-so-wide world of my web-based users. The cluster and the performance of components within it were my chief concern. I was also hoping that in tweaking each component for this specific situation, I would be able to illustrate the process of storage network component interaction generally.

Practical Application

From the background of the testing process and review of my specific requirements, I decided I was ready to design my own small storage network solution. Selecting MS Advanced Server 2000 cluster server seemed like the best way to proceed, given the requirements I introduced earlier. At this point, I'd like to review the MS cluster process and comment on the real-world experience I had with it.

After installing Microsoft Advanced Server 2000, I set up the Cluster Services. I should note that I encountered a few false starts in the process. For instance, I couldn't install Active Directory on the S/ATA drive when it was the boot disk. After substituting an IDE drive for drive C, the Active Directory installation process went reasonably smoothly. Alas, the importance of triple-checking the hardware compatibility test results from Microsoft became apparent, and Cluster Services refused to acknowledge my S/ATA drive. I was stuck with SCSI.

During the cluster installation process, I was presented with options for configuring the cluster as shown in Figure 10-6.

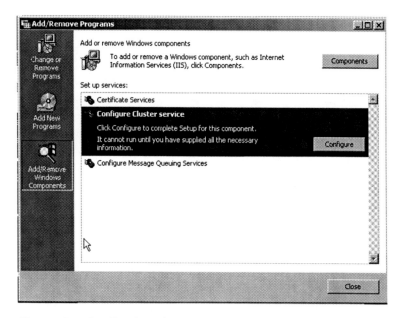

Figure 10-6. Configuring Cluster Services

There are fewer than a dozen configuration screens, and I'm not going to include all of them. However, there were a couple that provided interesting choices I was in a better position to make as a result of the experiments (see, for instance, Figure 10-7).

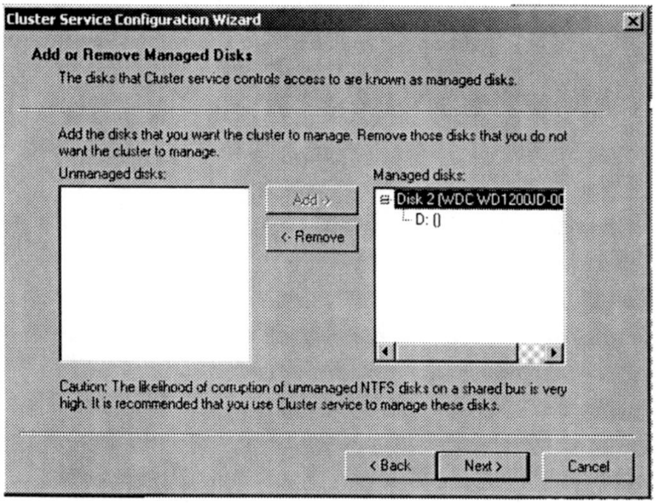

Figure 10-7. Assigning managed disks

It was at this point that I discovered that the MS Cluster Services didn't like my Serial ATA disk. Until then, it had worked swimmingly. That aside, I wanted to comment on the use to which cluster server puts this managed disk.

Each MS cluster node is synchronized. The primary node owns the disk they share access to across the same physical bus. In the event of a server outage, the secondary node takes ownership of the data resources. The mechanism by which this is arbitrated is a quorum disk on which the cluster database is maintained. The warning on this screen refers to the situation where two servers can access the same disk without arbitration. Unmanaged disk resources could be seen, mounted, and used from any of the Windows Servers on the bus; however, this would likely result in data corruption. Cluster Services are the way Microsoft controls the disk usage. It's worth noting that cluster server requires basic rather than Microsoft Dynamic disk formats, so I had to resist the temptation to click Yes in the Write Signature dialog box earlier in the server installation process (see Figure 10-8).

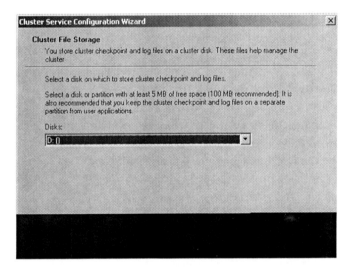

Figure 10-8. Selecting the cluster disk

As shown in the figure, the next step in the installation is to identify where Cluster-specific data will be stored. Given the importance of the cluster disk, it occurred to me that high reliability and isolation from application activity might be two criteria for selecting the disk type. An excellent opportunity to use my reliable, though somewhat smaller, Atlas SCSI drives, I thought (see Figure 10-9).

In this case, I opted for the D-Link 530T with jumbo frames and the Cat 6 cross-over cable for the private network. This segregated client communication coming in over the Internet from the server-to-server cluster-specific network activity.

A few clicks later and the installation of the main cluster node was completed.

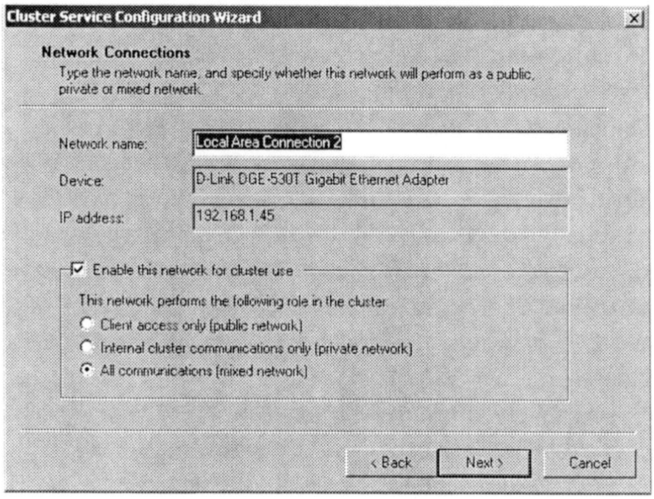

Figure 10-9. Public and private networks

Lessons Learned

A network storage environment is a complex arrangement of interoperating parts—any one of which can be the bottleneck for a given data transfer scenario. It's exceedingly difficult to pull generally applicable rules of thumb for the design and tuning of a network device as straightforward as a file server—let alone a more complex storage solution. However, the realities of increased disk capacities combined with network bandwidth and more varied software applications is that storage must be consolidated or it will be overwhelming.

From the ground up, you've seen that merely using faster disks provides no benefit if the other players in the stack aren't optimized as well. That was from the outset one of the value propositions of this book. By starting with simple examples and evaluating the factors that affect them, you can approach more complex SANs and comprehend them.

At this point, you should be comfortable visualizing the end-to-end connection of two applications that share data. I hope you can see how the approach to diagnosing bottlenecks can be applied to any collection of similar gear.

It's important to note that the relationship between capabilities is the key to understanding a storage network. A Serial ATA drive can boast a 250 MBps transfer rate, but without tuning the network connections, you can end up with little or no return. The way I approached this benchmarking exercise was to evaluate where to spend time and money first.

Some activities that I thought should yield performance gains in some cases did and in others did not. Striping, for example, was highly effective when using the SCSI bus, whereas it had an inconsequential effect on the throughput to the ATA/100 drives. To validate this, I went back to the system and configured a software stripe of four drives under the ATA/100 controller.

Anytime you can throw a gigabyte of data reliably around a network in less than a minute, I think it's fair to say you have the basis for building a consolidated storage facility. By showing the relatively small impact of journaling and mirroring on write performance, I think it should be clear that your approach to storage networks should be derived out from the services you want to provide your users. For some it will be the fastest possible recovery times; others will want their data always available. Still others need optimized file transfer time, so radiologists, say, aren't waiting for their images to load.

If you can work with a 1 gigabit a minute transfer speed limit, then you're well advised to look at Gigabit Ethernet and iSCSI solutions for your storage network. On the price/performance continuum this is going to be the absolutely lowest investment in capital equipment. You'll spend considerable time on the design and implementation of it, naturally. However, I think there is more than a little extra value in being that intimately acquainted with your storage network.

For those who require significantly more speed, distance, or scalability, the next chapters will review first NAS appliances and then fiber-based SAN solutions. There may be a temptation for some to look down on a DIY solution as being unsophisticated or unworthy of the label SAN. Regardless of the value you put on a shared SMB and NFS storage, their underlying principles are the same as those for any other storage network.

Summary

Now that you've gone through one specific example of how networked storage could be configured and optimized, as well as learning the specific performance metrics, you should be in a better position to relate the component concepts to a practical setting.

The main point to take away from this chapter is that when you treat storage network components like commodities, you get the slowest common denominator. With even a handful of components—cabling, network cards, bus, controllers, and disks, for instance—a tremendous number of potential interconnections and configuration variations arises. If anyone should be an expert in the behavior of your specific combination of storage and network components, it should be you.

CHAPTER 11

Vendor Offerings

THE PURPOSE OF THIS CHAPTER is to give you a tour of the Storage Area Network products on the market. Of course, specific model numbers, product characteristics, and attributes will likely have changed by the time you read this chapter. For this reason, I've tried to look at the history and strategy of the major players, all the better to round out the book. However, since I intended this book as a bottom-up primer for anyone addressing Storage Area Networks in theory and practice, I also added a specific requirement that was presented to me for a storage networking solution, and I relate those requirements to the specific product set I recommended in that case.

SAN Component Vendors

In this section, I want to review the market positions, strategies, and products of the major vendors in the SAN products space. These companies include Cisco, HP, IBM, and EMC for SAN solutions; Brocade and McData for switches; and Emulex and QLogic for HBAs.

Interoperability problems between sophisticated, high-performance, expensive components make it even more difficult to sort out the key players in any segment of the SAN market. However, like a lot of IT products, it can be easier to understand the market by looking at the vendors rather than the customers. SAN vendors have had to adapt quickly to changing customer priorities, new technological capabilities, and industry alliances.

In 2004, it was difficult to tell if Storage Area Networks represented a growing IT industry segment, or if a cannibalizing consolidation was underway. New offerings in the form of iSCSI and GbE opened up opportunities that were simply unavailable to the maturing but still complex and expensive Fibre Channel solutions.

My intent here isn't to do a feature-by-feature review of specific models of equipment as offered at the time of writing. (I do note some specifics where I think they highlight a larger point.) Instead, I want to take you on a tour of the vendors "most likely to succeed" in occupying a viable niche for the foreseeable future. Foreseeable by me that is, which means there is always the risk that my predictions could be off base.

With that caveat, you should be able to follow the SAN market and see where they are going.

Consumer NAS

On a walk through Fry's Electronics in early January 2004, I noticed a new offering on their shelves—a consumer plug-and-play Network Attached Storage device. By this I mean a real shared access, multifile system unit capable of storing 120+ gigabytes with client access over CIFS, NFS, HTTP, and AppleTalk.

Intended for the small office/home office market (SOHO), the Tritton ASA server line integrates a file server, firewall, router, and shared storage capability. It supports up to 20 IPSec tunnels concurrently, and at least at that time supported only 10/100 Ethernet links.

To me, there was a clear parallel between this turnkey NAS appliance and the plethora of Linksys-type Internet routers that replaced dedicated proxy servers for small businesses from 2000 onwards.

The main marketing message promoted by Tritton is reduced technical support. Complexity is expensive. Its browser-based administration console is, naturally, accessible from anywhere, which makes remote support not only plausible, but also preferred.

And speaking of Linksys, now that they are a division of Cisco, they are certainly in a position to ensure they aren't left behind. Their EFG120 is a 120GB Networked Attached Storage device with USB print server and router that also supports 10/100/1000 connectivity. With a second IDE drive bay, another 250GB can be added. If the original drive is upgraded, the EFGHDT2 (where do they get these model numbers?) can support a half terabyte of storage. Unfortunately, for those of us who like Panthers, the only supported clients are Windows based.

The main message I took away from this product is that Moore's Law, and its attendant drop in prices for yesterday's advanced capabilities, was about to hit storage networking. In the same way that DVD players were the expensive toys of a privileged few in the mid 1990s, and 10 years later you could get them with two cereal box tops, networked storage was becoming a consumer commodity.

Leaders of the Pack

Although a dead-simple assembly of NAS components might be a plug-and-play purchase from Amazon, and off-the-shelf bits and pieces could be assembled into a Linux-based storage cluster, the leading edge of storage engineering was still pretty sharp.

If you wanted to connect more than 64 devices, capable of handling 2 gigabits per second in and 2 gigabits per second out simultaneously in early 2004, you had to look to Fibre Channel. The National Center for Supercomputing Applications has long had a mission of maintaining a computing environment that is more than 5 years ahead of the processing power of current environments. In 2002, they upgraded their SAN technologies with a combination of Brocade Silkworm 12000 Core Fabric switches and Myrinet HBAs to support 200 connected servers. In October 2003, Myricom, the company that manufactures the Myrinet products, introduced the M3F2-PCIXE-2 fiber card capable of sustaining throughput of 950 megabytes per second. MSRP for the card when introduced was $1,195.

I mention Myricom because although they may not be a household name, they have demonstrated a consistent ability to lead with performance, especially in the arena of supercomputing clusters. On a marketing level, this quiet little company (48 employees in 2003) operates as an OEM selling 80 percent of the products it makes through companies like IBM, HP, Sun, and others.

The practice of buying technology from a manufacturer and rebranding it as part of a larger solution is prevalent in the networked storage industry. And it adds to the difficulty in determining which products you might choose. However, with their ability to acquire smaller companies, vendors such as HP, IBM, and Cisco are the 800-pound gorillas in this space. By watching the products they incorporate, companies they ally with, and lines they quietly "deemphasize," you can tell a great deal about the direction of a technology.

IBM

In 2002, Big Blue sold the hard disk division it created in 1956 to Hitachi Data Systems. Far from representing a strategic retreat from the storage arena, this action showed IBM's strengths when it comes to understanding where they can shine. Disk drives are a commodity, at least from a manufacturer's perspective. Higher production run rates, ruthlessly efficient manufacturing processes, and cutthroat pricing strategies are the order of the day. IBM has other fish to fry, including their largest storage array—the Shark.

From a storage perspective, IBM expects to generate what Wall Street calls *organic growth*—that is, the company is looking for an increasingly profitable revenue stream from a growing share of an enlarging pie. IBM isn't looking to the underlying hardware components to accomplish this alone. Instead, they have bet heavily on *virtualization* and *autonomic computing*. I'll go into more detail on these visions in Chapter 13, where you'll find my take on the future of networked storage.

At this point, it helps to understand the technologies that IBM develops and produces in-house. Within the storage networks arena this includes storage arrays (but not the drives), blade servers, Tivoli systems software, and two new offerings targeted squarely at the storage market: the SAN Volume Controller and the SAN Integration Controller. Both support integration with products from other vendors and provide device drivers allowing servers from HP, Sun, Wintel, and Linux to access their virtualized storage pools.

FAStT200

The Fibre Channel Attached Storage Technology (FAStT) combination RAID controller and disk drive enclosure is IBM's entry-level FC storage server. There are two models offered: one with single and the other with dual RAID controllers. Both incorporate redundant, hot-swappable power supplies. The enclosure has room for 10 half-height FC hard drives. Connecting additional EXP500 FC storage expansion enclosures supports additional disk capacity. Theoretically, you could combine as many as 10 enclosures before reaching the maximum 126 FC devices supported in an FC loop. However, for performance reasons, IBM recommends configuring not more than 30 drives with the single controller FAStT200 and 60 with the dual RAID controller model.

FAStT500

The FAStt600 Storage Server unit itself is available in two models, base and turbo. Turbo can be added to the base model as a later upgrade and increases the scalability of the system. Where the base model tops out at 400 MB/sec, the turbo feature scales up to 768MB/sec. Turbo also offers an increased cache, an additional 1Gbps auto-sensing Fibre Channel connection and VolumeCopy software for full replication of logical volumes.

Figure 11-1 shows a FAStT500 rack-mountable storage server.

A more informative perspective can be seen from the back of the unit in Figure 11-2.

In this view, you can see there are 8 Fibre Channel controllers installed on this unit, under which the two hot-swappable power supplies are located. In the center of the unit, a fan and communications module with serial and Ethernet ports is located.

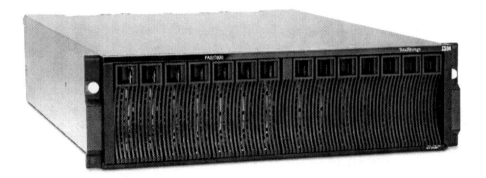

Figure 11-1. The IBM FAStT500 Storage Server

Figure 11-2. IBM FAStT500 connectivity

Both models allow expansion of disk capacity through external enclosures, including up to 28TB of storage capacity using Serial ATA disk drives under the EXP100 enclosure. By connecting up to 3 of the EXP700 disk enclosures, the base model can support as many as 56 disk drives while the Turbo model supports up to 112 fibre channel drives. This is depicted in the sample topology shown in Figure 11-3 with a FAStT600 storage server supporting two clusters and 40 disk drives.

In this topology the FAStT600 storage server is configured with one FC link to each of eight servers, organized into four clusters with two nodes in each.

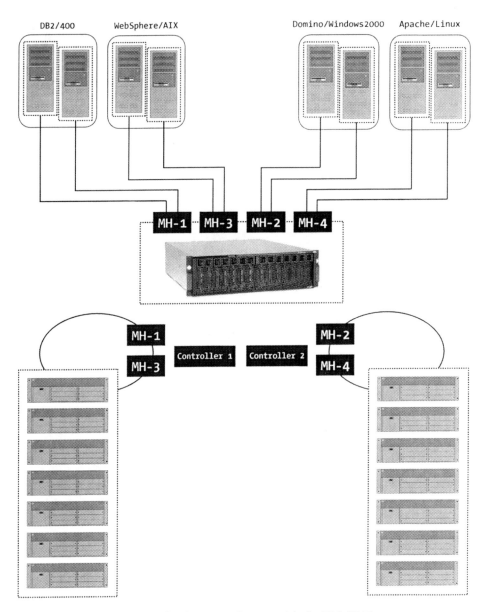

Figure 11-3. Supporting multiple server clusters with the FAStT500

SAN Volume Controller

This virtualization engine from IBM allows storage to represent LUNs to hosts in a typical SAN fashion. However, behind the scenes, the Volume Controller manages all of the disk resources independently through Volume Controller Managed Disks. Hosts connect to virtual disks represented by the SCSI LUN. The Volume Controller console handles discovery and assignment of disks. By consolidating storage pools and presenting these as virtual disks for HP-UX, AIX, Solaris, Linux, and Windows servers, the Volume Controller provides a single point of administration for managing disks and mapping storage to host applications. Note that although the preceding example depicts the maximum expandability of the FAStT600 without using a FC switch, much larger configurations can be supported. SAN Volume Controller also supports the Cisco MDS 9000, which I'll cover a bit later in this chapter when reviewing that company's storage network offerings.

Hewlett Packard

HP has a long tradition of not just acquiring companies, but successfully digesting them. Those of us who have some gray in our hair might remember their successful incorporation of Apollo Computing, which moved HP into the world of Unix and engineering workstations. I believe it's important to interpret HP's position on Storage Area Networks in light of their acquisitions of Digital Equipment Corporation (DEC) and Compaq Computer Corporation.

DEC was the second largest manufacturer of communications devices for many years. They pioneered development of TCP/IP networks in a long-pitched battle against SNA from IBM. Compaq, of course, brings desktops to the equation, but more applicably a large installation base of Novell and Windows servers. These now represent HP customers. In 2000, Compaq garnered a SAN and NAS market share in Europe of just under the 60 percent mark. In 2001, Compaq sold more storage hardware than any other competitor.

The third calendar quarter of 2003 marked the sixth quarter in a row that HP occupied the number one spot for revenue from disk storage under the StorageWorks banner. HP has a huge list of SAN and NAS products available in all three market segments—entry level, mid-range, and enterprise class. As noted, much of the momentum in this area was incorporated from Compaq. HP itself wasn't without products or a sales presence. They combined their systems management software, OpenView, with StorageWorks hardware in the Network Storage Solutions global business unit to promote HP as a provider of "storage as a utility."

Like the other big players in storage, the key drivers for future network storage growth is seen to be the fusion of SAN and NAS technologies, especially over IP networks, virtualization of the storage hardware platform, and storage resource management through software.

Still, with all that clout, HP has elected not to do everything themselves. For their high-end disk array XP, the company partnered with Hitachi. Likewise, router technology from Cisco and fiber-optic components from McData and Brocade form part of the StorageWorks product lines. Perhaps the most distinctive move HP has made was to build on their reputation in instrumentation and high degree of acceptance in the medical sector. Medical imaging is a vertical focus for HP, and they have selected Agfa, McKesson, and Cerner as key partners to bring an integrated solution to that market.

Entry Level

The HP StorageWorks NAS 1000s is positioned as their entry-level storage server. In keeping with the target customers for this technology, in late 2003 HP offered Windows Storage Server 2003 support on the 1000s product.

Capacities for the unit are 320GB, 640GB, and 1TB configurations. Similar to the Dell unit, the 1000s offers 2 auto-sensing GbE cards and hot swapping of ATA/IDE drives. The operating software for the unit is mirrored across two partitions and configured for automatic failover. Supported protocols include CIFS, NFS, NCP, AFP, HTTP, and FTP.

The 1000s is configured with a single Intel Pentium 4 processor (2.4 or 2.8 GHz) and is equipped with 512MB of SDRAM. The architecture is limited to four hard drives of either 80-, 160-, or 250GB each, which explains the three capacities offered in total.

A 1U form factor for the unit means it's designed to be a rack-mounted solution. An option kit is available for customers who choose not to rack the unit.

The single biggest differentiator in this product is quick recovery to factory default. Additionally, support for OpenView, the HP systems management offering, is included along with Insight Manager and Persistent Storage Manager, which allows online snapshots to be taken of the 1000s data sets.

By incorporating parallel ATA drives, instead of SCSI or Fibre Channel drives, the price point for the NAS 1000s is considerably lower than earlier SAN and NAS solutions. A key target area for deployment is for small and medium-sized business server consolidation and replacement of Exchange and Domino servers installed on dedicated HP servers under NT 4, as well as for servers of branch offices of large banks or retail stores within national and international chains.

Microsoft

As you might expect, Microsoft, being a software company, has a distinctly different approach to Storage Area Networks. When Windows NT came on the scene, Microsoft was clearly gunning for the Novell networking market, and they have done very well in that space. Then, as now, their primary competition was Unix. The variant of threat today is Linux rather than Solaris or HP-UX, but the dynamic remains the same. Microsoft wants to ensure that its installation base of servers grows, and Windows Server 2003 offers features that appeal to network and storage administrators alike.

Specifically, Volume Shadow Services (VSS) allow users to create shadow or backup copies of selected volumes across the network. If and when a change is made to a file, VSS ensures that up to 64 previous copies per volume are available. Perhaps the most attractive benefit of this feature is the ability for users to use VSS to restore accidentally (or not) deleted files using an interface built into Explorer. Additionally, VSS can also be used to extend the functionality of backup tools, allowing the creation of offline copies of online data stores for such servers as Exchange and SQL Server. Virtual Disk Services (VDS) allow the administration of disk partitions across servers with one storage administration interface.

In itself, this might seem a lightweight "me too" kind of offering, especially when compared to the ambitious potential of virtualization and heterogeneous file systems. With Microsoft's Storage Server 2003 and its attendant SDK, Microsoft is hoping to achieve with NAS appliances what it did decades earlier with DOS and Windows.

By providing an operating system for appliances, with special licensing that doesn't try to muscle in on the number of connected desktops, Microsoft is making a bid to become the NAS operating system vendor of choice. If able to gain the significant market share it enjoys with many of its other products, there would be no need to use any other disk administration utilities. The familiar disk manager approach works on all hardware that supports the Storage Server 2003 SDK.

Microsoft uses this approach to leverage customer investment in Active Directory, Exchange Servers, SQL Server, IIS, and, of course, Windows 2000 Server. Having surpassed the 100-million license mark with its Exchange Server in 2002, Microsoft is arguably the number one messaging software vendor. What with messaging driving disk consumption, and with server consolidation an ongoing phenomenon, offering Storage Server 2003 makes sense for many Microsoft-heavy shops.

As you might expect from a NAS-oriented solution, Microsoft Storage Server 2003 includes support for iSCSI. Another key strategic push for Microsoft is the definition of their TCP/IP Offload Engines (TOE) standard, code named Chimney. Microsoft certainly has the track record in pushing out APIs to a community of software developers. Their Chimney product may be the key to ascendancy for them in the iSCSI storage network. I discuss Chimney in Chapter 13 as a future direction, as it wasn't available when I wrote this.

NetApps

One of the early pioneers of storage network solutions along with EMC, NetApps has a range of offerings, including Fibre Channel, iSCSI, and, as you might expect from their name, NAS appliances.

Partnerships with Cisco and VERITAS round out their offerings to provide overall networking and software solutions to their customers.

Fibre Channel SAN solutions are supported for Windows, Solaris, HP-UX, AIX, and Linux hosts.

All Network Appliance solutions are based on the company's Data ONTAP operating system, which supports data access through either block or file access protocols over FCP or iSCSI and IP-based Ethernet, respectively.

Integration with database and other servers such as Lotus Domino and Microsoft Exchange is supported through their SnapManager product. This allows the company to provide a storage networking solution with value-added features such as hot backup, fast restore, and problem reporting.

SAN/NAS integration is supported through the FAS900, FAS200, and F800 series systems. These are offered as *unification engines* supporting concurrent multiprotocol access with a variety of LUN management features.

The NearStore product line features data protection, online archiving, and remote disaster recovery through SnapMirror and SnapRestore software. An additional product, SnapLock, is targeted at compliance and privacy applications with Write Once Read Many (WORM) volumes.

Virtualization of storage resources is handled through their Virtual File Manager (VFM) software, which use both Windows servers and NetApp devices as a single logical pool of storage.

Cisco

As a world leader in switch and communications technologies, Cisco is a natural contender of significant influence. For several years now, Cisco has articulated and promoted a vision of networking convergence under their Architecture for Voice, Video, and Integrated Data (AVVID) initiative. This facilitates an integrated strategy for IP, GbE, Fibre Channel, and optical network infrastructure. Cisco has the reach to pull SANs, NAS, MANs, WANs, and LANs into a unified infrastructure under common management.

One of the cornerstones of this strategy is the way Cisco has formed close working relationships with key providers of elements of the overall solution. Specifically, IBM, as mentioned earlier for storage arrays, as well as such companies as Alacritech, Brocade, EMC, Emulex, Intel, Network Appliance, and VERITAS are heavily involved with the creation of standards and testing for product interoperability.

Key applications and underlying technologies include

- *iSCSI:* The Cisco SN5428-2 Storage Router is an iSCSI-based communications device that works with TOE-enabled cards for optimized performance when moving large amounts of data over the IP infrastructure. FCIP is also supported by the Storage Router, and each port can be configured to support a combination of iSCSI and FCIP as needed.

- *FCIP:* Interconnecting FC SANs over long distances is supported by Cisco through their MDS 9000 Storage Services Module and FC port adapter products. They "snap into" the MDS 9000 family of multilayer directors and switches, allowing the integration of SANs, logical separation of storage resources into Virtual SANs (VSANs), and isolating hardware within a single SAN fabric. The Storage Service Module allows configuration on a port-by-port basis to support iSCSI and FCIP. As many as three virtual InterSwitch Links can be tunneled on a single Gigabit Ethernet port under FCIP, allowing better device connection through each port based on usage and traffic.

- *DS-X9308-SMIP:* Provides small form-factor–pluggable LC Gigabit Ethernet Interfaces supporting either short or long wavelength connections to extend the network reach to 550m or 10km, respectively.

Cisco competes with switch makers Brocade and McData. McData has committed to the iFCP protocol for linking, which wraps Fibre Channel data in IP packets and maps IP addresses to individual Fibre Channel devices. This is another approach to linking SANs that competes with Cisco's proprietary VSAN links. Brocade shipped more fabric switch ports than any other company (69 percent) in their last quarter of fiscal year 2003, bringing their overall market share to a reported 58 percent for the SAN switching market. McData, on the other hand, reports increases in their share of the SAN fabric switch market to 33 percent. When Cisco's share of this market is added into the mix, the total market appears to be divided into some 150 percent, which is unusual indeed.

Given that some numbers are restricted to 2GB Fibre Channel, others are based on port count, and still others are strictly dollars, the bottom line remains that there are three main contenders for the Fibre Channel switch business. Given interoperability concerns, once you have selected a switch supplier, chances are that's your supplier for the duration.

Dell

Dell enjoys a reputation as a tier one supplier of personal computers, servers, and related technologies to business. They didn't miss the opportunity to strengthen their product line to include network-attached and data center class enterprise servers several years ago. Dell provides entry-level networked storage with their PowerVault 725 offering.

The PowerVault 725 N is a GbE ATA drive network storage appliance. It offers two tightly coupled, fully redundant 10/100/1000 Ethernet controllers, JBOD, RAID 0, 1, or 5 and is based on a "streamlined" version of Windows 2000 Advanced Server. Disk capacities start at 160GB to a maximum size of 1TB. Two spare slots offer support for 64-bit 33 MHz PCI cards and one PCI-X 64-bit 133 MHz card.

Hot swapping of ATA IDE hard drives is accomplished through the front-loading panel. Additionally, there are four internal hard drives with matched capacities of 40-, 80-, or 120GB. The OS is mirrored on the first two drives, and the factory default OS is mirrored on the last two.

Supported processor types and speeds range from a 1.7 GHz Celeron to an Intel Pentium 4 at 2.0 GHz or 2.6 GHz. A maximum of 3GB DDR SDRAM is also supported.

It offers support for NT, Windows 2000, NetWare, Linux, and Macintosh clients without a licensing fee for additional clients. Network protocols include CIFS/SMB, NFS, NCP, AFP, WebDAV, HTTP, and FTP.

The value proposition for this box seems to be a lower cost, turnkey file sharing server with redundancy built in for critical components. However, it should be noted that Dell also offers integration with systems administration tools that allow it to be administered centrally through a web-based control console. Last, it's also worth considering that Dell's storage strategy allows integration of NAS boxes like the 725 to utilize SAN storage offered as part of their product line. The CX200 Fibre Channel–based storage solution is comanufactured between Dell and EMC. I'll describe this as part of the EMC offerings in the next section.

EMC

In the late 1990s, EMC emerged as the leading provider of networked storage solutions. While this segment of the IT industry has been highly competitive, EMC remains at the top as a solutions provider. The NetWin 200 Network Attached Storage System is an example of their entry-level products.

Designed to work with Microsoft Storage Server 2003 software or the EMC-provided ControlCenter, the NetWin 200 is a rack-mounted storage solution that uses a Fibre Channel connection to the EMC CLARiiON CX200 storage system. It provides RAID 5 on between 3 and 16 drives.

Supported file systems include NTFS and DFS. Communications supported include NFS, CIFS, NetWare, AppleTalk, and FTP. The two most important aspects of this network appliance are the QLogic host bus adapter and the PERC3 RAID controller. The Fibre Channel cards are addressed in the next section. Here let it suffice that a dual-channel HBA will support failover from one channel to another. That is, the fiber loop architecture protects against the disk resources being inaccessible due to a channel failure. Naturally, the single port implementation of the HBA doesn't support this feature.

The PERC3 RAID controller is built by LSI Logic Corporation, which acquired American Megatrends. As a 64-bit, 66 MHz, PCI SCSI –3, 160-drive controller, it's capable of supporting up to four SCSI channels, with each channel achieving a top throughput rate of 160 MBps. The controller is equipped with an on-board battery backup of 128MBs of SDRAM to ensure that data in the write cache is successfully transferred. RAID levels 1, 3, and 5 are supported.

Table 11-1 lists the operating characteristics of NetWin 200.

Table 11-1. NetWin 200 Operating Characteristics

Attribute	Model 1	Model 2	Model 3
Size	36GB	73GB	146GB
Transfer rate buffer to/from media	51–69 MBps	26.7–40.2 MBps	43–78 MBps
rpms	15,000	10,000	10,000
Average seek time	3.6 ms read	5.2 ms read	4.7 ms read
	4.2 ms write	6.2 ms write	5.3 ms write
Data buffer	8MB	8MB	8MB
Interface	Fibre Channel	Fibre Channel	Fibre Channel
Network support	10/100/1000	10/100/1000	10/100/1000
Processors	Up to two Xeon 3.06 GHz, 512KB, L2 cache, 533 MHz bus	Up to two Xeon 3.06 GHz, 512KB, L2 cache, 533 MHz bus	Up to two Xeon 3.06 GHz, 512KB, L2 cache, 533 MHz bus
RAM	Up to 3GB DDR SDRAM	Up to 3GB DDR SDRAM	Up to 3GB DDR SDRAM
Controller	PERC3–DI-D RAID controller (dual channel)	PERC3–DI-D RAID controller (dual channel)	PERC3–DI-D RAID controller (dual channel)
Dual Power Supply	502 watt	502 watt	502 watt
QLogic host bus adapter	QLA2340 (single port) or QLA2342-CK (dual port)	QLA2340 (single port) or QLA2342-CK (dual port)	QLA2340 (single port) or QLA2342-CK (dual port)

Hitachi

With the acquisition of IBM's disk drive business, Hitachi Data Systems (HDS) began consolidation of their high-end and mid-range offerings around disk arrays. In 2003, the company began to focus on creating momentum through bolstering their mid-range offerings by including the Thunder 9500V series with a new mid-range array, the 9580V. This product provides raw capacity of up to 64TB and supports connection of a wide variety of host operating systems. The Thunder array also supports ShadowImage, HDS's volume-based replication management software, as well as TrueCopy, which offers high-availability local and remote replication. QuickShadow provides fast disk-based restoration of data from snapshots.

The higher end Lightning 9900V series now supports serverless backup through e-Copy, which integrates ShadowImage with NetBackup from VERITAS. The Lightning 9900V provides ESCON and FICON ports, which are expected to work well with the z990 mainframe from IBM known popularly as T-Rex.

Hitachi also sees merit in the information life cycle management approach to positioning storage network solutions. They have defined a data life cycle management strategy designed to promote data protection and migration.

Sun Microsystems

This pugnacious company has picked price/performance as their key differentiator for strategic positioning of their storage products. Like IBM and HP, Sun offers a data center or enterprise class set of storage products through the mid-range to what they term *workgroup storage solutions*.

Long a champion of Unix, first under Bill Joy's BSD version, and then Solaris, Sun now offers Linux as an option. Sun acquired N1 in 2003 and is positioning a consolidated storage management software solution to compete with others in the market.

In November 2003, Sun compared their StorEdge 3510 Fibre Channel storage solution with the IBM FAStT600 with Turbo, claiming 17 percent greater performance and 33 percent better price/performance using 30 percent less disk. Earlier, Sun pointed to Storage Performance Council (SPC) test results showing the StorEdge 6320 system as delivering 46 percent greater performance than any competitors' mid-range storage offerings.

Sun has a long history of partnership with VERITAS and fully supports those backup and volume management tools while offering their own software to perform these functions as well. Additionally, Sun has a large and loyal installation base with a focus on database servers built up since 1982.

QLogic

QLogic is a leading manufacturer of controller chips, HBAs, and switch products for storage networks with an estimated 30+ percent of the HBA market in 2003.

Host Bus Adapters

QLogic offers a wide range of PCI-based cards supporting both fiber and copper. More recently they have brought iSCSI controllers to market, also supporting both transmission media. QLogic also develops embedded Fibre Channel products for a number of OEM customers including Cisco, Dell, IBM, and Network Appliance, among others.

iSCSI Cards

The key distinctions in QLogic's iSCSI cards are the single-chip offload engines for TCP/IP processing (TOE), Security Offload Engine (SOE), and iSCSI Offload Engine (iSOE). This circuitry takes on the processing of TCP/IP packets, ensuring the CPU isn't burdened with network traffic handling. By consolidating all of the logic on one chip, the iSCSI cards perform faster than a multichip solution.

Emulex

In 2002, Emulex was acknowledged as the American Electronics Association selection for outstanding public company and the largest manufacturer of host bus adapter cards for Storage Area Networks.

As the largest HBA provider, Emulex is, of course, partnered with everybody involved in the SAN marketplace. It offers a line of Fibre Channel HBAs targeted for small to mid-range SAN implementations, and Emulex has worked with EMC to ensure products like the LP952, LP982, and LP1050 are certified for integration with Symmetrix and CLARiiON storage arrays. Hitachi Data Systems incorporates Emulex LP982 HBAs into its Thunder 9500V series storage systems. The company also offers building blocks for the largest of SAN solutions.

Emulex works through channel partners to add value and support customers through the sales and installation process. Although not unique to Emulex, this emphasis on selling solutions through partners has been a strategic positioning that has paid off in market share.

Emulex is also working closely with Intel on research and development for an integrated architecture for Serial Attached SCSI, iSCSI, and Fibre Channel networked storage.

The overall approach for Emulex might be considered to be sticking as close to the hardware as possible and selling through others. The acquisition of Vixel in 2003 provided the company with a switching architecture to embed into their chipsets. Integrating switching into their Light Pulse (LP) HBAs allows Emulex to take more of the incremental SAN market for existing sites, with higher performance offerings embedded in Application-Specific Integrated Circuits (ASICs).

By moving switching into the adapter, disks can be accessed through switching rather than bus or backplane connections. The value of their InSpeed SOC320 (Switch On a Chip) for incorporation in other products has been demonstrated first by the Xyratex RS-1600-FC-SBD, which provides switch addressability for each drive in a single enclosure. This in turn improves performance and reduces latency for data transfers within the enclosure, much like the benefits switching provides for server connectivity.

Comparisons

As you can see from my coverage of selected areas, each of the major players has a different perspective and hence a unique proposition to make to the market. In spite of the number of startups funded a few years ago now bringing products to the market, and in stark contrast to the introduction of turnkey SOHO NAS offerings, Storage Area Networks aren't a commodity.

The key to sorting out the primary vendor to choose when creating your Storage Area Network strategy is to be very, very clear on the top priorities of your environment. IBM clearly sees consolidating mainframe and mid-range storage solutions. If you have an IBM mainframe in your world, it would be counterproductive to ignore them. Cisco has the telecommunications-intensive product line to support integration of voice and data over long distances. HP not only has a huge distributed installation base, but also offers attractive integration and migration options. On price point and distribution, Dell competes effectively with HP, and by partnering with EMC provides a solid path for growing storage requirements.

If you have a Fibre Channel infrastructure or are looking for a best-of-breed solution that combines the best on the market to achieve a high-performance goal, you might look directly at the QLogic, Emulex, Brocade, or McData products offered by a systems integrator.

Application-specific considerations, such as document imaging, video processing, and very large databases, also point to valuable niche-oriented solutions.

Whatever the key driver is for any given installation, a number of trends seem to have been adopted by everyone in Storage Area Networks. These include

- Virtualization of hardware resources

- Consolidation of direct-attached and other storage pools over IP

- More efficient management of storage resources by centralized, interoperating software consoles

- And last but not least, getting data and information assets under control through storage resource management

What Did I Buy?

At this point, it seems to me a good idea to introduce an actual buying decision in which my role was to assess the market and make recommendations for a client. I'd like to reiterate my statement that I'm not touting a particular vendor position and that every technology has a high applicability to some specific combination of requirements. Disclaimers aside, let me introduce the requirements.

I was approached to review an architecture and infrastructure plan for a web-based financial service that was preparing to move out of development and into beta testing with customers prior to "going live" in a production environment.

The application was an n-tier client/server architecture with the application logic residing in ColdFusion, the presentation layer handled by IIS, and the data accessed from SQL Server 2000 Enterprise databases. The primary consideration was high availability, with the secondary concern being performance, and the last scalability. A previous consultant had recommended a Linux-based load balancer as a front end to Microsoft 2000 Servers running IIS, ColdFusion, and SQL Server. Because the client had previous experience with ordering online from Dell, I was encouraged to evaluate that option first.

My inclination was to not mix operating systems to save up-front costs, especially since I firmly believe that ongoing expenses can skew the value of a given solution over time. It can be too easy to look at the up-front costs and overlook a key operating expense impact. I hate being "older and wiser" at the client's expense.

In any case, I found that by looking at Microsoft Advanced Server 2000, I could achieve both the network load balancing and the two-node clustering identified as a means of ensuring both high performance for the web application and high availability for the database server. In both situations, the hardware imprint was single or dual processor and 4 gigabytes of RAM or less per server. For this reason, it wasn't necessary to incur the added expense of a 64-bit operating system or buy the SMP support available as part of Windows Enterprise Server 2003.

However, as defined as the platform and vendor preferences were to the point of my involvement, there had been no thought put into whether the topology should support nondirect attached storage, or whether that should happen in the attributes of the switch. When I received the draft document for comments, a Cisco PIX 515e had been penciled in as the switch, and Dell 1750 and 2650 server configurations had been identified for the server platform. Since I was brought in as a replacement for another networking specialist who had a scheduling conflict, I didn't think it was appropriate to suggest going out to the market for another review of each of the components. Instead, I decided the best way to fulfill the objective was to look at the OS, as I mentioned a few paragraphs ago, and at the storage and switch configurations.

As you may remember from the topology in Chapter 8, I ultimately recommended the Dell PowerVault 660F and the Dell PowerConnect 6024 as the switch. Certainly there was nothing wrong with the Cisco recommendation; it just seemed to me to make more sense in this situation to keep all of the system management software in the same family, so that syntax and scripts would be identical. The command-line interface for managing the Dell PowerConnect switch is very similar to the IOS-based Cisco gear, but not identical.

The security considerations for this case were outlined in Chapter 8, but the performance and availability rationale is what I wanted to note in this discussion.

The PowerConnect 6024 supports Fibre Channel HBAs as well as Gigabit Ethernet links between the servers and outside world. Since the customer was moving from development to beta, and not working with known metrics, it seemed to make more sense to start with the less expensive copper technology until those benchmarks could be obtained.

However, in the event that server-to-server or server-to-storage connection became the bottleneck, an upgrade in the form of FC HBAs could be made with the existing switch and server technology. Each unit would have to be brought offline and upgraded physically, of course, but the clustered environment of both the logic and database servers meant this could be accommodated without application or service outage.

The PowerVault supports up to 14 hot-swappable 32GB RAID 5 SCSI drives, and we configured the order for 7, leaving room for growth. Under MS Clustering Services, I knew that one disk could be dedicated to cluster services and the other six managed by the primary server and taken over by the backup server in the event of catastrophic failure of the primary box. The synchronization of the two database servers was handled by creating an additional private network using a second GbE card in each. Through this selection of hardware and software, high availability and potential for performance increases were accommodated, without requiring the client to "overbuy" technology without knowing the real transaction loads to be supported.

MS Clustering was introduced in Chapter 10, as were performance statistics for Gigabit Ethernet configurations. With those characteristics in mind, and the vendor options discussed in this chapter, the potential value of new Storage Area Networks should be emerging. The decision matrix for relating the technology requirements to the products on the market is discussed in greater detail next in Chapter 12.

Summary

The Storage Area Networks market isn't a cleanly segmented one, and it's becoming increasingly confused as new players in hardware and software come into the market. The mid 2000s will be an exciting and interesting time for both customers and vendors, as the number of options increase, prices fall, and performance capabilities increase across the spectrum.

After reading this chapter, you should have a sense of where the market is conflicted. Clearly, there are no right answers for all settings. And equally evident should be the hedging of technical bets for protocols such as iSCSI.

The high-speed, high-priced Storage Area Network installations will continue to show the way. However, as more storage is added to keep pace with the insatiable demand for documents, images, and even voice applications, storage consolidation will likely increase dramatically.

Interoperability has long been the bane of SAN installations. In terms of fitness to task, you should have a better grasp on how each of the most well-funded, long-term players in the computing business see their storage network opportunities and where they are concentrating their strengths.

CHAPTER 12

Making the Business Case for Storage Networks

From **2001** to **2003**, IT shops overall saw a decline in the amount of growth in their budgeted expenditures. However, money allocated for networked storage solutions stayed flat. In other words, of all the things there were for a corporation *not* to spend money on, consolidating storage and administrative tools retained value overall for IT shops.

In this chapter, I'll identify scenarios that are well served by storage network solutions. I'll point out methods for presenting the business case and give you an overview of the justification approach. As an illustration, you'll get a chance to review a more detailed example of how a particular situation could be handled that shows the elements of a successful business case for reduction in total cost of ownership (TCO) as well as increases in administrator productivity.

Special attention is called to the nonquantifiable benefits of implementing a storage network, and this chapter shows you a way to direct attention to those while maintaining an accounting of the costs and hard-dollar benefits the storage network will bring. I'll define specific terms used by finance professionals for evaluating projects and their implications.

In this chapter, you'll learn the value that server and data consolidation brings to an organization. I'm going to explain this from the standpoint of a business case, complete with a review of the kinds of numbers that would apply to an example case. The intent is to provide you with a template for initiating a storage network project.

If you're the kind of person who feels they just received money when they get a credit card in the mail, you probably confuse justification with affordability. Unfortunately, sometimes an organization can't fund initiatives, even if the project would result in cost savings. That reality is at the heart of why I wanted to include this chapter in *Storage Networks*.

My goal is to take you through the "big picture" arguments for why this is an important thing to do and hopefully identify some "hot buttons" to help you make the case.

Use Cases

I'm a big believer in the value of story-based development. Whether in writing enterprise software or designing a networked storage infrastructure, the approach advocated by the creators of the Unified Modeling Language (UML) has proven highly effective. As you should remember from my discussion of logical and physical models for managing data storage in Chapter 9, UML provides a range of ways to depict information resources and describe how they are used. These are distinct from a business case, which details the value proposition for the costs and benefits of implementing technology, the function of which is described in the use case.

What I'd like to do here is describe several scenarios for the problem domain that could be addressed by networked storage solutions. Ideally, you'll find in them something that is similar to your own goals and challenges that will lead you to discover how to effectively present your own business case. I've elected to depict the scenarios in the UML use case format. Using this approach, you can describe the environment where a storage network could be implemented. The scenarios are frequently described as "best-case," "worst-case," "as-is," and "to-be" versions of a process flow, with a focus on the interaction of the user with the system. The main flow describes the events as they normally would occur, the exception flows are predictable descriptions of what goes wrong within the flow, and alternate flows describe discrete paths other than the main flow that wouldn't be considered problems or errors.

In this example, let's look at how you could treat the storage network hardware as commodities or basic widgets to be acquired and installed.

....

Hardware Replacement

Use Case Description

The following is a standard template for documenting use cases at Word N Systems, Inc.:
Version: 1.1
Version Date: July 21, 2003

Short Description

Hardware components supporting 24×7 servers sometimes fail and require replacement. This use case describes how a SAN supports component replacement without service interruption.

Scenarios

A systems administrator discovers that a hard disk in the storage array has failed and replaces it.

Actors

Primary actor(s):

Systems administrator

Secondary actor(s):

Service user, who requires uninterrupted access to the service

Data center manager, who needs to be updated of a hardware failure and component replacement

Use Case Goal

The goal of this use case is to respond to hardware failure without service interruption.

Postconditions

Notification is sent to DCM that an intervention occurred, identifying the component used for warranty replacement if applicable.
Notification is sent of component failure to systems administrator/operator responsible for maintaining resources at this location.
The new component is physically swapped for the old, and the data on that disk is automatically rebuilt by the storage array's RAID management software.

Trigger

This use case is triggered when a component fails, the management software flags the failure, and a systems administrator takes action to replace the component.

Preconditions

The systems administrator must be logged into the SAN management system.

Main Flow of Events

1. An alert is displayed on the console indicating a component failure has occurred.

2. The systems administrator reviews the console to determine the location of the failure and specifically identifies the component.

3. The systems administrator identifies that standard operating procedure for this component is a hot swap of the old device for a replacement.

4. The systems administrator locates the spare resource and prepares it for swap out.

5. The devices are exchanged.

6. The systems administrator verifies that the failure condition is no longer flagged by the management software.

7. An incident report is filed through the corporate messaging system.

Alternate Flows

No applicable alternative flows exist for this use case.

Exception Flows

- *E3.1:* The required component isn't in stock and must be obtained.

- *E3.1.1:* The system prompts the systems administrator to request shipment of a replacement component from the supplier of record.

Relationships to Other Use Cases

This use case is triggered by component malfunction and not related to other use cases.

Technical Requirements

The systems administrator must have the required training to be able to perform the swap out for the particular device that fails, or be able to contact the appropriate person and request assistance.

Open Issues

Notes

The Value of the Hardware Replacement Use Case

It could be argued that even server-attached disks, configured with hot-swappable RAID 5, would support this use case. Even without a single console view of all disk resources, it's possible to identify that a component has failed through server logs, or even when reviewing the status lights on the hardware itself. The business value that this use case points to is the inherent increase in systems administrator productivity, as well as the "proceduralization" of the process. With automatic notification and messaging, SAN administrative systems allow the automation of the monitoring process and streamlining of component replacement. Potentially, depending on the size of spare components, the system could enable a reduction in on-hand inventory of spare parts.

Let's take this approach to another case, specifically one in which previously departmental servers are being brought into the remote central management sphere through a wide area SAN and associated system management software.

Server Resource Administration Consolidation

Use Case Description

The following is a standard template for documenting use cases at Word N Systems, Inc.:
Version: 1.1
Version Date: July 21, 2003

Short Description

Distributed servers administered by various departments are being brought online with the remote SAN capabilities managed by Central Services. This use case describes the process by which a given server is integrated.

Scenarios

A Windows-based server with direct-attached storage is added to the SAN fabric. Upon successful connection of the server to the SAN, the file systems on the direct-attached disk are replicated to the SAN and designated as primary.

Actors

Primary actor(s):

SAN administrator

Secondary actor(s):

Departmental server administrator, who is responsible for monitoring user performance and availability of the service prior to recommending sign-off

Business unit manager, who must sign off control of disk assets to Central Services on acceptance of demonstrated performance

Use Case Goal

The goal of this use case is to integrate a new server into the SAN such that file sizes and resource utilization may be monitored by a single console and administrator.

Postconditions

The server transparently provides the traditional services to its users.
The disk resources of the server are managed by the SAN.
File system resource utilization and reallocation is provided by a central SAN administrator.

Trigger

This use case is triggered when a departmental server experiences an outage that can't be handled by local staff, disk capacity is reached, or a departmental administrator leaves the unit and can't be effectively replaced.

Preconditions

The central SAN must be prepared to integrate distributed servers of the required type.
Departmental management must be prepared to work through the process of transferring administrative responsibility.

Main Flow of Events

1. The distributed server must have a host bus adapter acquired for it.

2. Server outage is scheduled.

3. The HBA is installed and configured.
    E3.1: The HBA introduces instability to the system and the installation must be backed out.

4. The server is connected via the HBA and the SAN.

5. Disk resources are made available to the server.

6. The server-attached file systems are replicated to the SAN.

7. The direct-attached disks are taken offline.

8. Performance is monitored for agreed duration.

9. This use case ends with sign-off by the business unit manager that the service is up and running to acceptance criteria.

Alternate Flows

No applicable alternative flows exist for this use case.

Exception Flows

- *E3.1:* In the event that the HBA installation isn't successful, or "spurious results are encountered," the installation is backed out.

- *E3.1.1:* The reason for the incompatibility must be identified along with corrective action.

Relationships to Other Use Cases

This use case must occur after the Selection for Service Integration use case and before the Central Service Level Agreement use case.

Technical Requirements

Open Issues

Notes

The Value of the Server Resource Administration Consolidation Use Case

In this example, the SAN is up and open for business, and value is found in pulling management duties out from the field, where supposedly there is less control and a wider variation in administrative skills. Again, the argument from a business standpoint is one of productivity, but additionally, reducing the risk of data loss by performing regularly scheduled backups would be a desirable side effect of this scenario.

It's no accident that the previous use case refers to sign-offs by departmental managers and service level agreements from the data center. This level of commitment to predictability should be an explicit benefit of moving departmental direct-attached storage to a SAN, as it would be in any professionally managed IT service center. However, at the level of making the business case for networked storage, if this isn't something that is commonplace or in practice, it would certainly be an attractive nonquantifiable benefit to include in the request for funding.

Use cases are an effective way to describe any existing situation, and they can be used as data gathering techniques for a business justification. They can be reused as the basis for operational procedure guidelines, and also for inputs to setting storage policies. From here on, I'll address the considerations of building a business case or justification for expenditure, taking a full understanding of the environment as a given.

Structuring the Feasibility Study Template

In the same way that a template serves as a means of consistently representing process data, I've always used a logical breakdown of feasibility studies with the following format:

1. Objective

2. Terms of reference

3. Existing situation

4. Problem statement

5. Proposed solutions

6. Recommendation

7. Gross benefits

    a) Quantifiable

    b) Nonquantifiable

8. Estimated costs

9. Net benefits

This organizes the material to allow the reader to start from the goal of the proposal and move to a review of the constraints the solution must work within and a description of the existing situation. These are always simple, straightforward statements of fact. Save your diagnosis for the problem statement.

Take a look at the following sample, and you should see what I mean.

Consolidated Storage Feasibility

Objective

To review the storage requirements of Organization X, identify risks and inefficiencies in the current environment, and recommend technology and procedures to mitigate the risks and ensure access to critical data resources.

Terms of Reference

Any proposed solution will

- Leverage existing systems administration staff and not result in increased headcount

- Provide auditable "point-in-time" recovery for accounting and operational data

- Reduce departmental server downtime

- Eliminate the 50MB restriction on Organization X end-user mailboxes

Existing Situation

The Microsoft Exchange 2000 server was inaccessible on July 10, August 23, and September 5 for a combined outage of 4 hours due to having exceeded disk capacity. New hard disks had to be acquired, installed, and configured on an emergency basis on September 5, as all logs had been cleared and noncritical files (such as .hlp files) were cleared on the previous occasions. The Exchange Server also supports an Access database used by the sales department. This was unavailable during the server outage.

Problem Statement

Administrative support for key data stores is maintained at the department level. Recently experienced turnover in some departments has resulted in a lack of consistent backups and recoveries. Additionally, service packs for several of the servers have been recently published, but the upgrade hasn't been planned or performed due to manpower shortages and overutilized departmental resources.

Proposed Solutions

- *Training and certification:* All staff responsible for maintaining IT servers, whether centralized or departmental, should be required to achieve a minimum level of training and certification in the technology they administer.

- *Published standards:* The standards board should be asked to endorse the current IT Central Services standards for backup and restore of critical data services.

- *Administrative services:* Should be provided by Central Services; these include backups and upgrades to all servers whether maintained in the data center or remotely.

Recommendation

Server administration should be consolidated under Central Services to ensure consistency of practice and limit access to servers to staff with certifications in administration of the technology.

Gross Benefits

a) *Quantifiable:* There are currently seven departmental administrators whose job descriptions call for 20 percent system administration functions. By freeing these staff members up to do other duties, the equivalent of 1.4 full-time positions is made available.

b) *Nonquantifiable:* Consistent administration of servers, timely application of service packs including security upgrades, and reliable backup of data will minimize downtime and increase availability of services.

Estimated Costs

The Remote Administration Software in use by Central Service will require seven additional server licenses for a cost of $21,000. Training and certification of a Central Services administrator in the Microsoft 2000 Exchange technology is budgeted at $7,500.

Net Benefits

Given an average position cost for departmental administrators of $36,000 annually, including employee load factors, the return on investment will be realized in less than one year.

Building Business Cases

In the first part of this chapter, I showed you the elements of use cases and feasibility studies and gave you a quick tour of how the pieces fit together. At this point, I'd like to go into more detail on how to review your situation, extract a description of a viable solution, evaluate vendor offerings, and build a financial case to support your recommendations.

This is really the heart of the ground up approach to storage networking. Through the case studies, you should gain insight into the kinds of criteria that make one solution superior to another for a given situation.

Begin at the End

The very worst approach to take is to become fixated on a key technological feature or attribute and then look for ways to put it to work. This phenomenon is pithily described by the old saw, "When you only have a hammer, every problem is a nail." True, to successfully apply storage networks products, it's certainly important to understand each component, what it is, and how it works. But success is defined by how well those features and functions address a specific job of work, including the priorities and constraints of the environment in which that work takes place. These must be understood, articulated, and agreed upon first.

The Objective

It has been said that very few achievements are the result of aimless luck, and that to get somewhere you have to first define a goal. That is the whole point of defining an objective in the context of applying storage network technology. One problem that I've frequently encountered when defining objectives results from the misuse of vocabulary. This is exaggerated in a business and technology setting, where jargon makes up a significant percentage of everyday communication and where terms are thought to be uniformly understood by all. They are not.

Mission, goal, purpose, and objective aren't synonymous; they have precise meanings. Mission and purpose are strategic intents. Goals and objectives are tactical ends. Although a goal is a "state of affairs that a plan is intended to achieve" (according to Dictionary.com), an objective is something that is worked for. An objective is a tangible realization of effort, whereas the goal is the desired outcome of that effort.

This is a key point. You may achieve your objective, but not reach your goal. It's quite possible to successfully implement a technology that doesn't provide the desired effect. To do that, you must have matched the objective to the outcomes required. I think of the outcomes as desirable side effects of succeeding at the task.

This matching process occurs in the definition of the terms of reference.

Terms of Reference

If the objective helps you define when the task will be complete, the terms of reference define the rules under which you must perform the steps that make up the task. It's in the terms of reference that you nail down the concerns that must be addressed by your proposed solutions. When these terms are correctly identified, it becomes much easier to select appropriate technologies, because the selection criteria are rooted in those terms. Prior to reviewing the available options, the terms of reference set the stage for sorting the optimum solutions from those that will suck up time, effort, and money but not yield the needed effect.

Server Consolidation

Let's look at a specific (though hypothetical) example of an objective and some terms of reference for a storage consolidation project. It's worth noting that if you're working within highly structured methodologies for describing projects, this approach can be easily adapted to different filing formats. It's the definition that counts.

Objective: To consolidate server storage across the enterprise.

You should be able to see how this is highly focused on the work to be done rather than the outcome expected once the work is completed. The value of performing this work isn't left as some undefined but somehow desirable goal. Instead, the side effects are identified within the terms of reference, such as the following for the server consolidation project:

Any recommended solution will

- Maintain or enhance existing levels of server uptime, availability, and recoverability.

- Support all servers currently deployed within the company.

- Result in a net reduction in the number of staff hours required for systems administration.

- Provide for recovery from disaster potentially affecting mission-critical data stores.

- Allow uninterrupted operation of divisional systems in the event of network failure.

Note that a recommended solution isn't the same as a proposed solution. In this feasibility format, you may elect to propose a solution that doesn't actually meet all of the terms of reference. You would then, of course, not recommend it, though you might raise the issue for consideration. This is an effective way of incorporating "suggestions" from internal factions with a different agenda. By structuring the review of the problem and potential solutions in this fashion, the range of discussion can be supported while keeping firmly focused on the optimal solution—in this case, one that meets all of the terms of reference.

Because of the realities of organizational politics, it's frequently necessary to satisfy concerns of one high-ranking official, even though they seem at odds with the wishes of another.

By focusing on the job of work, and the rules under which it will be planned and executed, this fine line can be walked and not crossed. In the terms of reference listed for the server consolidation project, there are several caveats that would likely be the result of accommodations between business and IT management. Specifically, the current service levels will be maintained, and divisional systems must be network failure proof. The net effect of the last term of reference might be to eliminate total centralization of servers as an architectural constraint. Or it might call out a need for a replication strategy to be supported in order to meet the objective. Support for all servers in the company also sets a critical success factor for any workable solution. These terms of reference are set in advance of further work on the case study, and it's possible that they are renegotiated as implications are uncovered. To accomplish this, the existing situation must be reviewed in detail.

A Tale of Two Companies

Because the proposed solutions outlined earlier will likely involve a set of vendors, I want to be as fair as possible in the coverage of various potential strengths and weaknesses. To illustrate the relative merits of different component combinations, I'm going to apply the same objective and terms of reference to two very different situations. One is a highly centralized organization with a big investment in mainframe systems, and the other a highly decentralized organization with 500 stores, regional distribution centers, and multinational head offices.

Company A operates more than 500 stores in the United States supplied from four regional distribution centers located in Nashville, Tennessee; Denver, Colorado; Ontario, California; and Atlanta, Georgia. The company has opened new stores at a rate of approximately 30 per year for the past 3 years. Store systems include online inventory of in-stock and special-order products, and Point-of-Sale (POS) systems for processing cash, credit card, and debit card transactions as well as customer loyalty cards. Cycle counts and inventory checking are both conducted using wireless bar code scanners that update a local database replicated each evening to the head office over a frame relay network connection.

Figure 12-1 shows this layout. For the purposes of these examples, I think the topology will be sufficient to work up a set of solutions.

Any differences between stores would also be noted in the existing situation for special case treatment. The POS system is listed as a black box, as it isn't in scope for the proposal other than as a data feed for the inventory database.

Now, let's look at Company B, which operates an insurance underwriting service sold through a network of independent brokers throughout North America. Although many brokers use computers in their offices or take laptops to their clients' homes, some still complete manual forms and submit them via mail and courier. A staff of 800 clerical workers, managers, and actuaries use the company's 43 software applications built using a combination of COBOL, CICS, ISAM, Oracle, and Delphi. The company supports an ES390 mainframe and 500+ PCs running Windows 98, 2000, and XP (see Figure 12-2).

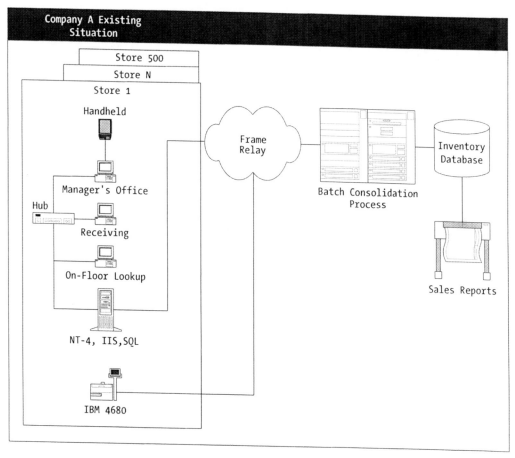

Figure 12-1. Company A's existing situation

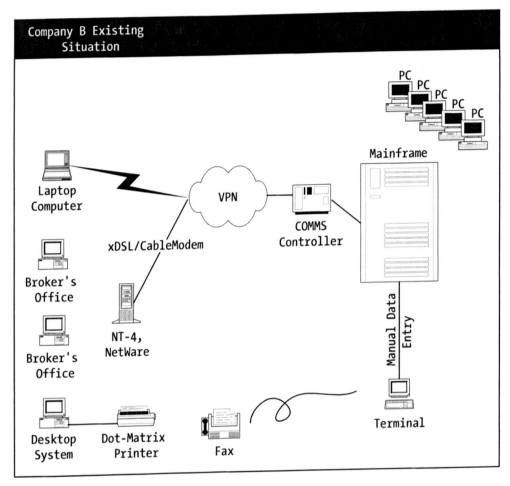

Figure 12-2. Company B's existing situation

Analyzing the Existing Situations

In both cases, the existing situation is described as a collection of verifiable facts. If there are any contentious assertions, vague or ambiguous descriptions, or allusions to problems without the underpinning details, the existing situation isn't adequately described. In the example of Company B, arguably the number of brokers who process forms manually might be required, or the rate of automation and increased acceptance of technology. However, for purposes of this case study, you'll see that the main point introduced is that some provision for supporting a manual documentation process is required, rather than an assumption that total automated support is possible. That point is generally made in the problem statement, which distills the facts presented in the existing situation and narrows the issues down to the ones that must be addressed by any proposed solution.

Company A's problem statement might look like this:

Inventory changes made by sales through the POS system, as well as the receipt of new inventory during the week, aren't reconciled or reflected in the in-store inventory used by customers and staff to search for available products. The frame relay network links between the stores and head office don't permit a full database transfer within the 2-hour batch window required for updating the head office database prior to running the daily sales analysis reports. As a result, sales reports submitted daily frequently don't accurately reflect actual sales, as returned products aren't calculated until month's end. This weakness is especially critical during the Christmas sales season, when the stores do more than 50 percent of their annual sales transactions.

Company B's statement could read like this:

To support processing of any given application, the data is rekeyed into applications twice, downloaded, and transferred from the Oracle applications to the CICs customer data file and back in a batch process. Overall, the processing time for a new application is 3 days before an actuary is able to review the application prior to its approval. During this interval, more than 15 percent of new applications are withdrawn by applicants.

Analyzing the Problem Statements

As the preceding problem statements represent problems both posed by and potentially solved by information technology, I believe they will serve to illustrate the way to build a business case effectively. The specific examples may not be realistic, because I don't have domain expertise as a business user in these areas. With that proviso, let's zero in on both the cause and effect for both situations.

Company A has a data latency issue resulting in incomplete information communicated to executives during peak transaction periods. The actual net dollars produced by the stores isn't known for 30 days. Anyone who has to balance their checkbook (or reconcile their web accounts) on a daily or weekly basis can relate to how much difficulty an organization might get into if they had no precise idea of how much money they had made, lost, committed, or freed up over the course of a month. Certainly many businesses use imprecise metrics and do just fine— profits cover a multitude of inadequacies, but the reality of providing information services to enterprises today is that timely information is a valuable commodity. Notice that in the problem statement there is no attempt to quantify the amounts of money represented. This is broken out in the quantifiable benefits equation based on the recommended solution. At this point, the idea is to remain focused on the nature of the underlying problem; in this case, consolidation of data can't be achieved within the batch window for updating the sales database.

Company B also has a data latency issue. The overall processing time from initial receipt of the data, which may also include a few days for the USPS to brave the sleet and snow, to the point where the business decision to take on the account is made causes a loss of opportunity. In this case, the rejection or fall-through rate was identified in order to draw attention to the size of the problem.

As a note on organizational politics and the effect they can have on your storage networks proposals, let me add that in the Company A example, you can assume that this study has been commissioned by an executive sponsor who already knows this problem exists. The focus of this case will be on how to solve the problem, rather than identifying that there is a problem. In fact, it's quite possible that some technology projects will be planned and approved to solve business problems that are perceived by executives to be priorities when in fact more pressing problems exist. That is sometimes the way of the world, and it has even shown up here, a hypothetical justification for a storage network solution.

In the example of Company B, you see a more bottom-up example. Imagine the frustration of an IT manager responsible for all this rekeying and transfer of data laboriously from one application to another. Here the storage network is likely to be the answer to a question that management hasn't asked themselves, so the case study points out how this format can be used to elevate a business issue while at the same time promoting a solution to address it.

The Problem in Context

At this point, you've only seen the problems facing each organization described, put in context, and any constraints within which any potentially acceptable solution must fall identified. You should note that generally an existing situation review isn't going to consist of a paragraph or two. Instead, the detail review of the "status quo" should be the result of a solid fact-finding exercise and should identify as close to all of the attributes of the problem as you can get. The outcome of this process is a solid description of the task to be met by the proposed solutions. In this example, you want to look at storage networks technologies to remedy the business problems posed by the two situations.

You're only now ready to begin looking at potential solutions that might be suitable to the task.

Proposed Solutions

Here I'll list several ways to address the issues identified in the problem statement.

Doing Nothing As an Option

Generally, I don't recommend doing nothing as an option. It more or less defeats the entire exercise and begs the question, "Why did I read this report to this point if you don't want to do anything about it?" Remember, you aren't going to review the estimated costs and anticipated benefits of each and every proposed solution. You do those as part of the recommendation you present in the report. In this case, then, doing nothing isn't likely to be recommended (although it might be easier to have that option approved), and there isn't going to be a discussion of the consequences of doing nothing. Therefore, you should leave it as an unstated option.

Unless . . .

There is always a "but" to these kinds of guidelines. In a situation where a significant faction would prefer to have nothing to do with your recommendation, you can throw "do nothing or next to nothing" in as a proposed method of dealing with the situation. Then, as part of your benefits case, you can call attention to the point that only by doing something will the existing cost/pain/problem be resolved, and that left to its own evolution, things will go from bad to worse. This is a positioning issue that differs from case to case. I mention it here to explicitly draw your attention to the point that this plan is the meeting of several forces: financial, organizational, and technical. Since the tripod is a most unstable structure, it's critical that you balance the three legs of the review and don't overdevelop one at the expense of the others.

Proposing Storage Solutions

So with the caveat that your proposed solutions won't be successful if you overfocus on technical issues, and because this is a technology book, let's look at storage network tools that can help you solve these problems.

Segregating the Impact

First, consider where the bottleneck occurs. With the reference to batch windows and file transfer times, clearly the network should be considered a candidate for an upgrade. However, in the real world, services like that have contracts with penalties for buyout. As part of the existing situation discovery, you would know exactly what terms were contracted for with the service provider. This could mean you want to consider shrinking the processing time by upgrading the mainframe as compared to the network. Or you could opt for one, the other, or both to make up three proposed solutions. However, one key factor is the growth rate the company has sustained. Perhaps a two-tier network, with a migration strategy for the established stores, would make sense. New sites would go on the newer platform, the size of the project limited to the number of new stores opened, and the value demonstrated to managers of new stores and of old stores alike. If that were to be the recommendation, no doubt you would want to include a note that opening new stores is a time-consuming process, and the innovative new approach might introduce risk, but the company can deal with that a little later.

Generally, a storage networks installation isn't going to serve as a means by way of which an overhaul of your entire system's architecture is innocuously introduced. At the same time, a Storage Area Network represents a demanding consumer of data networks and as such it may not be appropriate for the existing architecture. In this case, I would assume that in order to comply with the terms of reference regarding uptime, a distributed storage strategy would work best, with replication of data on an as-changed basis to minimize data exchange and network usage.

To validate that notion, you're actually finally ready to do some comparison shopping.

The Decision Matrix

In order to compare offerings from different vendors, you need to have a breakdown of required characteristics and a rating for each factor relative to its importance. For example, in the existing situation for the distributed retail organization, you would have noted the number of employees on average accessing the system throughout the day. Since this is a case study I've concocted, I can be a little arbitrary and say that, in each store, there are no more than three concurrent users throughout the day, with peak usage of five people accessing the database. For the purposes of this example, the POS system is isolated from the operational system, and integration isn't advisable. From the benchmarking of GbE data transfers, you saw the impact of processor power on throughput. More concurrent jobs consume more CPU. Fewer users consume less CPU. You don't necessarily need the big V-8 engine in this configuration. What is important here is per-unit price. You have 500 stores, so the potential cost of a unit for each quickly becomes a staggering requirement for capital. Remember, executives have to pick and choose between competing proposals. The more bang for fewer bucks, the more likely your proposal gets the green light.

Since you're leaning towards a replication strategy, software also becomes an important factor. Management generally doesn't want to look at a "rip-and-replace" proposal; instead, you want to show you can leverage existing assets. Software licenses are assets, even though they're frequently depreciated in the first year. For instance, what I didn't say in the treatment of the existing situation was that the local database in each store has a five-user Microsoft SQL Server database license running under Windows 2000. Of course, if the existing situation had Oracle or DB2 in its place, that would tend to influence the recommendation.

In this case, I've decided that it's most appropriate to focus on Windows Storage Server 2003–based entry-level NAS offerings that will provide database backups and scheduled replication to the head office for SQL Server transactions that result in changed data. However, instead of the current system (aha—another existing situation fact that wasn't in the description), the replication strategy to be supported is one of pulling the data from the NAS. This replaces the current process of pushing the data from the store to the head office on a set schedule basis. An additional reason for moving in this direction is technically strategic. Rather than recommend upgrading the 200 boxes, you elect to move the databases over to NAS files, where they will be protected, as well as more readily available for timely data integration.

The criteria list would begin to look like Table 12-1.

Table 12-1. Rating Relative Importance of Criteria

Criteria	Rating	Importance	Score
Windows Storage Server 2003 support		10	
Price/Performance		10	
Regional HW support		5	
Web administration		5	
Integration with central administration		7	

After surveying the market, the following vendor proposals were received and shortlisted:

HP StorageWorks 1000

EMC NetWin 200

Gateway 860 B NAS

Another product that could be evaluated for the scenario shown here includes the NetApps Network Appliance products. However, these are based on their Data ONTAP operating system, not Microsoft Windows Storage Server 2003, and so weren't short-listed for this case study. Linux-based solutions and others weren't considered for the same reason. However, if you think that position is arbitrary and unfair, don't forget that you have another case study with a different set of constraints.

Proposed Solutions for Company B

Of course, one of the most immediate ways to decrease the processing time required for insurance applications would be to insist that they were all filed electronically. Unfortunately, what is convenient from a data processing standpoint sometimes runs afoul of the marketing folks who might actually enjoy a relationship with established independent brokers who aren't about to change the habits of decades. As expressed in the terms of reference, allowances need to be made for the processing of manually created records, which in turn means the focus of the proposed solution must be from the moment the data is captured.

The technical strategy in this case is completely different. With the server infrastructure creaking at the seams, in order to accommodate the growth rate in the data, it's inevitable there will be some investment made in new storage. The question to be addressed in this case is how to achieve that while providing additional capabilities beyond increasing capacity. Of course, the secondary question to be answered first is how to tie those new capabilities to business benefits to justify the increased investment.

Unlike the remote access issues facing Company A, this case can benefit from a storage consolidation solution. By moving data to a centralized storage array, the large-scale movement of data can be speeded up, and the amount of processing increased in the same batch window.

Recommendations

The recommendation is generally a short statement designed to set up the financial case section, which holds the justification. For example, in the case of Company A, the following recommendation might be submitted:

> *This proposal recommends the installation of a xDSL replacement to the frame relay data communications network. To maximize technical support coverage across all of the company's stores, and to ensure the best ongoing vendor relationships, a split award of half the stores each to HP and Gateway for their StorageWorks 1000 and 860B NAS products is recommended.*

Don't get distracted by the need to justify your recommendation. State your piece for the record and move to the next section.

The Financial Case

Having decided on the specific strategy and vendor products to recommend, you're now ready to build the detailed financial case. The financial terms of reference will vary from organization to organization and change to reflect the economy and situation. This means that you need to talk with someone from Finance before going too far down the road of building your financial case.

For Company A, let's assume that your heart-to-heart with the CFO showed that capital dollars were in short supply, and that investment in new technology would have a better chance of being approved if it balanced out in operating dollars budgeted and saved. This leads us to look for three kinds of expenditures:

- *Obviated costs:* These are new expenditures that may be budgeted for and expected but can be avoided through the successful implementation of the system.

- *Eliminated overhead costs:* These are expenditures that are built into the operating base and allocated either to a business unit as a direct or shared cost. Centralized IT services are frequently allocated to revenue-producing business units on a percentage basis. This is one of the reasons why IT is so popular with operating managers. (Not.)

- *Reduced carrying costs:* In a retail, distribution, or manufacturing setting, inventory is an asset that has certain costs associated with it. These can be quantified by cost of capital, storage and handling costs, and inventory risk.

Quantifiable Gross Benefits

For Company A, the recommended storage strategy will support better inventory stocking decisions, and this is where the key business benefit and financial justification can be found. Naturally, the operating division has to be brought into this equation, both as a customer and in providing validation that the numbers can be realized by better information. In this instance, reduced, returned, or overstocked inventory is estimated at .5 percent of all inventory, amounting to $1,000,000 annually.

In terms of obviated costs, the position I would take in building this justification is that a certain number of store systems require replacement each year—

based on historical installation and mean time between failure (MTBF) rates, let's project 50 problem sites resulting in replacement. This is 10 percent of the store base and obviously works out to one a week. As a note on the existing situation, you should be able to see that in some cases you'll want to go back to your report, dig up some statistics, and articulate those in the existing situation. In some cases, you let the data drive your solution, but because there is no such thing as a perfectly informed decision, sometimes you have to go back and determine numbers that support your case.

The strategy recommended for Company A is to hold the line on upgrades to store-based application servers and move data, and the subsequent replication, over to storage network software over new xDSL networks.

The cost of each intervention and server troubleshooting exercise averaged out to $3,500 per store over the past 2 years. This generates an additional savings of $175,000 per year.

As the xDSL network is installed, the frame relay connections can be retired. The strategy calls for this to occur over a period of 3 years, managing a network migration project of 15 stores per month. The net difference in communications fees, even allowing for the increase of traffic, is estimated at $100 per month, or 15, 30, 45, 60, 75 stores and so on, for a total estimated cost savings of $990,000. Because this is cumulative, you have to multiply the first store's savings by the number of months of the project period, in this case 36, the next number of stores by 35, the following month's total number of stores (45) by 34, and so on. By the end of the conversion, the frame relay network is no longer in service, and the new network costs represent a savings of some $50,000 monthly. For cost-justification purposes, you can assume that once you've successfully converted to the new technologies, savings have been realized, and any further justification would have to come out of the new network costs.

However, over the course of the conversion project, the network savings amounts to a further million dollars to add to the justification. The total quantifiable gross benefits of this storage network proposal come to $4,525,000.

Nonquantifiable Gross Benefits

What is the prevention of store downtime worth? That is a question that can be very difficult to put a number to, even if management agrees that there is a real cost to it. You can avoid a discussion over whether a number came out of the air by moving the benefit to the nonquantifiable column. Granted, there is real money involved, but it's too difficult to say precisely (or even roughly) how much that would be. The primary nonquantified benefit in this case study is data protection through replication. By having a centralized copy of the database, a store system could be re-created in the event of a catastrophic data loss.

Estimated Costs

Clearly, a NAS implementation for each store, as well as the coordination of the network transition, is going to have hard dollar costs. Because you have equipment costs and staff time costs, you have to start with estimates for both operating and capital expenditures. As you'll see later, the capital numbers may be converted to operating costs, but first that number has to be nailed down. Based on your shopping around for competitive quotes from Storage Area Network vendors, the per-store NAS configuration has been identified as $4,500 for the hardware, software, and shipping. For all 500 stores, this totals $2,250,000.

The staff required to pull together a network migration, NAS installation, and configuration at a rate of 15 per month is a rollout team of four plus a technical supervisor. Assuming average salary and overhead dollars per technical resource at $50,000 per year, and you have a staff budget of $750,000 over the life of the project. Even if at least one of these resources was expected to be redeployed from the "troubleshooting" team that currently supports the servers in the stores, it might be wiser to avoid trying to claw that cost savings into the justification. The reason for this is, given that in the first year there will still be a preponderance of nonconverted systems, the support requirement likely won't go away until after the project is nearer to completion.

xDSL network installation, scheduled as part of the NAS project timing, carries with it a setup and modem cost of $100. Although the frame relay connection is replaced by the xDSL, for protection from configuration and other problems, redundant service is recommended for 1 month after the xDSL installation. Since the same volume of data isn't moved through the frame relay link, the $100 fee is reduced to the connect charge of $25 per store. For all 500 stores, this means the network transition fee is $125, for a total of $62,500.

Ultimately, no one really knows what the costs of a project will be exactly. The estimated costs serve as a budget according to which you will manage, and against which your performance and the value of your solution will be judged by management.

Net Benefits

In this case, justification for storage network technology would indicate that for an operating lease commitment of $4,275 monthly, 10 percent of the chain's stores could be moved to NAS devices, proving the value of the technology, showing the abilities of the rollout team to make their deadlines, and consolidating the data for selected stores for immediate reporting. The internal rate of return for the entire project would be calculated on the estimated net savings of $1,462,500 on project costs of $3,062,500 and total (quantifiable) savings of $4,525,000.

Add in a go/no go decision point for further rollouts, and I think it would be a relatively safe bet to assume this proposal would be approved.

Company B: Another Set of Requirements

I'm not going to go into the same degree of detail with a justification for Company B, as many of the considerations, such as internal rate of return and financing options, apply to any scenario. However, there are several differences in the justification for a storage network that involve a server consolidation strategy, and I wanted to call attention to those here.

Virtualization allows the migration of database and application servers from one environment to another. An Oracle database might be on, say, a Sun, HP, or IBM platform, and that specific vendor may no longer be part of the company's architecture going forward. By introducing a virtualized storage pool into the shop, such databases can be not only moved off the direct attached-storage but also redeployed to a new Oracle instance running on a completely different server platform. The OS and hardware for the application is swapped out from under the virtualized database. This becomes an especially attractive option when considering migrations from one environment to another on the basis of licensing costs. Some applications become less useful over time as they are replaced. By incorporating a virtualization engine into the centralized storage environment, a reduced operating cost profile by moving the server to, say, a Windows- or Linux-based processing engine might be possible. Administration of multiple environments and the troubleshooting (let alone risk) required as a result is a potentially rich vein for justifying the introduction of storage network technology.

Taking advantage of existing investments in networking expertise and toolsets, such as IP, SAN, and NAS solutions that weren't available even 2 years ago, can open new doors. Organizations that until this point have been content to "stoke the engines" of their established application platforms are now facing tremendous new opportunities and options as a result of storage network technology.

Clearly the prices for NAS solutions have dropped to the point where they must be considered for nearly every server that requires disks. For organizations with significant investment in legacy systems, large centralized data stores, or a plethora of platforms, a SAN/NAS combination sets the stage for managed growth.

Vendors offer examples of customer case studies for each of these configurations. Having provided a format for interpreting the options and their implication for business benefits, I'll assume you're in a better position to interpret those results.

Is IT Feasible?

As you can see from the template, the key to making a solid business case for a SAN is to segregate the solution and its cost from the problem and benefits of solving it. The format I recommend here tends to structure that very logically and allows a nontechnical decision maker to follow the rationale without getting bogged down in the "techie" details.

It's worth noting that information technology frequently carries with it an impact on the political landscape of an organization, regardless of its size. The fundamental case for Storage Area Networks is centralized control with the corresponding efficiencies and economies that go with it.

Part of the role of the feasibility study is to directly address the expected workload increases and service levels. It will help to be realistic about the perception your departmental users have about the ability of the data center to support distributed users. On the other hand, specialized skills are required to effectively manage complex technologies. Although the past two decades have seen an incredible increase in the number of departmental and regional servers, experience has shown that this is an expensive way to support technology from the perspective of total cost of ownership.

An argument about skills specialization and TCO will generally not go very far if the end result is that one senior corporate type feels they will be losing to another. The point is that you can use this template to make a rational and logical case, but in my experience, approval is often obtained for other, softer, reasons.

This template supports these "undocumented decision criteria" by allowing you to state your case objectively and describe the technology in the context of the service and value it provides—quantified and nonquantified.

Virtualization As a Benefit

One problem with developing a justification for networked storage is the inherently technical nature of the underlying components. However, given that virtualization is a key virtue of managing a SAN, it can also be used as a valuable tool for justifying it.

It shouldn't be difficult to arrive at anecdotal (and perhaps apocryphal) horror stories of server outages or near misses. Explaining the value of networked storage as a means of moving towards commodity disks—scalable, replaceable, interoperable, and heterogeneous in light of new systems integration—is a key attribute from a management perspective.

In an era of corporate consolidation, it makes sense that if your organization is an acquirer, technology that allows new systems to be added and administered more easily is strategic. On the other side, the value is just as apparent. If the disposition of the enterprise is ultimately to be merged or otherwise folded into another outfit, anything that eases that process will increase the value of the company. Not to put too fine a point on it, but even firms that get acquired against their preferences often find units of excellence that end up in a "reverse takeover" position relative to their acquiring colleagues. Simply put, it's a career enhancer to be better organized, and storage networking allows you to do just that.

Summary

In this chapter, you've been introduced to a well-proven structure that demonstrates the financial and operational feasibility of implementing a storage network. By using the administrative tools that allow the virtualization of storage across all servers, organizations have achieved economies of scale that allow a single administrator to manage more than a terabyte of data. Compared to the more restricted productivity limits per administrator for server-attached storage, this can make for a compelling business case.

However, you should also have taken away a sense that while enabling centralized control, there is a political "turf" dimension to systems administration that should be addressed head on to ensure your business case is approved.

Although the technology supporting a consolidated storage network is complex, the most easily approved business plan shows that it improves service to the organization, and alleviates complexity rather than adds to it. By using the documentation techniques recommended in this chapter, you can be sure you make those points in your request for new resources.

Storage networks involve the cutting edge of technologies. Network speeds, distances linked by fiber optics, and historically unparalleled increases in storage capacities combine with new software techniques to change the architecture of systems large and small. That being said, it's still all about the business supported by the data, and ultimately your investment in storage networks is just that—an investment.

Because part of the aspiration of this book is to provide the end-to-end coverage any administrator, manager, or technology architect might need when considering storage networks, I thought it vital to include a treatment on exactly how to calculate return on investment. And, for you as a technologist, one key nonquantifiable investment in any system is the amount of time you spend to learn the tools. I hope from this chapter you gained a better insight on how to calculate and balance that cost.

CHAPTER 13

Future Directions for Storage Networks

I ONCE ATTENDED a conference where an information scientist employed by NASA spoke on some of their activities. He said, "At NASA, we tend to break things into two groups, 'down and in' or 'up and out.'" He went on to explain that the focus of their engineers and scientists was on the details of the interaction of molecules, chemicals, and the environment. Astrophysicists were preoccupied with what was out there and how to get to it. In this book, most of the focus has been down and in. In this chapter, I'd like to look up and out at some of the things that could make the future of storage networks fascinating indeed.

It was the first half of calendar 2004 as I wrote this. At various times in this book, I've referred to my tour of duty in the systems world over the past 20 plus years. One of the key lessons I've taken away from that experience is that forecasting information technologies is about as reliable as predicting the weather or stock market. The other side of that argument is that there is a need for, and there are professionals who work as, meteorologists and financial planners. So with the caveat that I'm completely aware of just how wrong I might be, in this chapter I would like to share with you my impressions of areas ripe for radical changes in Storage Area Networks and their components, and their utility over the coming months and years. These include

- TCP/IP offload initiatives by Microsoft

- Microdrive technology from Hitachi

- Silicon-based optical processing from Intel

- Quantum cryptography and computing

- Ubiquitous, constant-connected mobile devices

- Grid and autonomic computing architectures from IBM

Of course, there are plenty of other companies doing great work in labs all over the world, but buckle up and let me take you on a tour of some of the ones I think have great promise for significant impact.

Third Chip from the Sun

Moore's Law is at heart the proposition that transistors per real estate on silicon will roughly double every 18 months or so. But what if that law broke out of the clean room where chips are made? If the network is the computer, and the World Wide Web is a network, does Moore's Law apply more widely? My observation is that equating connected computing devices to NAND and NOR gates on a CPU chip, the rollout and upgrading of these nodes, and the associated increase in compute power is occurring at a rate commensurate with Moore's Law—and has been from about the mid 1990s. The difference being instead of transistors, these nodes represent integrated processing units with their own storage and connectivity.

Consider the rollout of broadband to consumers worldwide over the past few years. In 2000, the number of broadband-connected (xDSL or cable modem subscriber) homes was 20 million. By 2003, it was 60 million. Now, you would be correct to observe that there isn't quite a doubling there in 18 months. But the observation incorporates more than just one technology; it applies to compute nodes including storage. Even though I'm setting aside discussions of 3G networks and the eruption of hot spots, I believe those statistics reinforce the general idea. Worldwide integration of systems is occurring at a rate in keeping with Moore's Law.

An overlay of the rates of high-speed Internet penetration, increases in CPU, sales of new systems, as well as storage capacities, is shown in Figure 13-1.

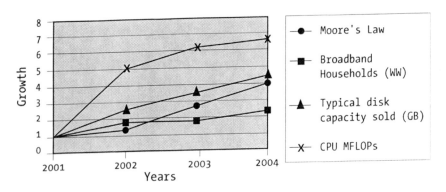

Figure 13-1. Compute node growth patterns

It's worth noting that 2001–2002 didn't see the robust markets for technology that had been enjoyed in previous years; however, capacities continued to increase.

One net effect of this incredible increase in the amount of storage and the number of users is, naturally, an increase in demand for managed storage resources. Another is a dramatic increase in the complexity of systems and a pressing need to automate administrative tasks.

I'll talk about administration and software for managing complexity a little later in the chapter. First, let's look at some of the technologies emerging to assist Storage Area Networks to keep up with demand.

ASICs Get the Job Done

One of the themes in the early chapters of this book was the idea that higher network performance resulted from moving logic closer to the hardware. For TCP/IP processing, this means a TCP/IP offload engine (TOE) needs to be incorporated into the network card to really make GbE+ fly. And to do that, the operating system has to be ready, willing, and able to relinquish that work. Hence the Microsoft Chimney project for building TOE capabilities into Windows Storage Server 2003 and, I'll assume, operating systems beyond that.

When Microsoft announced the Chimney Offload Architecture for Windows in May 2002, their stated intention was to offer a standardized way to interface TOE hardware with the Windows OS stack. This would allow iSCSI host bus adapters or TOE network cards to perform TCP/IP connection and transmission processing at the hardware level for performance gains. Concurrently, the design calls for enough processing in the operating system to ensure that data integrity and IP security isn't compromised.

The target for Chimney general availability is mid 2005. By that time, hardware vendors will have had an opportunity to look at the spec and decide how to enable their server GbE ports and NICs with it. As a result, Microsoft will be able to offer a storage software platform that provides significantly better performance for IP-based storage networks.

Inarguably, Microsoft has the installation base and the marketing muscle to make this happen. As hardware vendors offer next-generation MS-OS compatible devices, Linux and other software platforms will want to take advantage of the capabilities of the gear. This will likely lead to a de facto standard around TOE processing for GbE-based Storage Area Networks.

Microdrive Technology

As I wrote this, the smallest-footprint–largest-capacity microdrive was the 1-inch drive with 4GB capacity. Originally developed by IBM, the microdrive technology was transferred to Hitachi with the sale of that division in 2002. In 2004, the single biggest application of these drives was for MP3 devices. With this kind of footprint (1 inch) and with the light power draw for operation (< 5V during writes with 314 mA current), it's easy to see how mobile devices will be increasingly enabled with data storage capabilities. Mobile means wireless, and anyone can foresee the rapid and inevitable increase in the number of hotspots and synch zones for users and their information.

When I used an early Pocket PC device (2001) to play back a movie during a long flight, I became convinced that personal viewers would someday become a popular handheld application. As the cell phone companies move from snapping low resolution images to recording and transferring DIVX movies, it isn't difficult to see how this will take up and push demand for storage networks.

Silicon Photonics

As indicated elsewhere in this book, Fibre Channel has a tradition of leading the push of the performance curve for Storage Area Networks. In 2003, the CTO of Intel made an announcement that could pave the way for a revitalized Fibre Channel price/performance calculation.

As you'll remember from Chapter 3, although fiber-optic cable and devices represent the high end in performance, they also represent the high end in complexity and cost. It's hard to compete against solutions that, while slower, represent 80 percent or more of the installed base of networks (copper IP). To that end, Intel is moving to put optical processing into silicon.

At a technical conference where he discussed Intel's strategic initiatives designed to open new markets, CTO Patrick Gelsinger indicated that Intel envisioned chip-based optical processors that handled all aspects of photonic communications. Of course, Intel sees this as a way of bringing down the prices currently paid for optical filters, for example, from $10,000 per unit to $1 each. This would radicalize the telecommunications equipment market for high-performance photonics. An example of products that work toward this goal include Intel's quasi-planar packaging components. These can be used to support 10 Gigabit Ethernet and Fibre Channel communications using fiber-optic lasers and receivers.

The quasi-planar packaging doesn't eliminate the need for light pulse components. However, it does provide a less-expensive and reliable means of packaging tunable laser optical communications components over current methods. Tunable lasers allow wavelengths to be dialed on demand, resulting in a more flexible communications network. This is especially applicable to long haul networks and Metropolitan Area Networks as data users and storage assets are linked at high speed over increasing distances.

Even with a tremendous rise in adoption rates for copper IP–based networking, it's developments like these that will continue to position fiber optics as the numero uno contender for data communications networking speed and distance metrics. The main point I want to draw attention to here is that when these technologies reduce component costs by several orders of magnitude, suddenly what was previously out of reach becomes commonplace. Silicon-based photonic operations have the potential to do just that in the coming years.

Quantum Cryptography

Of course, with all this sharing, something must be done about security. In Chapter 8, I discussed the role of public and private keys as they relate to encryption. Clearly, scrambling transmitted and stored bits of data in ways that can only be unscrambled by authorized parties is a growth industry. Limitations on the export of encryption and encoding software, such as 128-bit encryption, are based on the idea that cryptography is a function of warfare. That some countries should be prohibited from taking advantage of features of products developed by citizens of another country for whom they've declared or undeclared hostilities isn't really my concern (I'm Canadian). What is interesting to me is the idea that randomness, and as such, the security of the encrypted data, can be virtually guaranteed by the use of keys derived from quantum physics.

As you should remember from the discussion about private keys, the way to get around having to manage distribution of defined keys is to be able to derive a private key from a public discussion via the Diffie-Hellman key exchange protocol. The way this is done, of course, is by multiplying prime numbers together to make a suitably large product, where guessing which primes were used (and required for decryption) would require a Herculean effort. It should be noted that brute force isn't the only way this encryption technique could become undone. As noted by the character Avi in Neal Stephenson's book, *Cryptonomicon* (an outstanding read), it might also be accomplished by a great leap forward in mathematical theory.

Quantum cryptography is a highly efficient means of distributing secure secret keys. It has already been used in fiber-optic networks and takes advantage of the fundamental uncertainties inherent in quantum physics. Sender and receiver have to agree on the state in which the photons will be placed and observed. The sender encodes the message in quantum states—for example, the polarization of a photon. The receiver observes the states and through a public (in the clear) discussion of the observations determines which of the states to use for decoding. For example, polarization of photons can be expressed as rectilinear, circular, or diagonal. An interceptor without knowledge of the basis for that observation randomizes the other quantum information known as *conjugates*. The act of observing changes the quantum states. To help you understand this concept, consider the analogy of bidding in the game of bridge. Two partners discuss out loud specific, though not explicit, values reflective of the contents of their hands. Anyone listening in on the discussion would, unbeknownst to them, change the convention under which the bidding was made, to the point where "Go Fish" might be the bid they hear.

The main point here is not my lack of comprehension of quantum physics—however impressive that lack may be. Rather, that in the realm of fiber optics, photonics, lasers, and the other constituent components underlying Fibre Channel Storage Area Networks, there is considerable room for further gains in security as well as performance.

On that note, let me take a quick look at the state of the photon as a means of storing and retrieving data.

Quantum Computing

As you've seen elaborated in the discussion of electronic components in this book, the transmission of high and low signals through networks married to the writing and reading of up and down polarity fluxes on disks has given us tremendously powerful Storage Area Networks. As the decades march on, we make components smaller and smaller, wavelengths shorter and shorter, and frequencies higher and higher. All this is based on having put in place layers of control on a binary foundation.

Quantum computing doesn't use the classical binary digits—bits. It works instead with a quantum bit, or qubit. Reflecting the nature of quantum physics, a qubit may be in a 0 or 1 state (so we can still use 8/10b encoding), but it also may simultaneously express a superposition of these states.

A fundamental law of quantum mechanics is the Heisenberg Uncertainty Principle, which says that quantum measurement affects the observed system—the idea that the act of looking for a location of a quantum particle changes its location. However, just because you can't be certain where it is doesn't mean that its location is random. The result of measuring the path of a photon, for example, allows it to be consistently detected in the same place.

Experiments with photons have shown that mirrors can be used to direct each single quantized packet of light (a photon) towards, say, two detectors, A and B. The key term is "single packet," which means the photon isn't actually split. Quantum theory provides for the counterintuitive notion that the packet travels down both paths at the same time. The photon is never split, but when measured at the detection point there is an observable change in the photon, referred to as *quantum interference.*

The quantum state can't be fully established by any measurement, but information about the state can be communicated without having that knowledge. This is the basis for quantum cryptography, as I discussed earlier.

The point here is that single photons can be directed and controlled, in spite of the uncertainty as to how they might precisely travel to the detection point. That which can be controlled can be put to work, and quantum computing does just that.

So what is the practical application of these sometimes mind-boggling theories? Flash memory for storage devices becomes ineffective when paths for electrons to travel are reduced below 65 nanometers in width, as the path starts to "leak" its contents. For a physical analogy, let's consider translucently thin plumbing pipes. There is a point at which the contents aren't maintained by the containing walls of the pipe.

However, by reducing the number of electrons required to represent a bit of information, effective channels have been demonstrated at even 2 nanometers in diameter.

This means that future increases on storage sizes and access rates will probably contribute to the next generation of advances in storage technologies. (I had to throw that "probably" in there because, after all, we're talking about quantum physics.)

Invariably, software lags behind hardware in the revolutionary/evolutionary process. This makes sense, I suppose, from an enablement perspective. Software requires hardware, and faster hardware supports new and (sometimes) improved software. More processing power means more software capability, and, as you've already seen, the potential for architectural changes around distributed computing to make more effective use of the processing capacities that you already have, let alone what you may enjoy from a quantum leap forward in technology.

Exploding Demand from Shrinking Devices

This leads to future directions for the way you interface with your computing infrastructure. There are two distinct avenues along which these developments are occurring: one where you off-load more processing to the machines, and the second where you increase the ease and speed of your access to computing resources.

Communication first occurred, as Marshal McCluhan said, in acoustical space. That is, two people interacted and conveyed messages through body language, eye contact, tone of voice, and words. At some point, that communication was frozen, or cooled into a set piece of cave drawings, hieroglyphs, cuneiforms, alphabets, and numbers. This allowed people to communicate over time and distance. The telegraph was the first application of adding electricity to messaging, and we humans used our time-honored ability to codify a message and transmit it from a sender to a receiver some distance and time away. As our collective experience and abilities grew, radio broadcasts became prevalent, creating a one-way real-time link between one sender and many receivers over distance. The telephone became established, allowing real-time bidirectional interaction in acoustic space, and then television.

This is significant in as much as it points to the way in which we apply technology to interaction as more capability is made available to us. First stored messages, then real time, then interactive, always moving towards enriching the content of the message until we're finally interacting as much as possible with body language, eye contact, words, and tone of voice—real-time acoustical space.

In the past decades, we've also followed this model in dealing with computing devices.

The richest content is still offline, a stored set of video, text, sound, and words. Our real-time sharing of content is moving towards sound bites and snapshots, with clear words and sounds transferred anywhere in the world to handheld devices.

It might surprise you to find that I'm not going to point to virtual reality or holographic imaging as the significant contributor to the human/machine interface. Instead, I think a clear picture of the cell phone, as an interface to an interconnected grid of computing devices, is a more powerful, more immediate model.

The heads-up displays used by the military to display information can also be adapted to convey instructions—drilling down a level of detail, bringing up, or activating a dormant meter. Voice instructions are already used to navigate through computers acting as switchboard operators. Taken together, the future seems to hold a command-driven interface not unlike the disembodied voice of Majel Barrett on the various NCC-1701 versions of *Star Trek* fiction.

Online users will drive demand for online storage. And there should be no question that searching the hard drives of PCs around the planet isn't within the response time expectations of most users today. The potential for increases for integration of data storage resources can't be overestimated, at least using Moore's Law as a yardstick for the next 10 years.

Virtualization

At the heart of the push to virtualize the physical assets of a Storage Area Network (or for all aspects of IT hardware for that matter) is the notion of encapsulation. This allows the segregation of components (or layers) from the operation of others. Messages are exchanged with the ones located immediately next to any given component. The way to regulate the messages (and when considering interoperability and multivendor realities, this regulation is critical) is through definition and adherence to standards. In short, the only way to continually increase capacity and throughput within a heterogeneous environment is either by multiparty development and adoption of standards at all levels, or through compliance to a single vendor specification pushed onto the marketplace and backed with sufficient numbers of buyers to make it the de facto standard.

There are several key technologies over which this battle for hearts and minds (and wallets) will play out in Storage Area Networks. Not the least of these is iSCSI. For now, let me start at the ground level and work up.

Organizing the Circus

Anyone with a background in records management, including the classification and retention of data according to schedules, can't fail but be frankly terrified at the idea of all that information floating about. The technological capacity to generate, store, and transfer information has vastly outstripped the ability to classify and index it. Luckily, search engines have made some strides in using brute force to accomplish this for you. While an individual user might have to dedicate their personal computer (and a significant amount of time) to a search for "*.mp3" or "%resume%" across a significant number of storage devices, Google accomplishes a similar result using a huge cluster of Linux machines. The net effect is a huge increase in performance. What I want to introduce here is the idea that clusters of processors, dedicating to searching data or otherwise processing it, won't be centralized, and that the virtualization of hardware has a tremendous potential when harnessed in a peer-to-peer networking scheme. This isn't a new idea, of course. It has already been proven effective in such experiments as the Search for Extraterrestrial Intelligence (SETI), in which people volunteered unused cycles of their PCs to search the sky for intelligible signals.

What is new is the software regime for making that kind of collaboration a part of our daily lives.

Work on efforts such as PAWN and SHARK have shown the value of coordinating distributed computing resources into a grid. The overlay of mobile software agents onto an extended peer-to-peer network has tremendous significance for storage networks of the future.

Let me describe a hypothetical, but practical, example of how this could work.

A tourist involved in an injury accident is admitted to a small city health center. An MRI indicates that there may be internal bleeding; however, the attending physician wants an independent review. Four time zones away, a qualified specialist is preparing to go to work. As part of her duties, she has elected to participate in a peer-to-peer network for medical consultation. A software agent identifying her qualifications and availability status is operating on her PC. When the health center, also a participant on this network, requests assistance, the autonomic software agent ripples through the grid, looking for a match. Once found, the specialist is notified that there is a request for consultation, and if accepted, the two nodes can be directly linked, and the MRI transferred, evaluated, and discussed.

Having worked with medical oncologists, I know there are significant organizational issues (not to mention insurance) to be addressed before the preceding example becomes practical. Apply the scenario to SAAB engine mechanics with access to a digital camera, however, and you should be able to see the commercial implications. The point is that models for data processing are moving away from centralization, just as server storage is becoming consolidated.

Regulated data, such as patient information or sensitive defense project files, may not be the first common implementations of grid and autonomic software agents that enable distributed processing, storage, and access. However, this architecture represents both a significant departure and tremendous opportunity for storage networks, where the network is the computer and the grid is the network.

Autonomics

Earlier in this chapter I referred to the creation of mobile software agents that could be made "aware" of changes in situations and take action dynamically. This is a function of a new model for computing, which IBM calls *autonomic,* HP calls *adaptive,* and Microsoft calls *dynamic.* I had the opportunity to work with some early prerelease software from IBM on their autonomic computing toolkit, so I would like to use that as a basis for my last set of observations on the future of Storage Area Networks.

I referred to virtualization a little earlier in this chapter, but there is another aspect to virtual storage that is worthy of note: utility computing. The combination of the grid architecture, virtualized server assets, autonomic software agents, and virtual storage pools have the potential to transform the way we provide access to stored data over networks.

It would be difficult to argue that the current levels of efficiency provided by IT shops worldwide is sufficient to support an explosion in demand. Those of you who already support ever-increasing demand with stretched budgets no doubt shuddered at the idea of an explosion. But the trend towards ubiquity of access and an online world represent that sort of "hockey stick" graph of devices, connected and querying.

The vendors predict this too, of course, which is why they all offer to varying degrees products and services to support utility computing, or what IBM calls *on-demand computing.* As I've been working with some of their autonomic products prior to their release, I'm more familiar with how IBM intends to "productize" this model than I am with the plans of, say, Sun, HP, or Microsoft. Let me describe for you here how a couple of those products will fit within an autonomic storage network environment.

Virtualization is a prerequisite. If your environment requires a physical cabling change, configuration of settings by hand, and a reboot, autonomics don't enter into the equation. You can't automate with software something that you don't actually do with software (you could use robots, I suppose, but that is beyond the scope of autonomic computing).

So let's assume that precondition is in place. Your environment is physically installed and configured to be one big interconnected pool of resources—bandwidth, RAM, CPU, and storage devices, all of which can be assigned and allocated on the fly.

Concurrent with that evolution of hardware is a corresponding enhancement in the way administrators interact with software. I say "administrators," as this is a key group in the move towards autonomic systems. The promise of this approach is to allow administrators to specialize, to really get to know how to tweak a system for performance or security. The idea is that too much time is spent doing administrative "grunt work" and this takes away from the resources needed to turn the computing infrastructure into a "well-oiled machine."

Solution Install (SI) is one example of this. Solution Install is an autonomic tool for taking the software installation process to the next level. Again, this represents building at the foundation level, rather than a great leap forward. Solution Install itself is aware of the software installation process. If a node doesn't have the necessary installation resources, the SI process installs them. These resources include "touchpoints" for servers that are tiny-footprint databases maintaining information about installed applications and their dependencies. Through this mechanism, any newly installed software can establish whether the components it requires are already in place, and if not, whether any other application would be affected by an upgrade.

You should be able to see from this how the trial-and-error, consulting-the-innards-of-the-goat approach to software upgrades becomes a thing of the past. Dependencies not only include identification of software components, but of other prerequisites such as hardware and connectivity.

Let's marry the autonomic software installation process with a virtualized hardware environment. Under this regime, if the application being installed requires more physical memory than is currently available, it's empowered to request more from the virtual environment. This means that without human intervention, the platform on which the software is being installed reconfigures itself (in compliance with the policies previously set by the administrator) to be able to run the application. This autonomic provisioning or "self-configuring" aspect of the process isn't limited by location. As we tie more organizational assets together, we can also create accounts and linkages that cross organizations. Under a utility computing model, the assets added to the virtual pool, whether they are hardware or software, may be acquired from third parties. This means that the system itself can buy (lease, rent, or borrow) the resources needed to fulfill its mission.

Another tool within the Autonomic Toolkit is the Integrated Solutions Console. This tool allows a single browser-based console to be used to administer a huge range of different processes, including log analysis and event notification. Through integration with a credentials vault, it's possible for an authorized user (or software process) to acquire the user identification and passwords required to authenticate in other systems—without actually obtaining that information. This centralization of authentication provides a means of control across a number of heterogeneous assets, including, as I'm sure you can imagine, the credentials required to obtain new assets. Working together, Solution Install uses the touch-points to gather and register information about processes; when necessary it can obtain credentials needed to make changes from the vault. The installation routine doesn't have to be aware of the credentials; it need only be an authorized process to access the vault. And it accesses a complete, up-to-date picture of the environment where it is being installed through the information maintained by the touchpoints.

It's worth noting that autonomic monitoring can be performed on the logs generated by various servers and thresholds set for potentially threatening warning levels, such as disk free space. Combined with the process I've sketched here, you should be able to see how this autonomic monitoring need not necessarily page some administrator for help—it could simply request the needed resources itself, staving off a potential systems failure. Other conditions can be monitored such as the number of port accesses from a particular IP where the threshold is set to identify potential Denial of Service attacks. The response to this threshold might not be acquiring more resources; instead the reaction could be to deactivate that port or deny access to that IP. Under that scenario, the autonomic system becomes self-protecting.

There are similar initiatives underway across most of the storage networks vendor community. This tells me that these services are likely to show up in the next generation of software and that it makes sense to start to plan for them. Autonomic computing isn't a fad. It's a critical step on the path to organizing your computing infrastructures to be able to handle the data storage and access explosion that shows no signs of letting up.

Summary

Just as our storage devices shrink in size, the reach of our networks grows. We pack exponentially increasing megabytes stored and compute cycles available into each square foot of real estate, then find faster and more reliable ways to increase the connection between geographic centers.

The trends I've identified in this chapter aren't the only important ones. I'm positive there is groundbreaking work being done in research labs somewhere about which I have no idea. The purpose of this chapter is to go up and out into what will be possible.

Yes, predicting the future can be a mug's game. But still, you should be able to see the potential directions for Storage Area Networks on the horizon.

Clearly, it isn't yet time to stand pat. Too many things are in the works, and the status quo simply doesn't provide the foundation needed to keep up with increases in demand. *Jetsons*-like flying cars aren't likely part of the near future (or even the far future, for that matter). But wristwatches you can talk into, store the Library of Congress on, and beam pictures around the world through are fast becoming realities.

The traditional roles of data managers throughout history still must be fulfilled—keeping the information secure, making it available to the right people, at the right time, in a format they can use. This is one mandate for storage networks.

There is a vast challenge facing those of us who work with networks and data storage. We must continue to investigate, evaluate, and apply technologies that allow us to fulfill our mandate.

After reading this chapter, you should see that there is quite literally no end in sight. The potential application of physics to computing for storage, transmission, and cryptography is greater, not less, that it has been in the past.

Afterword

I TOOK AN advanced Local Area Networks course from Digital Equipment in 1982. At that point, when the instructor took us up through each layer of the ISO OSI model, I thought I had never seen anything quite so brilliant in my life.

To this day, the model and its separation of concerns, interfaces between adjacent layers, and ongoing process of elaboration and adaptation is to me a wonderful example of how humans collaborate to make the abstract applied.

That same year, I bought my first hard disk. It was a 5MB Winchester disk, contained within a Convergent Technologies IWS workstation. The CTOS operating system, documentation, and a COBOL compiler took up 4MB. It communicated over a 300/1200 baud modem to the Multics system at the university. I loved every bit of it.

I mention this not to present myself as a fossilized veteran of IT gear from history, rather to demonstrate that although the model numbers and vendors of yesterday don't necessarily apply, the principles and standards most certainly do.

This was the approach I wanted you to take through this tour of Storage Network technology—setting aside the specific vendor offerings and models that can change from one quarter to the next, and focusing on the role played, even today, by each layer in the stack.

Yes, storage networks can be fiber optic or copper based. That is the province of the physical media, and I hope that you learned something of value about that from Chapters 2 and 3. The fiber build-out across Europe and North America is there and waiting to be taken advantage of. Wireless technologies provide different options for Asia, India, and places in Eastern Europe.

Yes, there are innate differences between accessing block devices and files across a network. As we progress, however, those lines blur and ultimately will converge for many applications. It was my hope the discussion of bus, switch, and router connections would demonstrate how to identify where performance bottlenecks can occur.

Regardless of the underlying network connectivity, there are standards to be embraced and interoperability to be achieved. I tried to go into enough detail to help you gain insight into the process by which these are defined and the products that result from efforts to comply with these specifications.

The trade-offs to be made between investing in the infrastructure, cost of managing resources, and rip-and-replace vs. ad hoc integration will be different for each organization and specific project within organizations. My intent was to provide you with a framework for evaluating the various technologies, in light of your own specific requirements, which only you can know.

The mission, as opposed to the goal or objective of this book, was to take you, the reader, from the bottom of the stack, through each layer, up and out to where you could apply what you've learned. All too often, evaluating IT options is a process of being hosed down by details and jargon. If, by reading this book, you're better prepared to sort through and classify these details into layers, allowing you to focus and ask better questions, then I've succeeded in my mission.

—Daniel Worden

Index